YESTERDAY'S MASHED POTATOES

THE FABULOUS LIFE OF A HAPPY HAS-BEEN

PATRICIA WILSON

For Rebecca,
with love and
thanks —
Patricia Nelson

First published by Dog Ear Publishing
4010 W. 86th Street, Ste H
Indianapolis, IN 46268
www.dogearpublishing.net

ISBN: 978-160844-125-9

This book is printed on acid-free paper.

Printed in the United States of America

FIRST PLACE WINNER FOR EXCELLENCE IN WRITING
(Santa Barbara Writers Conference, June, 2007)

"THE WRITING SURPRISED ME...NOT JUST FOR THEATER BUFFS!"
...Harold S. "Hal" Prince

"IT'S A HELLUVA STORY...WRITE IT!"
...John Steinbeck

"PART DRAMA, PART COMEDY, PART HISTORY—<u>ALL</u> HEART."
,,,Warren Lyons

For my family, past, present, and future:
not just for those touched by Fate
to be actors, but for those touched
by Common Sense not to be.

ACKNOWLEDGMENTS

*"Think where man's glory begins and ends, and say
'my glory is that I   had such friends.'"*

...Keats

Without my friends and their encouraging enthusiasm and patience I might have given up all this writing, researching, and re-living long ago. Margie Gray and Sheldon Harnick, Pat Stanley Matthews, Barbara Ann Grimes, Beverly Dixon Wills, Jerry Bock, Marilyn Tyler, Nancy Fox, Elena Giordano, Ellen Hanley, Pat and Carol Fagan, Ruth Lampert, Jane Klain, Tony O'Dell, Pat Hanley, Rebecca Robins, Anne Jackson Barry, Mark Levine, Bill Slater, Sherri Long, Al Checco, Barnaby Conrad, Marcia Meier, sister-in-law and friend Joan Wilson. I love you and thank you all.

My daughters, Kate and Penelope —two better friends a Mom could never wish for— have offered unfaltering love and support in my "outing" of the family secrets, as well as supplying the best of expertise, each in her own field: Kate is a genius in communications and public relations—getting the message out!—and Penelope scholarly in the detailed, mind-bending work of helping to refine and define words- on- paper. I thank you and love you both with all my heart.

Mara, just "Mara," far more beautiful than any of the actors you photograph professionally: thank you for making me look good on these covers and for the past twenty years.

Miles Nelson, Amber Ortner, and Matt Murry at DogEar Publishing: you are newer friends, but have my deepest appreciation for putting up with my endless questions, anxieties, and computer illiteracy.

Mike Quinn, Kate's husband, offered suggestions that helped shape the book, and James Flemming, even in the early months of his marriage to Penelope, relinquished precious time with her so that she could be of help to me. Good fellows, my sons-in-law.

And to anyone young or old who might pick up this story of my life-journey, I repeat one of the favorite phrases my brother David and I heard as we huddled next to the old crystal radio set on our grandmother's Ohio farm many years ago. It was simply:

"Thank you for listenin', folks!"

With author Ray Bradbury, one fabulous inspiration in my fabulous life. Taken at the writer's conference in Santa Barbara, CA, in 2008. (photo by Carol Fagan)

Seven-year-old Rory and three-year-old Liam catapulted into the house, rattling kitchen window shades like maracas in a Latin band. Their neighbor-pal, Karl, the only shifty-eyed six-year old I've ever met, slunk in after them.

"Grandma!" Rory shouted. "You're an actor! We're watching a baseball movie at Karl's house, and you're in it!" Rory was talking about A League Of Their Own. I play a character named "Marla Hooch" in that film.

"Ac-TRESS, sweetheart. That's girl for actor."

"But no one else's grandma is an ac-TRESS!" Rory and Liam live in a small town in Connecticut. In New York and Hollywood I know plenty of grandma-actresses, whether they own up to it or not.

"Are you a star then, Grandma?"

Shifty-Eyed Karl spoke up. "My dad sees you on Nick-at-Nite," he announced. "He says you're a has-been!" I couldn't help myself. I snorted with laughter. Liam, his brown eyes reflecting a grandma's-lost-it expression, patted my arm

"Is a has-been something bad?" Rory asked. I wiped laugh-tears from my eyes.

"No, honey, nothing bad—just yesterday's mashed potatoes!" Rory was relieved, hearing our family expression applied to this intense moment. His friendship with Karl was on the line. He laughed with me, exposing pink gums where baby teeth had been the week before. Liam joined in, flashing smiley-dimples. I gathered my grandsons into a hug.

Shifty-Eyed Karl stood aside, staring at us. Rory broke away, grabbing up his ball and glove from the kitchen counter. On impulse, I reached for Karl and put my arms around him. His small bony body stiffened, then relaxed into the hug. He sighed, laying his cheek against my waist.

"C'mon guys, let's go!" Rory, impatient.

"Yeah, let's go!" Liam echoed, following behind, lugging a baseball bat.

Karl, his too-big ball cap falling over his shifty eyes, stopped and turned back to look at me. He managed a smile.

"Know what, Rory-and-Liam's Grandma?" he said. "I'm gonna tell my Dad— you're sure a happy has-been, anyway!"

The boys trooped out the door.

ACT ONE

FROM THE PUMPKIN SHOW
TO THE BIG APPLE

"Throw your heart over the bar, and your body will follow."
...Norman Vincent Peale

scene i: December 1960, New York City

Smack-dab in the middle of "The Golden Age of Broadway," Ethel Merman held audiences hostage in *Gypsy;* Jackie Gleason starred in Robert Merrill's musical, *Take Me Along;* Mary Martin charmed the world in *Sound of Music;* Richard Burton and Julie Andrews debuted in Lerner and Loewe's *Camelot.*

And I was singing my heart out as the leading lady of the hit Pulitzer Prize-winning musical, *Fiorello!*

It was Wednesday. Matinee day. I hurried across snow-blustery West 44th Street to the Broadhurst Theater. As I pulled open the stage door, the familiar smell of dancers' sweat and the sounds of warm-up tootles from the orchestra pit greeted me. Brona, the regal Russian who took care of my show wardrobe and helped me dress, was already preparing for the day's matinee, her elegant fingers busily picking lint from the blue wool skirt of my first act costume.

"Gosh, Brona, sorry I'm late!" I plunked down at the dressing table mirror to dab on stage makeup.

"Too bad you have to cover those rosy cheeks with that goo," Brona said.

"Mom's Welsh/Irish complexion. I got lucky with genes."

"Yes, my dear. And with her auburn hair, too. But those soulful brown eyes are your father's. If I didn't know better, I'd swear he was Russian." I'd never thought of my eyes as "soulful." They squinted up and disappeared when I laughed.

Brona sighed. "It's a good thing you have me to get you onstage on time." A former ballerina, Brona was imperious. "I hope you're late because you're working on that book. If John Steinbeck had told *me* to write a book, I'd have done it long ago."

"Ah, yes, Brona." This was an old conversation. Five years earlier I'd met the icon of American literature, John Steinbeck, when I was in Rodgers and Hammerstein's *Pipe Dream,* a musical based on Steinbeck's novels, *Cannery Row* and *Sweet Thursday.*

"He *mes-mer-ized* you," Brona drew the word out like a midnight cat's wail.

"Cut it out, Brona. I'm sorry I ever told you I had a crush on John Steinbeck. I can't resist those older, dark, foreboding types."

2

The finale of Fiorello! Tom Bosley was Fiorello LaGuardia. I was his long-suffering secretary but I got him in the end.

Brona batted her eyes. "You fantasized enticing him to run away with you, to some remote desert island, where you'd spend a lifetime listening to him spinning stories! Too bad you're not much of a seductress."

"Now you've gone too far, Brona! You're dealing with the star of a hit Broadway show here. Have a little respect."

We laughed. We both knew it was not I, but my show business genealogy that intrigued John Steinbeck: my grandparents' showboat life in the early 1900s, my father's birth on the showboat, my mother's career as a monologist on the old Redpath Chautauqua circuit.

"Your family is pure Americana, Patrish. Fun stuff. Promise me you'll write about it," John Steinbeck had said.

"Oh, Mr. Steinbeck, I promise." I blushed at his attention.

"It's a helluva story, Pat. It's the story that counts. Trust me!"

After that day's *Fiorello!* matinee, I mulled over both Brona's and Steinbeck's words as I crossed 44th Street to Sardi's Restaurant. Medium-rare prime rib was also on my mind, and I missed seeing an icy patch on the December sidewalk. Down I went. A strong arm attached to a mellifluous voice brought me to my feet.

"Oops, Miss Wilson," said Richard Burton. Musn't get hurt. You're a *splendid* actress." Then he strode on his way, hands protected from the cold in the pockets of a well-worn tweed jacket.

"Thank you!" I shouted through the falling snow. "So are you! *Actor*, I mean!"

Richard Burton smiled and winked in a glance back over his tweed shoulder. John Steinbeck was gone from my thoughts.

Fiorello! had opened just a year earlier, on November 23rd, 1959. From the moment the curtain came down on that magical premiere night, the Broadhurst backstage swarmed with well-wishers, signaling that we were a major hit. Tom Bosley, a then-unknown actor, had given a tour-de-force performance in the title role of Fiorello LaGuardia. Hal Prince, our young prince of producers, caught me in a bear hug, exclaiming, "Pat, you saved your best performance of 'Marie' for opening night!" Actress Peggy Cass and her husband, Carl Fisher, who was our *Fiorello!* company manager, chimed in, "Patty, did you hear the applause explode when you took your curtain call?" I remembered very little about the performance itself, only whispering the opening night prayer my mother had taught me to say when I was three: "Lord, let Your light shine through me!"

Brona stood in the wings, smiling and beckoning like a bossy older sister. "Pat, hurry! It's time for you to dress for the opening night party."

She helped me into the gown I'd wear, a Balenciaga, black-flocked silk taffeta with a scoop neckline, cinched waist and short train, bought at the designer's discount outlet in Canada two years earlier. "That dress makes you look as if you stepped out of a Goya painting, Pat," said my dresser/friend. Rr—ip! The zipper on the Balenciaga gown chose that moment to give out.

"I don't have a back-up dress!" I wailed.

"Stop whining. I'm sewing you in." Several needle jabs and fifteen minutes later, I made my opening night star-entrance into legendary Sardi's Restaurant.

"What a shame you have no one special in your life to share this night with," Brona had said. Her comment was an unintentional wound, but it hurt far more than those inflicted with her wayward needle. My escorts on this important night were my professional manager, and an attorney friend who happened to look good in a tuxedo. And my mother and father, who had flown in from Cincinnati that day.

"I could have gotten someone *wonderful* to accompany you!" Brona said.

"Oh, you mean like some swell, muscle-y fella from the Bolshoi, Brona?" I shot back, immediately wanting to swallow the bitter words. I took her hands in mine. "Thanks, my dear, dear friend. But I *wanted* my parents here. This night belongs to them as much as to me." *And my grandparents, those scandalous showboat folk,* I thought. *To all three generations of us.* I swept unescorted into Sardi's that night in my stitched-on Balenciaga, head high. I sat at my parents' table.

"You blew it." my father hissed. "You should have arrived fifteen minutes earlier." Poppa, ever the showman, always the critic. He and Momma had sat laughing, applauding, and weeping, in two of the best house seats for the performance.

"Fourth row center, Pat? The Wilsons have come a long way!" my father said. They touched my heart when I saw them dressed for

I was sewn into my Balenciaga gown for the opening night party, but Vincent Sardi didn't seem to notice.

the occasion. Momma, ever beautiful, wore a lapis-blue velvet gown with white beading around the neckline, her skin glowing, her graying auburn hair a frame of soft curls. Poppa, still dapper and handsome, was geared in a spiffy new tuxedo, carrying himself like the proud military man he'd once been.

"He gave that poor tailor back home *hell* to get his tux just right," Momma said. I could well believe it.

Producer Hal Prince invited my family to the private opening night celebration in Sardi's upstairs dining room. *Kind, Hal!* I thought, grateful. There the opening night reviews were read aloud as they arrived hot off the presses, the cast raising champagne glasses for each accolade.

"Exciting!" wrote Brooks Atkinson of the New York Times. "*A great big YES for the LaGuardia musical!*" said McLain of the Journal American. "*Fiorello! hits with one hammer whack after another!*" declared Frank Aston of The World Telegram. *"A beaut! Director George Abbott is younger than springtime!"* raved Walter Kerr in The Herald Tribune. And Walter Kerr wrote about my character of Marie: *"Miss Wilson, who has the mistiest eyes I've seen in many a month, is creating a fond, forlorn game little chick with a spine of her own, and when she comes to sing I'll Marry The Very Next Man she has ten-tenths of a characterization going for her."*

As the reviews were read, I watched the shining faces of my parents. Pop had tears in his eyes. He brushed them aside with a show business joke I'd heard repeated in my family for all the years I could remember:

"There wasn't a dry seat in the house tonight, Patty...not a dry seat!"

Mr. Abbott, an actor's best friend.

Our legendary director, George Abbott, held court at a corner table with his date for the evening, movie star Claudette Colbert. Tall, handsome, silver-haired George Abbott was imposing in his tuxedo. *If God chooses to walk the earth in human form*, I said to myself, *He'll undoubtedly choose George Abbott's.*

Miss Colbert was ravishing in a full-length chocolate brown chiffon gown. We dressed up in those days. Mr. Abbott's and my relationship during rehearsals had been stressful, but the grievances

6

and disappointments of a long rehearsal and out-of-town tryout period now melted away. It was Thanksgiving week, a time for gratitude.

"Mr. Abbott?" I excused myself. "I just wanted to say thank you."

His face lit. "You were good tonight, Pat. How does it feel to be one of Broadway's newest stars?" He introduced me to Claudette Colbert, who offered her slim hand and familiar, dazzling smile.

"Miss Colbert, I'm such a fan!"

"And I of you, Miss Wilson."

An amazing night.

Journal: November 24, 1959: Slept late this AM—woke Mom and Pop up in their room at The Wyndham Hotel. We met at The Carnegie Deli for breakfast. Waffles with maple syrup...forget the diet! Yummy! If Fiorello! had flopped last night, would they have tasted so good?

My dressing room in the Broadhurst was filled with flowers and telegrams. There hadn't been time to go through them the night before, and Mom and I headed to the theater after breakfast to read and catalogue the messages. I wanted to acknowledge them all. My mother's excitement lingered. "Patty, look who this telegram is from! My goodness! " She read it aloud: *"Dear Pat: You are where you belong and wonderful. Congratulations. Dick Rodgers and Oscar Hammerstein."*

Momma read on, riffling through messages and cards accompanying floral bouquets. My dressing room was delicious with fragrance. Telegrams were from Ohio pals and childhood buddies, from John Steinbeck, composer Jule Styne, and my friend Carol Burnett. There was a special note from Journal American columnist Liz Smith, whom I'd met when I was playing my supper club act at New York's posh St. Regis Maisonette a year earlier.

Dear Patty: I just want to tell you what a great thrill it was last night to see you onstage, and to say how much I loved your performance...you have guts and character and a sense of humor. And of course everyone knew you had the talent! I loved Fiorello! and I loved you. Warmest congratulations, Liz Smith. I watched my mother in the dressing table mirror, her still-young complexion rosy with pleasure and pride. I leaned across the makeup jars and kissed her soft cheek. She took my hand. "This is a dream come true for all of us, Patty! But you should have someone special—besides Pop and me, I mean—to share this time with!"

"I know, Momma." I'd tried not to think about it.

My parents stayed over for Thanksgiving Day. I took them to Stouffer's on 57th Street for an old-fashioned turkey dinner with all the fixin's, Ohio-style. We'd been celebrating in Gotham glamour all week, in Gallagher's Steak House, and Downey's, and Sardi's. Mom and Pop glowed with the reception given to us everywhere we went. A new hit show benefited all of the Broadway community. But Pop picked up every check. The simplicity of Stouffer's family-style restaurant felt right for our holiday dinner, and I didn't feel guilty about my father's pride as he emptied his wallet. When I returned home from seeing them off at the airport the next day, I found a note Pop had left for me at the front desk of my apartment building.

My dear Pat: 'With many a growl of tooth and jowl, we talked the marvel o'er.'

(Pop loved quotes.) *And it has been a marvel. Your grandparents must be smiling along with your mother and me. That you have given us such a thrill has been better than seeing you come home with all As on your report card. This is my bread-and-butter letter, thanking you for allowing me to pick up the tabs, walk your dog, share a beer, and sit in the audience watching you become famous. Thank you for bringing home all As. Thank you for being my daughter. Love, Pop.*

Pop. In his good moments, my father was the best. But Ross Howard Wilson was a complicated man, the product of an unstable childhood as the youngest member of a family of actors known as *The Touring Wilsons.* His tyrannical parenting, though designed to protect my brothers and me from the fearsome instability he'd experienced in his early years, was a source of melodrama and dysfunction for us all. I'd worked hard to understand him. After many years I forgave him. And loved him.

Wrapped in my timeworn, comfy chenille robe, Pop's note still in my hand, I lay down on the sofa in my West 58th Street apartment. Charlie, the Yorkshire terrier, scrambled up and snuggled in close. I scruffled his neck.

"Hey, little buddy! Know what happened this week?" The small dog opened one brown eye and yawned. "I opened on Broadway, that's what! In a big hit show called *Fiorello!*" Charlie was already deep into dog-snoring. I sighed. "Swell audience," I said, closing my eyes. The heavy sleep of a pre-show nap displaced my thoughts, and dreams carried me to a different place, to a place of earliest memory, to my Ohio childhood.

scene ii: December 1932, A small farm outside of Columbus, Ohio

"Hurry on in before you freeze, Patty!" Grandad Ben called out behind me. The snowdrifts on either side of the pathway leading to my grandparents' kitchen door were above my head. I slipped and

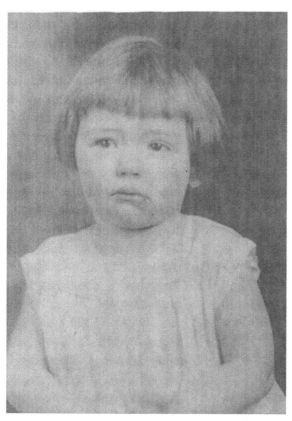

No, Mr. DeMille, I'm not ready for my close-up.

slid on the icy path, struggling to stay on three-year-old-barely-past-toddler feet. Step—slip—shiver—step. The kitchen door seemed far away, like a long walk through a narrow igloo.

"Grandad, could you carry me?"

"You'll be okay, honey," Grandad Ben said. "Your father needs help here." He slipped his beefy hand under Poppa's elbow. "Hang on, Ross, I won't let you fall again!"

Poppa had broken his leg the

9

week before. He'd lost his mobility and everything else that year, 1932: first his job and our nice home on Walhalla Road in Columbus, then another job and our not-so-nice home in Huntington, West Virginia. He'd left his life as an actor to work in marketing and sales, but during the Great Depression, when people had no money to buy things, salesmen weren't needed to sell, nor marketers to market. Like his leg, Poppa's proud spirit was broken, for on this day, we were all moving in with Momma's parents. It was survival time. The gloom of the Depression hung as heavy over our family as the weather itself.

At the head of the treacherous ice-path stood a short, plump, cheerful pink-cheeked woman, dauntless against financial tribulation and cold alike in a wooly cardigan sweater over her flowered apron. This was my maternal grandmother, Grandma Daisy to us all. She grabbed my outreached hand and swept me into cozy, comforting arms.

My drawers drooped, but the pups didn't care.

"Welcome, Patty-girl! I have hot cocoa inside for you." My mother and older brother David were already toasting next to the big, iron coal stove in the kitchen, along with newborn puppies snuggled close to their mother in a wooden crate. Coffee steamed in a pot for the grown-ups, and the oven's apple pies suffused the air with cinnamon deliciousness.

In two of the four bedrooms upstairs were built-in beds where David and I would sleep, covered with down mattresses to sink deep into, topped with our grandmother's handmade quilts. And in what would be our living room for the indefinite future—a big room, about thirty-by-forty feet—burgundy-red wool carpet covered the plank floors, and soft, down-cushioned sofas in glowing gold-and-orange tapestries faced each other across a circular furnace grate. My grandmother was an artist, and her color choices had no problem announcing the fact. Her hand-painted china pieces were housed in curios and niches around the room, and her paintings and tapestries hung beside ornate Tiffany sconces on the walls. The Depression made life everywhere seem drab, but Grandma Daisy made certain we were colorful.

"Look what's here, Patty," Momma called from the living room. She sat down at her scarred, old, upright piano, and patted the bench beside her. "We'll still have our music!" The big furnace grate in the center of the room poured forth welcoming heat. "And we'll be warm." That wasn't always the case in our ramshackle Huntington bungalow. Momma often had to rub her fingers to warm them before striking the keys. "The piano will stay in tune. Aren't we lucky?" My mother and I sang together every day to her rollicking ragtime accompaniment. My father scowled for reasons I didn't understand then, but Poppa often scowled. His disapproval didn't matter. If Momma wanted me to sing, I'd warble like Grandma Daisy's pet canary, Enrico. Somehow I knew my mother was planning my future with our songs. "Sing, Patty, sing. God's given you a voice. Ask His light to shine through you, and sing, no matter what!"

We weren't a religious family, in the church-going sense, but I understood about God. One day earlier that autumn, before Grandad Ben drove his old farm truck over to West Virginia to move us all back to Columbus, I rode my tricycle on the crumbling sidewalk outside of our dingy, Huntington bungalow. At the far end of our street was a kaleidoscope of color, a towering hill, orange and scarlet and gold in the fall; black-and-icy white in winter; shades of sweet green in spring and summer.. On the hill that day, through a blue-gray mist, appeared a gentle, smiling face. I smiled back. We continued smiling at each other, the Hill-Face and I, before it morphed into amber light, washing over somber tree-skeletons on the mountainside. I decided the Hill-Face was God. I wasn't frightened. I kept riding my tricycle. I'd tell my older brother David about it, as soon as he came home from school.

"Oh, yes, it was God," David said.

My brother and I sat on the sidewalk, our skinny behinds numb on the cold cement.

"That's where He lives, God—" David said, his eyes on the Hill.

"Is it Heaven, then, Davey?"

"Oh, no, it's just His hotel. It's where He stays when He's in Huntington."

David, almost seven, was my authority on everything. Three-and-a-half years earlier, after our mother told him a baby would soon join the family, "in the spring, Davey, when the flowers grow," she'd found him digging in the snow.

"I'm looking for the flowers, Momma," David said. "So Baby Sister can come." He knew I'd be a sister, and that he'd look out for me. His certitude that the Hill-Face was God was all the assurance I needed that the Heavenly Father was visiting the Wilson children in West Virginia.

Now Momma and God and I sat at the only piece of her furniture that had been loaded onto Grandad Ben's truck for the Huntington-to-Columbus move. Her piano. We sang songs from her days as an entertainer, and looked out from the piano over the sweeping acre of grass that fronted the farm. The birds in the lilac bushes sang with us, as the blossoms sweetened our spring days. We sang as we gathered berries—blackberries, loganberries, blueberries, raspberries—to eat for summer breakfasts, or to be simmered into rich jams for wintertime toast. We sang with the breezes that gently moved the blades of the windmill at the side of the house, delivering cool mineral water from the depths of its well. We sang sitting in dirt furrows of the garden together, eating tomatoes, peas and snap beans picked fresh from their vines, hot from the sun. The blue Ohio skies wrapped our voices in white cloud-puffs and carried our songs far away, to the land of my mother's dreams.

My grandparents had bought the little farm just before we all moved in, several acres bordering Oakland Park Avenue on the northern outskirts of Columbus, for $7,000. Before my father lost everything, Grandma Daisy and Grandad Ben had lived in a stylish house on East North Broadway, in the north end of Columbus.

"I hope you won't miss that fine house too much, Daisy," Grandad said.

"Hell's katootie! That's all yesterday's mashed potatoes, Ben," she answered. "Now we have to take care of this family!" She wasn't

Grandma Daisy and Grandad Ben were survival for us all.

about to let any of us starve. We'd all move onto the farm together, under her wing. We'd raise vegetables in the fields, and fruit in the orchard, and chickens in the coops. We'd milk Jess, the cow bought from the neighboring Simpson family.

And Momma would teach me to sing.

It was a few days before Christmas, 1932, when we Wilsons moved to my grandparents' farm. The only toy left for me under the tree that Depression year was a wooden doll bed, hand-made by Grandad Ben, and painted in the same soft lavender paint as Grandma Daisy's art deco bathroom. I was only three, but I knew, on that Christmas morning, that there wasn't a Santa Claus. I decided it best not to tell the grown-ups.

scene iii: May 1953, Twenty-one years later, New York City

"Pat! Wake up!" I startled into consciousness, sitting upright in the passenger seat of the new Chevrolet.

"I'm sorry, honey," my young husband said. "I couldn't let you miss this view!" Rick's face was one big grin.

Our Chevrolet coiled down the New Jersey hill that borders the Hudson River, heading towards the Lincoln Tunnel and New York

City. Manhattan's skyline sparkled across the water, lights winking throughout the night-time panorama, the river catching their glimmers and tossing the reflections back into the automobile.

"Oh, Rick, it's beautiful— so *alive!*"

Snuggling close to him, I studied his classic, clean profile. High forehead under thick, baby-fine brown hair, long eyelashes shading soft hazel eyes, straight nose over a sensitive mouth and even, white teeth. I watched his slender hands on the steering wheel, and reached to touch them.

"I fell in love with those talented hands," I said. Rick smiled. He was a pianist and conductor. We'd met at Ohio State University almost six years earlier, in the fall of 1947. Rick was an upperclassman conducting a student musical show called *Strollaganza*, and I was a terrified freshman auditioning for him. For me, it was awe at first sight, with love fast on its heels. Rick, five years older, a serviceman returned from the Pacific, was slower to display his feelings.

The Chevrolet eased to stop at a toll booth, and I kissed Rick's ear. The rotund man in the booth stared at us.

"It's okay," Rick said. "She's my wife. We're on our honeymoon."

The fat man smiled. "Greatest town in the world for a honeymoon!"

"Couldn't agree more," Rick said, and we maneuvered into the tunnel under the Hudson River. I giggled.

"Liar, you neglected to mention our honeymoon has been a little delayed. We've been married for two years."

"So what. We're in New York for the first time together, and that makes it a honeymoon, doesn't it? I'm just mad that Jonathan beat us here."

Jonathan Winters. Our friend and co-worker from WBNS-TV, the CBS outlet for Central Ohio in Columbus. Jonathan Winters was an announcer and show host at the station, Rick a director/producer. I was the staff singer, and the spokeslady for the Ohio Fuel Gas Company on a nightly newscast. Johnny Winters had left Columbus for New York a month earlier to try his talent as a comedian in New York. He'd honed characters like "Maude Frickert" on personal appearances we'd performed together in and around Columbus. During one, the annual Circleville, Ohio Pumpkin Show, Jonathan stood in the wings, scoping the audience for new characters, while I sang *Won't You Come Home, Bill Bailey?* onstage with Louis Armstrong. Mr. Armstrong was the star of the show, and he couldn't believe a white girl from Ohio knew that song. I told him Momma had taught it to me. His rich, raspy guffaw continued unabated for a full minute.

Jonathan Winters (back row, C) and I (C, in dark V-neck dress) helped WBNS-TV celebrate a birthday before we both left for New York.

"I'll bet it's pretty quiet around WBNS-TV without the three of us there," Rick laughed.

He revved the Chevy up the slight incline, out of the tunnel into Manhattan, and headed north on Eighth Avenue. I glanced at the dashboard clock. 11:10 PM. Broadway shows were just letting out, and the street teemed with theater-goers. At Forty-fourth and Eighth, we passed the marquees of the St. James and Majestic theaters bright with lights. *The King and I,* starring Gertrude Lawrence and Yul Brynner, was at the St. James, and *South Pacific* held forth after four years, at the Majestic. I was spellbound. Two Rodgers and Hammerstein hits, playing across the street from each other! Under the excitement bubbling inside me lurked a deeper feeling, a "knowin'," as Grandma Daisy called such feelings. I'd had knowin's all my life, and the knowin' this time, as we skirted the New York theater district, was *here is where I belong—here is where I belong.*

"We have to call Doraine and Ellis in the morning to let them know we arrived okay," Rick said. I nodded. Our friends Doraine and Ellis, a husband/wife singing team, lived on Long Island.

"Did I ever tell you Ellis says you belong in New York?" Rick asked.

"Nope, but I hope you told him Ed Sullivan said the same thing," I'd met Ed Sullivan in 1950, while I was still a university coed. The Ohio State football team was victorious in the Rose Bowl that year, and I sang at the celebration welcoming them home. Ed Sullivan, well-known for his popular CBS Sunday night variety show, *Toast of the Town,* was a guest at the gala.

"You have some voice, kid. So what are you doing in Columbus? You belong in the Big Apple," Sullivan had said. I later wrote to thank him for his comments. He wrote back to tell me he'd meant them.

Rick and I checked into our hotel and decided to take a walk. We wanted to savor the post-midnight vitality of the incomparable city. Meandering up Fifth Avenue, we passed Bonwit Teller and Tiffany's, ogling Bergdorf Goodman, the Plaza Hotel, and the patient carriage horses and nodding drivers waiting for tourists to hire them for a ride through Central Park. We strolled hand-in-hand until three in the morning.

"Would you ever want to live in New York, Rick?"

"Are you kidding? I've always dreamed about it."

Our hotel room telephone jangled us awake at nine the next morning.

"Well, thank the Lord you're here!" our friend Ellis said. "Why haven't you answered my calls? I've been trying to reach you since yesterday. Where in *hell* have you been?"

A stack of messages from the hotel operator sat unread on the dresser top.

"Ellis," Rick said, "we didn't get into our room until three this morning." Not a lie. "We were going to call you today."

"Well, what I have to tell you couldn't wait!" Rick held the phone away from his ear. I could hear Ellis's voice across the room.

"I have auditions set up for Pat all this week! Tomorrow at three she sings for the most prestigious little club in New York, The Blue Angel. Tuesday at eleven she'll sing at the Winter Garden Theater for the Rodgers and Hammerstein casting office. Wednesday afternoon at four she auditions for Arthur Godfrey's *Talent Scouts* at CBS. God, don't tell me she has a cold!"

"She's fine, Ellis," Rick said. "What did you do, apply for your agent's license?" He winked at me.

"I just got going," Ellis said, impatient. "I called everybody I could think of. I told them Pat is a special talent, and in New York for just a few days. I said they'd better see her or miss out. I didn't know I was such a good salesman. I'll feel like a jackass if you kids don't follow through!"

Rick hung up. The hotel room was decorated with pale yellow-and-white striped wallpaper, and the stripes rippled before my eyes. My always-nervous stomach performed a flopover.

"Did you put Ellis up to this, Rick?"

"No, I sure didn't." He was solemn. "You're supposed to be on vacation. What do you want to do?"

I reached for Rick's hands. Years earlier, while we rehearsed for an Ohio State show, he'd taught me to breathe properly, to support my voice on the flow of breath. His hands pushed hard against my midsection.

"Breathe from *here*, Pat—your diaphragm!" he'd said. I'd nearly fainted from loving him so much.

My first New York professional picture, 1953. 100% sequins.

Now I laughed. "What do I want to do? Heck, I want to sing! And you'd better be ready to play for me!"

Within a week I'd opened at the chic East Fifty-sixth Street nightclub, The Blue Angel. The owners then moved me to their downtown club, The Village Vanguard, where I was held over for several weeks.

The producers of Arthur Godfrey's *Talent Scouts,* as hot on TV in 1953 as *American Idol* is today, auditioned me live at The Village Vanguard.

Journal, June 15, 1953: I'm on Arthur Godfrey's Talent Scouts tonight! Johnny Winters was on last week. Good things are happening for all of us Ohio kids!

The *Talent Scouts* audience voted me winner of the competition that night. I was booked to appear on Arthur Godfrey's CBS radio show, with singer Julius LaRosa and the McGuire Sisters.

Rick and I went to Lindy's Restaurant after the *Talent Scouts* performance to celebrate with corned beef sandwiches. John Wayne, sans toupee, wearing his wispy hair in a comb-over, was on his way out through the revolving door as we were on our way in. He was a hero of mine, a girl-time crush. I gawked at him, and he smiled at me. *A good omen,* my knowin' told me.

A young girl approached our table. "Excuse me, Miss Wilson, could you sign this for me?" She handed me a pen and a Lindy's napkin. "My parents and I are from Iowa. We were in the *Talent Scouts* audience tonight." She pointed to a couple beaming at us from a nearby table. "They discovered a real star tonight, as far as we're concerned!"

Rick and I were learning what Andy Warhol's "fifteen minutes of fame" could do to one's heart and psyche. Within a week, we'd found an apartment in the Riverdale section of New York. We asked for an extended leave of absence from our WBNS-TV jobs in Columbus. My mother supervised the packing of our belongings there (including Rick's eight-foot, Steinway concert grand piano) and had them shipped to us in our new Riverdale home. Our blue Chevrolet had brought us to a new life, and to what would be called in theatrical history books "The Golden Age Of Broadway."

We didn't return to Ohio.

scene iv: Later that summer, 1953, Enter Bob Fosse

"Rick, is it me, or is it hotter here than in Columbus?" It was sizzling in our Riverdale apartment.

"Calm down, honey, you won't stay cool by getting all riled up. You're like a racehorse at the starting gate." Rick was right. We sweltered, I stewed.

Journal, July 28, 1953: Bought two fans this AM. Sat in front of one all day. Guess I have to get used to being "between jobs." Ellis is on tour with Doraine again. Ellis can't decide if he's a manager or not—and I need one!

Journal, August 2, 1953: Restless, restless. Hot, hot. An agent called. Brad somebody. How did he find me? The Vanguard? He handles theater people. Wants me to audition for an industrial show. Is that good? Rick says call Ellis.

Journal, August 6, 1953: Ellis says sure, why not? Industrial shows are a big deal. I sing for them at the Majestic Theater tomorrow. Now that is a big deal! I'll be singing from Mary Martin's very own stage!

"Just what is an industrial show?" I asked Brad the agent.

"Manna from heaven for theater people," he said. "Big corporations spend millions of dollars presenting shows to their clients and staff all across the country. They're Broadway-happy. They parody or even plagiarize current musicals. The Oldsmobile show, the one you'll audition for tomorrow, is patterned after *South Pacific.*"

"Doesn't sound ethical to me."

"The songs and libretto are different. It's the *theme* they copy. Your show has a bunch of macho sailors and pretty Navy nurses. And even though you're auditioning for the lead, don't kid yourself! The new line of Oldsmobiles will be the stars. The whole purpose of the show is to introduce the 1954 models across the country. The productions are tax deductions for corporations, and bonanzas for theater people. Money is no object—they pay top dollar for the best writers, directors, choreographers. Everybody wants to do 'em!"

Skeptical as I was, being cast in the 1954 Oldsmobile Show, *The Mighty O!* was a dress rehearsal for New York theater, for Broadway during its "Golden Age." It's hard to say exactly when that golden age began or ended, but in 1953 it was in full swing. I asked my new friend and cast mate, Jetta MacDonald, how close the Oldsmobile show was to the real thing. Jet had done several Broadway shows, both in New York and on tour.

"Pat, it's *exactly* the same," she declared, "only we're singing about wonderful Oldsmobiles instead of wonderful guys!"

It was mid-September when *The Mighty O!* left New York's Grand Central Station for Chicago, where we were to rehearse and perform our initial presentation. We traveled by train, each of us in a private roomette. Rick came to see me off, and as we hugged on the train platform, I noticed another couple lingering over their goodbye. I recognized the young woman from the MGM musical, *Good News.* She was dancer Joan McCracken, the original "fall-down" girl in Rodgers and Hammerstein's *Oklahoma.* The young man was small and compactly built, apparently a dancer as well, with blond, thinning hair. When I located my roomette on the train, he was opening the door next to mine. He had a cigarette, which seemed a permanent fixture, dangling from his mouth.

"Hi," he said around the cigarette, which bobbled up and down as he spoke. "I guess we're neighbors." He thrust out his hand. "I'm Bob Fosse."

Later, in the dining car, my new neighbor plunked himself down across the table from me. "I'm sorry, is this okay?" I wondered why he was so self-effacing. Wasn't I the one who felt awkward and out-of-place?

"So who are you in this thing?" he asked.

"Well, getting the job happened so fast I'm not sure of my character's name. But I was hired to sing a song called *A Mechanical Minded Gal.*"

Bob whistled. "Hey! That's the big specialty in the second act. You must sing pretty well." I blushed, and he continued. "I'm a dancer. Nobody can hear my voice past the orchestra pit." He added, in what again seemed like an apologetic tone, "I think we play opposite each other." He was right. Our roles were a sailor and a Navy nurse who fall in love. Bob could dance, I could sing. Counter-balance. That was creative casting in those days.

Bob Fosse carried a script under his arm throughout our tour. "It's a new musical George Abbott is producing with Bobby Griffith and Hal Prince, and co-directing with Jerome Robbins," he explained. I tried not to let my jaw fall open. George Abbott, Broadway's legendary hit-maker, and Jerome Robbins, master choreographer! Bob smiled. "I'm gonna do the choreography. 'Course, if I goof, Robbins is there to fix it!"

"What's it called, Bob?"

"It's from a book, *Seven-and-a-Half Cents*, but they're thinking about a new title." He explained the show would go into rehearsal early in 1954, at the conclusion of our Oldsmobile tour, then open late that spring. Bob was plotting parts of the innovative choreography for the new show between rehearsals of scenes for *The Mighty O!* He became famous overnight when *Seven and A Half Cents* hit Broadway that spring as *The Pajama Game.* Fresh, amusing musical numbers like *Steam Heat* and *Hernando's Hideaway* catapulted my Oldsmobile leading man into theatrical history.

"Do I honestly have to dance with you, Bob? Can't we talk Max out of it?" Max Hodge (who later wrote and directed TV's classic *Batman* series) was our writer/director.

"Aw, c'mon, Patty! It's like I'm dancin' with Cyd Charisse! Besides, you dance with your *face!* Nobody's lookin' at your feet!"

"Don't make me laugh, please, not on top of these spins!" Bob Fosse was wiry, amazingly strong as he whirled me around. "Remember I have a weak bladder, too." We laughed a lot. But for all our jokes, there was an underlying sadness in Bob Fosse, a melancholy strange in such a young man.

At one point our dance was staged to get me out of Bob's way. I perched on a prop, an overturned rowboat, and gazed at him adoringly while he performed fancy footwork around me. I didn't know it at the time, but his style was to be reflected soon in an explosive career. Later, towards the end of our romantic waltz, Bob lifted me off my rowboat/perch, and we dropped to our knees, grasping each other's hands and swaying backwards in an acrobatic backbend, our heads finally touching the floor. Very sexy. I was young and flexible, so my bones could take it, but Bobby's knees were another story. He'd damaged them doing dramatic knee-slides from the time he began his professional dancing career in Chicago at the age of thirteen. I watch him periodically in films like *Kiss Me Kate,* and marvel that he managed those knee-slides with a smile on his face. In every performance of *The Mighty O!,* when we dropped to our knees to begin that section of our dance, Bob would mutter "ouch" under his breath. *Hot stuff,* I thought.

Most theatrical love scenes are illusion. Almost always they're uncomfortable for one reason or another. Bob wore knee pads, but they were of little help. Ever self-effacing, he said, "Well, you know what they say: when you can't dance any more, choreograph! And if you can't choreograph, teach!"

We filled the long train jumps from one city to another with games and banter and food. That was the beauty of traveling with a company. You made friends. You didn't have to be alone unless you wanted to be. I thought of my father's family, *The Touring Wilsons,* and my mother in her glory days in Chautauqua, a generation before me. I knew from the stories they told of their theatrical lives that they did their traveling by train, just as we of *The Mighty O!* did. According to their journals, the camaraderie of their companies was similar to ours. My father, age seventeen, journaled in 1913: "Long, boring hop from Chicago to Salt Lake. Ma says I'll burn in Hell for playing cards most of the trip…"

Arriving in a city, we'd go to our hotel to unpack and rest while the crew set up the show scenery. *The Mighty O!* was performed in the late afternoons, so our audiences could be wined, dined, and further entertained later by a big nightclub-style variety show. My ability to double as an actress/singer in the musical comedy, and then perform in the variety show presented at the dinners, was one of the reasons I was hired. I was glad to have the opportunity to be myself, entertaining with my own songs and arrangements at the dinners. There was no getting around the fact that we competed with Oldsmobiles as stars of the musical comedy. Bob and I wrapped up our love story in the finale with an embrace, but then turned to salute the 1954 Oldsmobile as it was driven onstage to wild applause. A happy ending for all.

Bob thought I was being exploited, doubling as I was in the dinner shows. "They'd better be paying you plenty for knocking yourself out," he growled through the ever-present cigarette. His protectiveness made me smile. It reminded me of my older brother David.

While we were playing New Orleans, Bob mentioned that he wanted to see stripper Lili St. Cyr at a club on Bourbon Street. I asked if I could tag along.

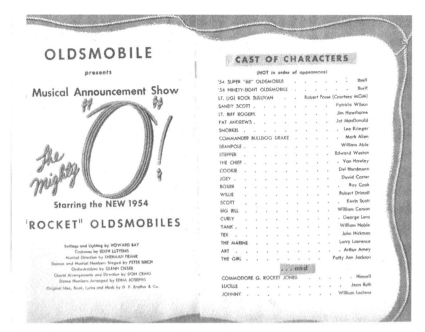

Bob Fosse danced, I sang. We were both second fiddle to the cars.

"We—ll…" He said he'd think about it. As it turned out, several of the cast members went as a group, so the decision was taken out of his hands. Even then, Bob took pains to explain to me how Miss St. Cyr's moves were balletic, even poetic.

"Yeah, right, Bobby. I'm from Ohio, but I'm a married woman," I said. "I get it!"

Fred, the handsome young stagehand/carpenter who toured with us to supervise the crew, made no secret of the fact that he was attracted to me, though he knew I was married. He pressed his case in a very straightforward manner. Bob snarled at him. "Knock it off, Fred. She's not like the rest of us."

During one of the rehearsals, a dancer said to Bob, "How come you never invite her to one of our parties?" He nodded toward me.

"My God, no! She's so sweet," Bobby said. Later, as he evolved into the most important choreographer/director of our generation (and of generations to follow), several of my friends, both well-known and not-so, had erotic encounters with him. He—and they—freely acknowledged them. His autobiographical film, *All That Jazz,* more than merely alludes to his proclivities. They infuse all of his work, affecting the raw, erotic brilliance of musicals like *Cabaret* and *Chicago*, and undoubtedly contributed greatly to the sexy romp of Gwen Verdon's performance as "Lola" in *Damn Yankees.*

But no, I was never invited to one of Bob's alleged revels. To me, Bob Fosse was a friend, my first leading man in New York, one who happened to become more and more famous as his innovative imagination fired the souls of audiences.

Our paths crossed many times in the years after the Oldsmobile tour, after he became famous, before his tragic death from a heart attack on a Washington sidewalk in 1987. One hot September day in 1964, I was waiting for the light to change at the corner of 75th and Broadway. I wasn't moving fast. It was a sticky-humid Manhattan day, and I was eight months pregnant with my first child.

"Hey, lady, dancin' much these days?" said the soft voice behind me. There was the familiar smile, the familiar bobbling cigarette.

"You're a beautiful sight, Patty!" So said my friend, Bob Fosse, as he tenderly patted my protruding belly.

scene v: Early 1954, Los Angeles and New York

Journal, January 29, 1954: Today's the last day of the Oldsmobile tour. It's sad to see our tour ending. I've made friends. But I've also missed Rick terribly.

We performed *The Mighty O!* at the Shrine Auditorium in Los Angeles, where we lived in the Ambassador Hotel, which also housed the famed Coconut Grove nightclub. As a kid movie-fan in Ohio, I'd read *Photoplay* and *Modern Screen* magazines until the pages wore thin. The Coconut Grove was pictured as the hangout of my favorite film stars: Clark Gable and Carole Lombard, Humphrey Bogart, Judy Garland. Our dinner shows following *The Mighty O!* were performed in The Coconut Grove. There, Bing Crosby had sung, years earlier, on the very stage on which I was performing every night. I was exhilarated to be singing on that stage. No teasing from my cast mates, Bob Fosse or anyone else, could diminish the thrill for me.

Jet MacDonald and I flew back to New York from Los Angeles together. The rest of the cast scattered, some staying on in Hollywood, others departing to visit friends and family after our long tour. On our coast-to-coast plane trip, I confided to Jet that I was worried about professional management.

"I don't really have anyone, Jet. My friend Ellis got me started in New York, and wants to be a manager, but he's always on the road, working. If this Oldsmobile tour hadn't come up for me in a fluke-y kind of way, I'd still be sitting in New York worrying about the rent." I told her that Ellis and Doraine had signed on for yet another long tour, this time through college campuses. Ellis wanted to book me into colleges, too. "You and Rick can travel together. You can *concertize!*" Ellis said with his usual enthusiasm.

"That's ridiculous," Jet said. "How does Rick feel about leaving New York to play colleges?"

"He's against it, for now at least." Rick had earlier flown to New Orleans to join me for a week. "We both think we should stay in New York for a while. But college concerts seem to be all Ellis has to offer."

Jet shook her head. "It sounds like Ellis is a great friend, but you need someone with clout who can help you in New York. *Theater* people—producers, directors— have to hear you, and I don't think Ellis can open those doors for you." She paused before she mentioned the name of someone who would become a major part of my life.

"Gus Schirmer. You need Gus Schirmer," she said.

Gus, Jet explained, was the son and heir to the Schirmer music dynasty. His father, Gustave Schirmer, Senior, the company's founder, still ran the Manhattan store.

"Gus Junior is one of New York's top talent agents. He knows everyone in theater, from Ethel Merman to Rodgers and Hammerstein. And he's not intimidated by anyone!"

Jet was as frank about her career as she'd been about mine.

"Gus likes new people, discovering and molding talent. I'm with another agent."

Jet confirmed that after making a small inroad in New York, I needed to stay close by the big city, ready to pop into auditions as they came along. Even my husband and father agreed on this point, although Pop had not wanted me to marry Rick, and the tensions between them were always ready to surface.

Pop said, "A tour of colleges? You won't end up on Broadway, and that's where you belong. You don't need to go traipsing around the country. I'll pay your rent in New York for a few months."

Rick's ears turned red. "Thanks, Ross," he said, "I can do temporary office work, if my coaching and music aren't enough to support my wife. Practicing scales and playing concertos have made a helluva typist of me."

I called Gus Schirmer's office the next morning.

scene vi: Spring 1954, Enter Gus Schirmer

Gus Schirmer. Without question one of the most unique people in my lifetime of meeting unique people: blunt, sentimental, irascible, tasteful, generous to a fault, and masculine, but candidly gay in a time when "politically correct" was forty years in the future. He had a built-in radar for talent, and one of the biggest hearts I've encountered in show business. We remained friends for all of his life, he, the elite young man raised on Park Avenue and the Hamptons, I, the kid from Ohio. It made no difference. Our spirits were the same. We'd fight and not speak, then we'd collapse into giggles and tears, gathering each other into huge bear hugs. "Patty, I can be both brother and sister to you," Gus would say. And he was.

Our meeting was a long time coming, for Gus was elusive. It was weeks before he answered my almost-daily calls, and then only because new Broadway Golden Boy Bob Fosse recommended me to him.

On a warm May afternoon at the Nola Studios on 57th Street in New York, Gus listened to me sing Gershwin's *But Not For Me* from *Girl Crazy,* and the wistful *Ohio* from *Wonderful Town.* He had a half-smile on his face, and tears in his eyes. It was the first time I knew I'd met my match when it came to cry-babies.

"Can you sing a rhythm song?" he asked. I belted out *I Got Rhythm.*

"Where did you learn to sing like that?" Gus asked. I pointed to Rick. "My husband is a vocal coach," I said. Gus's face fell.

"Your *husband?* Oh, well. Good work." I was to learn Gus hated husbands, feeling they interfered with his management of clients. He scowled at Rick before turning to his assistant to ask a question. "Should she play Luciana, Forrest?"

Forrest Carter nodded. "Absolutely," he said.

Gus hired me that afternoon to play the ingenue lead, Luciana, in his revival of Rodgers and Hart's musical, *The Boys From Syracuse*. Rick and I spent our last dollar so I could join Actors' Equity that same day, for rehearsals began the next.

The Boys From Syracuse toured all that summer of 1954, playing theaters up and down the east coast: Boston, Ogunquit, Maine, Chautauqua, New York, Skowhegan, Maine, Barnesville, Pennsylvania —so many I've forgotten. During the tour I learned to love and respect Gus, though he often teased me about my recent arrival from Ohio and lack of New York sophistication.

"You jumped a foot when you heard someone say 'shit' during rehearsal."

"Maybe so, but I'll bet I'm the only one you know who grew up shoveling it."

Before our first performance, Gus appeared onstage to address the cast. He'd lamented that I was skinny and needed building up, particularly in the chest department. He asked the wardrobe mistress to install "falsies" in my costumes. "Well," Gus informed the assembled company, "I stopped by Patricia's dressing room and saw her new figure hanging on the rack—it's quite an improvement!." The company applauded, and I blushed and took an exaggerated bow.

Our *Boys From Syracuse* cast included Jack Weston, who was soon to become a movie star, and Pat Wilkes, who'd left her job as Rosalind Russell's understudy in *Wonderful Town* to play the comedy lead. That summer, in Barnesville, Pat gave me my first taste of beer. I never drank, not even in college. I wasn't a goody-two-shoes. It just didn't occur to me to drink. No one in my family did. I didn't smoke, either, though everyone else puffed away. I'd heard it could damage my voice.

"What, you don't drink? Not even a beer? Here, have a sip," Pat Wilkes said one night that summer. "It tastes great after a show." I felt like the hick of the world. And Pat was right, a cold beer did taste good on a hot night.

Pat was dead within five years. Of acute alcoholism.

Blonde and bosom-ed for my first Equity show. I'm fourth from L, Pat Wilkes is between Jack Weston and Al Checco.

By the time our tour ended in September, Rick had attracted several new voice students. He was happy and busy, and I could relax a little. Often I drove the blue Chevy into Manhattan to meet Jet McDonald. We'd window-shop the splendor of Madison Avenue together, feeling autumn breezing in, and stop for hot chocolate at Rumpelmeyer's.

"I'm treating," I said. "I can never thank you enough for telling me about Gus Schirmer!"

"I had a hunch you two would click. Someday you'll be able to do something for me." I nodded. Networking was a part of our lives. There was little backstabbing. We all pulled for one another. But auditions were few that fall, even with Gus as my new manager, and by Christmas of 1954, there was little for me to do in New York.

"I can book you into Schirmer's music store if you need holiday money," Gus joked. "My father asked if I know any pretty young actresses who want a job demonstrating musical toys at the store for Christmas."

"I might enjoy that, Gus. Rick is busy. I need something to occupy my time, and we can certainly use two incomes."

"Well, I'm authorized to officially offer you a job for the Christmas holiday at Schirmer's music store. I warn you, though, my father loves young women! Never let him catch you alone in the stock room!"

I took the job for the holidays. From Thanksgiving to the New Year I fended off Papa Schirmer's attempts at advances. He was short and round as Santa himself, and delighted in cornering me whenever he could. It was like playing hide-and-seek with a toddler, in one door of the stockroom, out the other. Today it would be called sexual harassment, but then I couldn't take offense. It was like a game to Papa Schirmer, and my knowin' told me nothing terrible could ever occur in such a beautiful setting. The store was a Dickensian Christmas card come to life. As snow fell outside its multi-paned windows, I reveled in holiday music and the fresh scent of lavish pine decorations. I loved watching customers arriving with snow on their coats, their faces lighting up when I showed them beautiful German dancing-ballerina music boxes and hand-carved Swiss cuckoo clocks.

"I warned you," Gus laughed when I told him Papa Schirmer had lived up to his reputation. "But someday I'll tell you how much my father likes and respects you." Years later he told me the rest of the story:

"Dad thought Rick was the wrong man for you, Patty. He offered me $50,000 to break up your marriage and have a child with you, to carry on the Schirmer name."

"Gus, you're kidding, right?"

"No, I'm not kidding. My father meant it. He always refused to accept the fact that I'm gay—his only child. I love you dearly, Pat, but there's only one way that scenario could have worked. Tell me, would you have been willing to wear a Cary Grant mask to bed?"

scene vii: Early 1955, Enter new opportunity, New York City

Journal, January 11, 1955: Rick and I have moved into Manhattan! Our new apartment is at 87th and Riverside Drive, next to the park.

"Folks, this big piano ain't gonna fit into that elevator," said our moving man. He seemed happy to make the pronouncement. Our new building superintendent joined us on the sidewalk. Rick's eight-foot concert grand blocked all foot traffic.

"You hoist it up the outside of the building, and in through the big front window," the super said. He looked annoyed with the moving man. "That's how it's done every day in Manhattan."

"That'll cost extra," said the moving man, squaring off.

"No, it won't. You took the job. Now get it done!" said the super, fighting our Big City battle. The piano hoist went without a hitch and we settled into our new home. It was practically empty, save for the piano, but we were ecstatic to be in our first Manhattan apartment.

Gus submitted me for two new shows.

"One is a revue, a revival of *Meet The People.* The original was a big hit."

"How long ago was that, Gus?"

"About ten years. But get this—the new version is opening in the old Diamond Horseshoe. That could be a lot of fun, and it'll generate interest. The place has been closed down since Billy Rose abandoned it and his wife, Fanny Brice, for the Aquacade and that swimmer Eleanor Holm!" Gus loved gossip.

"All I remember about the Diamond Horseshoe are Billy Rose's 'long-stemmed beauties' they wrote so much about."

"Yeah, those showgirls," Gus sighed. He loved the days of the *Ziegfeld Follies,* and *Earl Carroll's Vanities.* He was certain to break into a showgirl strut at parties, his big frame instantaneous grace and posture.

"The second show is *Damn Yankees,* the new musical being prepped by *The Pajama Game* team. Your buddy Bob Fosse is doing the choreography again."

"What's this new show about?"

"Baseball. Your role would be that of a fan, waiting outside the stadium. It's a small part with a big solo called *For An Autograph.* They want you to sing the song for them. They sent it over to the office. Can you pick it up?"

"I guess the sooner the better."

The auditions for the two shows fell on the same day. I sang *S'Wonderful* for the *Meet The People* producers at the Diamond

Horseshoe, then hurried to the St. James Theater on 44th Street, muttering the words to *For An Autograph* under my breath. It was a raw, bone-chilling day, and I'd worn my best audition outfit, a green-and-white gingham shirt and green cotton velveteen skirt, under my heavy winter coat. Good onstage, especially for a redhead, but not so good in the raw Manhattan cold. It was a brisk four blocks to the stage door of the St. James Theater.

Bob Fosse was standing inside when I tugged the stage door open. We hugged hello, and I congratulated him on his *Pajama Game* success. "And thank you for saying nice things to Gus Schirmer about me. He's my manager now."

"Good casting. Are you singing for them today?" He nodded towards the front of the house.

"Yep—any tips?"

"Just do your thing. I was on my way out, but I'll hang around until you sing, if that's okay." Bobby. After all the accolades, still self-effacing. He disappeared through the door that led to the theater seats, where director George Abbott and producers Robert Griffith and Harold Prince waited to hear the day's auditions.

For An Autograph was full of long, sustained notes, the wail of a young fan waiting for her hero. I sang to the balcony, as usual, from the St. James stage. There were whispers from the front. Suddenly Hal Prince, very young and very energetic, bounded onto the stage.

"We have a job for you, Pat. This scene in *Damn Yankees* may be cut. It may not even make it to rehearsal. The show is long. But we've lost two girls from *Pajama Game*. If you can rehearse and open in ten days, we'd like to put you in that show." Bob Fosse gave me a high sign from beyond the footlights.

Rae Allen was leaving the role of "Poopsie" in *The Pajama Game* to play the sarcastic lady reporter in *Damn Yankees*. Shirley MacLaine, Carol Haney's understudy in the comedy role of "Gladys," had already left for Hollywood. Shirley was a real dancer, so I knew I wouldn't be following in her footsteps. But I thought I'd be replacing singer Rae Allen in the minor speaking role of "Poopsie." During rehearsals, I learned about pecking order in the Broadway theater. Poopsie's lines were taken one by one and distributed to the ensemble girls who'd been with the show from the start—a line here, a line there, until there was no more Poopsie for me to play. I was left with ensemble singing. I look back now and see it as fair. I was a newcomer. The hard-working girls who'd been with the show from the start deserved the plums. I bit my tongue, but I was miserable. The mythology I believed was that an ensemble girl never became a leading lady, and that's what I was in a hurry to become. As ashamed as I am today of my childish ingratitude, then I felt betrayed. I wailed to Gus about my misgivings.

"It's not true that ensemble girls never become leads, Patty, particularly with these producers," Gus assured me. "They're loyal to their people. You've got a job on Broadway, in a big hit show. You're working, and work begets work. Don't make waves."

"I could go back to winding musical toys in Papa Schirmer's store," I sniveled.

A week later, Gus called. "I almost hate to tell you this, Pat. You've been offered a lead in *Meet The People*. If you decide to take it, you'll have to give your two-week notice to the *Pajama Game* office tonight."

"Tonight? But tonight is my first performance! I go into the show tonight!"

Gus sighed. "You think I don't know? The timing couldn't be worse. It's up to you. But remember, if you leave *Pajama Game* like this, you'll never work for George Abbott or producers Griffith and Prince again." I was guaranteed a long run in *The Pajama Game*, a steady paycheck. *Meet The People*, though a revival of a former hit, was an unknown quantity. But *Meet The People* would be reviewed by the New York critics, and I would be one of its leads. At seven-thirty that evening I hurried to the St. James to begin my run in *The Pajama Game*. And to give, simultaneously, a two-week notice.

My worst nightmare was realized. I ran into Hal Prince. I liked Hal very much. Giving my notice under these circumstances was one of most difficult things I'd ever done.

"Are you okay, Pat? We haven't rehearsed you too hard, have we? We need your voice on that stage tonight! Are you excited?" *Right, Hal, be nice. Make it tougher on me.*

"Gosh, Hal, excited isn't even the word. I'm thrilled. Thank you for the opportunity!"

He beamed, uttering Broadway's good luck mantra: "Merde!"

"But Hal, I have something to tell you," I gulped. "Today I got a call from *Meet The People*. I auditioned for them on the same day

I sang for you, and they've offered me a lead. They start rehearsals in two weeks. I have to give you my notice tonight."

A quiet "wow" from Hal. Then, brightly: "Well, congratulations! You know we wish you the best of luck. A lead in this revue might be the showcase you need. We hate losing you, but you have to do what's right for your career."

Class always tells. And Gus was wrong that I'd never work for Hal Prince again.

One incident remains in memory of my brief, two-week run in *The Pajama Game*. John Raitt, the leading man, the original Billy in *Carousel* (and father of latter-day singing star Bonnie Raitt), had not seen me prior to my first performance. His understudy rehearsed with me. During the dramatic first act finale of the play, all sewing machines in the pajama factory are smashed and rendered useless in a union action. John Raitt, playing the factory manager, turns to my character, one of the seamstresses, and says: "Get Charley in here! He'll fix these machines, and we'll be workin' around here again in no time!"

John turned to bark out his line on my first night onstage with him. He saw me, a stranger, in front of him. His handsome face went blank. Stammering, he finally picked up his line:

"G-g-get Charley in here!! He'll fix these machines, and we'll be—uh-hmm-uh—*bangin'* around here again in no time!"

What was in John's mind? Rick told me later I should be flattered.

scene viii: Spring 1955, Enter a flop, New York City

Meet The People, 1955, was touted as "the return of continental theater to the United States." Rows of audience seats were removed and replaced by bistro tables and chairs, where light eating, drinking and smoking were allowed. This form of theater was popular in Europe, represented in a sleazy way in the production, *Cabaret.* And that's exactly what it was—cabaret. *Meet The People* was called "continental theater," but it was, honestly, a cabaret revue.

Billy Rose's Diamond Horseshoe, located on the lower level of the Paramount Hotel on West 48th Street, was the perfect venue for this form of entertainment. The horseshoe-shaped stage that inspired its name allowed performers to move out and—hey!—*Meet The People.* The producers and investors of our show hoped to establish a new old-style revue, evolving into sequels featuring bright new talents, like a latter-day *Ziegfeld Follies.* Lionel Stander, the actor known for his gravelly-voiced roles in many films, and later for his character of "Max" in the television series, *Hart to Hart,* wore a new hat as producer. Lionel's partner, Jay Gorney, was the original lyricist, and much of the material in our show was from the original show of 1941. That should have been my first clue that we were not going to set the Broadway world on fire. Pre-show publicity made much of the fact that I'd left *The Pajama Game* to join the cast, and that was a second clue.

Let's cut to the chase. We were a catastrophe. Robert Sylvester's headline in the *Daily News* said it all: "INTIMATE REVUE FALLS DOWN THE CELLAR STEPS." The critics lambasted the material. Brooks Atkinson of the *Times* called it "ludicrously hackneyed."

Walter Kerr said, "This is battered terrain, an embarrassment to even the authors of Jokes For All Occasions." Most of the reviewers, mercifully grouped the cast as "fresh young talent," granting us anonymous distance from the over-all calamity. William Hawkins did, however, single me out in his review in the *World Telegram*: "An extraordinary talent is that of Patricia Wilson. A big-eyed, calm-tempered lass, she sings with a fine, resonant throb—"

Michael Callan flies into theater- bomb history. I'm in the middle, R.

We played out our brief run to empty houses. One night, TV

star Steve Allen and his wife, Jayne Meadows, sat alone in the theater. A few of the performers dropped out. I stuck it through to the end, picking up the slack for those of the cast who abandoned ship. I had nothing else to do. It had been seven weeks since I'd left the sanctuary of *The Pajama Game*.

scene ix: Summer 1955, Enter more opportunity, New York

Journal, April 28, 1955:   Out of a job again! "Up again, old heart!"

It seemed an appropriate time to drag out my favorite spirit-lifting mantra. Someone once said that promising talent often falls by the wayside, the sensitivity that sustains their talent making them unable to handle the vicissitudes of a theatrical career. That spring of 1955, after *Meet The People* disintegrated, I was disappointed, but it didn't occur to me to fall by the wayside. I'd gambled and lost. So I reminded myself: "Up again, old heart!"

"Well, honey," my father chuckled, "welcome to show biz. You've always been a sturdy rat. You'll get past this." Leave it to Poppa. It was little consolation to be called a sturdy rat.

"Go ahead, Pat, cry. You've had a big disappointment." Good, gentle Rick. He comforted me, but I was worried about my husband. He was playing a lot of Bach lately, sitting for long periods of time at the Steinway. *He's just meditative, isn't he? Surely not unhappy. I love hearing him play!* The rest of the world would, too, someday soon.

"Things seem to be moving too fast, then not fast enough, don't they, Rick?"

"My life stays the same. I work with you, I work with pupils. I play for people."

"But Rick, that's not enough! You've played with symphony orchestras!" While he was a Princeton student, before he was drafted into World War II, Rick had played concerts with Toscanini in Carnegie Hall. Once, during an air-raid warning, he'd calmed a jittery New York concert audience by playing "Three Blind Mice" in the styles of different classical composers. "And you've helped write shows, the Princeton Triangle show, our shows at Ohio State!"

"Is what I do now not enough for you, Pat?" He stopped playing.

"You know that's not what I mean! What else can we do to get your music going in New York? You're always helping me. What can we do to help you?"

Rick spoke softly. "Just keep singing, Pat. Just keep singing."

Journal, May 1, 1955: Gus says, "Pick yourself up! Even Ethel Merman can have a flop." He says there are still roles open in summer stock. I was so inspired by the sermon in church this AM that I snapped out of my doldrums. I feel good about auditioning for summer theaters.

Rick and I belonged to The Marble Collegiate Church at Fifth Avenue and 29th Street. We'd met its minister while we were working at WBNS-TV. The charismatic man came through Columbus to publicize his recently-released book, and Rick was the director of an interview show on which he appeared. The minister autographed a copy of his book: "For Rick and his wife, Pat: May your lives always be positive! Norman Vincent Peale." The book was *The Power of Positive Thinking.*

Our acquaintance with Norman Vincent Peale was a blessing, hearing him speak a privilege and education.His face fronted by old-fashioned, rimless spectacles, Dr. Peale by-passed the hellfire-and-damnation rhetoric of his clerical peers. Instead he mesmerized his congregations with the truth of the higher spirit living in each of us, awaiting purposeful fulfillment. He wove stories and humor throughout his oratory, reaching out to his audiences with a divine common touch. On one of his visits to New York, my father openly wept after hearing Dr. Peale give one of his sermons.

"Pop, are you okay?" I asked. We made our way down the Marble Collegiate Church steps.

"There wasn't a dry pew in the house, Patty! Not a dry pew!"

Journal, May 2, 1955: Dr. Peale inspires me every time I hear him. He makes me feel I can do anything. What a gift he has! I sing this afternoon for the Pittsburgh Light Opera, then for St. John Terrell and the Lambertville Music Circus. Gus tells me St. John also owns Neptune Music Circus in Asbury Park. He hasn't cast "Nellie

Forbush" in South Pacific yet —my DREAM! Gosh, how I want to play that role!

Later, 4 PM: The Pittsburgh Light Opera seemed to like me. I sang I Don't Care and Ohio— opera? Ha ha! Everybody else was trilling Victor Herbert and Romberg, operetta-style. So glad Rick is with me. I don't sing like everyone else, and I don't feel like I can sing right without him. What would I do without Rick? My love, my mate—

Journal, May 9, 1955: St. John Terrell wants me to do Me and Juliet in late June, then come back in August to do Wish You Were Here. Both are ingénue parts—gotta jazz 'em up! I don't mean to sound ungrateful. I'm thrilled, even though I have to parade around in a bathing suit in Wish You Were Here. Maybe there's a way to camouflage my lumpy legs.

Later: Gus says I have to be cleared by the Rodgers and Hammerstein office to do Me and Juliet. Oh, dear!

Gus didn't know about my first audition for Rodgers and Hammerstein, and it was time to confess the awful truth. My manager had to know the worst.

"Gus, I auditioned for the Rodgers and Hammerstein office my first week in New York—but I—"

"They don't seem to remember you—for whom did you audition? John Fearnley is their chief casting director, a very intelligent, respected man."

"O, hell's katootie, Gus. I really blew it."

The morning of our third day in New York, before auditioning for John Fearnley of the Rodgers and Hammerstein office, I'd said to Rick, "I've saved my *best* hat to wear, just for an occasion like this!" I arranged the huge Milan straw hat on my head, admiring the pink cabbage roses covering its wide brim. *It's so lovely, and perfect for New York,* I told myself. The stage of the Winter Garden Theater was lit by a work light, and my face was totally shadowed by the huge hat brim. Then there was the fact that hip young theater performers in New York never wore hats. My hat *was* perfect...for the Easter Parade! John Fearnley stopped me during my song, and cleared his throat.

"Uh, Miss Wilson, would you mind taking off your hat and beginning again?"

I removed the cabbage roses and swung with gusto into the venerable Al Jolson favorite, *Rockabye Your Baby With a Dixie Melody.* Another blunder. I wanted to show that maybe I'd been a little dumb about wearing a big hat, but listen! I had a voice to fill the theater. Theaters didn't have microphones then. My song selection proved I could belt it out, but lacked the sensibility to show I was a Rodgers and Hammerstein leading lady.

John Fearnley and I became friends later in my career, when I *was* a Rodgers and Hammerstein leading lady. I once asked him if he remembered that audition. He was astonished that I was the same person.

"OhmiGawd, Patricia! No!" he said, "That cornball was *you*??"

scene x: May 1955, Enter Rodgers and Hammerstein, The Winter Garden Theater, New York City

"You'll be singing next, Miss Wilson," the stage manager said. I grabbed Rick's hand.

"Just pray it's someone besides John Fearnley out front, Rick," I whispered.

It was. There was no mistaking who sat fourth row center that day in the Winter Garden Theater. I recognized Richard Rodgers and Oscar Hammerstein immediately. Rick followed me onstage and sat at the piano to my right. I could sense his surprise, too. We had no idea these great men personally supervised auditions to clear singers for stock roles.

I'd decided against singing songs from *South Pacific.* One of Rick's students had related a horror story. Richard Rodgers was a perfectionist, protective of every quarter note he wrote. A hapless star took liberties with a Rodgers melody during an audition. The actor received a tongue-lashing and failed to win the part he was hoping to play. Oscar Hammerstein was equally protective of his lyrics. I knew I could get carried away in the dramatics of a song, extending a note, as I did in phrasing "pop" songs, or making up a lyric, if I forgot one under pressure. My racing heart and rubber legs told me *this* was pressure. Rick played the gentle, legato introduction to the song we'd chosen, Harold Arlen and Johnny Mercer's *I Had Myself A True Love* from the 1946 musical, *St. Louis Woman.* That show had not been a hit. It ran only 113 performances. But the score, which included *Come Rain or Come Shine,* was beautiful. *I Had Myself A True Love* was almost an aria, ranging from guttural chest tones to a high, wailing soprano, an emotional marathon, joyful, angry, bitter, wistful. I used several voices to highlight different aspects of the character I sang. It wasn't studied. I performed on instinct. My knowin' set a character, and I went with it.

It was a long piece. John Fearnley told me later he'd never seen Rodgers and Hammerstein sit still for such a lengthy audition. Director George Abbott said he knew within eight bars whether or not he liked a singer, and Abbott was known to stop singers, even major stars, dead in their tracks. Yet in my naiveté it never occurred to me that I wouldn't be allowed to finish my song that day. This was a story song with a beginning, middle, and end. The story had to be told. Rodgers and Hammerstein listened. I finished the last notes and stood waiting to hear what I was expected to do next.

Oscar Hammerstein said from the fourth row, "Miss Wilson, we're coming onstage to talk to you. Would you give us a moment?" Now I could glance at Rick, still seated at the piano. His face told me what I needed to know: we had performed well.

Richard Rodgers and Oscar Hammerstein came on the stage. An assistant moved two stools and a chair into the work light. "Sit down, Pat," Rodgers said. He and Mr. Hammerstein perched on the stools. I could see the curious expression of another actress, Polly Bergen, just offstage in the wings. I'd seen Polly in *John Murray Anderson's Almanac* when I first arrived in New York. I couldn't believe such a star was required to audition.

Oscar Hammerstein said, "Miss Wilson, Mr. Rodgers and I are impressed with your work. You're fine to play any of our leading lady roles."

"Yes," said Richard Rodgers. "In fact, Oscar and I have something else in mind for you. Are you aware we're preparing a new show to go into rehearsal in September?" I was aware. "Our new show is based on John Steinbeck's characters from his sequel to *Cannery Row.* Have you read *Sweet Thursday*?" I gulped, cutting off a nervous hiccup.

"No, Mr. Rodgers. I studied John Steinbeck in college, though. I know the *Cannery Row* story and its characters." John Steinbeck had written from his early life in Monterey, California, during the 1920s. The area was called "Cannery Row" for the companies that processed catches netted out of Monterey Bay. The picturesque characters in Steinbeck's novel were based on people the author knew during those years, local citizens, from flophouse residents to heart-of-gold whores. *This will be one colorful musical,* I thought. *Rodgers and Hammerstein? John Steinbeck?* I was playing the entire production in my mind when Richard Rodgers interrupted my thoughts.

"Our show, *Pipe Dream,* is based on those characters. And there are new characters Steinbeck added for *Sweet Thursday.* A young girl, Suzy, becomes a prostitute to survive, then falls in love with Doc—remember him from *Cannery Row?* She turns her life around."

Doc, a marine biologist based on Steinbeck's real-life friend, was a bitter drop-out from big-city life. He moves to Cannery Row to set up a small laboratory, and becomes a combination guru/father-figure to the unconventional locals.

Richard Rodgers continued. "Henry Fonda has been studying singing so that he can play Doc. The part requires a strong actor. We also need a Suzy who can act as well as sing. Oscar and I think you'd be very good in the role." I looked at Mr. Hammerstein and he nodded. "Are you available this fall?" The graying, good-looking stage manager stood behind the two men, his arms folded. *He looks more like John Barrymore than a stage manager,* I thought. *Am I dreaming this? Could they possibly think I wouldn't be available for the new Rodgers and Hammerstein musical?*

"Thank you. I'm pretty sure I'm available." *Dumb!* Rodgers and Hammerstein stood, and Hammerstein smiled. "Good, Pat. We'll be in touch."

Rick and I left the stage door of the Winter Garden and walked up Seventh Avenue.

"That was amazing, Pat! Your ancestors must be smiling down on you! There you were, talking to Rodgers and Hammerstein about playing the lead in their new Broadway show!"

"Oh, Miss Wilson!" We turned to see the stage manager, Charlie Atkin, sprinting up Seventh Avenue. "Could you come back to the theater for a moment, please? Mr. Rodgers would like to see you again." We returned to the stage door. Polly Bergen and the other auditioners were still milling in the wings as Charlie Atkin walked me back onstage.

"Oh, Patricia," said Richard Rodgers, "Could you tell us your vocal range, please?"

I looked to Rick, who stood by the piano. "She has a solid G below middle C, Mr. Rodgers, even an F. Then she has a D above high C. She has quite a range."

"And it all seems to fit together, too!"

"It does. She has an imperceptible break, a natural blend."

"Yes, so I heard. Thank you for coming back."

Once more Rick and I headed up Seventh Avenue.

"Oh, Miss Wilson!" Charlie Atkin again. We turned and he beckoned us back to the stage door. One more time I walked past the line of waiting singers and onto the stage.

"Pat, could you come to our office this afternoon at two?" asked Richard Rodgers.

There wasn't time to go home. We had tea at the Carnegie Deli and talked about our future, as we waited for two o'clock. Rick, solemn and thoughtful, nibbled a pastrami-on-rye. "It looks as if a wonderful thing is about to happen for you, Pat."

"For *us*, Rick! This is what we've dreamed about, isn't it?"

He nodded and looked at his watch. "It's almost two—you'd better go."

"You're not coming to see Mr. Rodgers with me?"

"Of course not. It's you he wants to see." We left the deli, heading in opposite directions.

Rick turned to wave. "Good luck with Rodgers!" he called down Seventh Avenue. Standing in the warm May sun, I felt a sudden chill as I watched him walk away.

scene xi: Later that day, Richard Rodgers office

"Pat," Richard Rodgers said, ushering me to a chair in front of a corner window, "Oscar and I were truly impressed with your audition this morning." He was a slight, near-handsome man in his early fifties, brisk, pleasant, and forthright. His office was unpretentious and businesslike, which I thought suited him perfectly

"We see many talented young people, but when someone like you walks in from nowhere, we want to know more. Where are you from? Why haven't we seen you before?" Blushing, I described my first audition for John Fearnley. Mr. Rodgers laughed, then got down to the nitty-gritty.

"Patricia, Oscar and I feel you are the perfect actress to play 'Suzy' in *Pipe Dream*. Our director, Harold Clurman, is on the west coast for a few weeks. Do you know him? *Pipe Dream* will be Harold Clurman's first musical," Mr. Rodgers continued, seeming as impressed as I. Harold Clurman, one of the founders of Group Theater, was a director of several hits, and had just staged William Inge's successful new play, *Bus Stop*. "We felt we needed someone with a reputation in dramatic theater for *Pipe Dream* because it's a musical *play,* a departure from traditional musical comedy." I nodded. Harold Clurman! I thought about my acting professor and mentor, Roy Bowen, at Ohio State. *Roy—in fact the whole theater department—would be so impressed!*

"Oscar and I have spoken to Harold in California and told him about hearing you this morning. He's anxious to meet you, as soon as he gets back to New York." My stomach was spinning, and my blue linen blouse felt damp with perspiration against the back of the chair. Mr. Rodgers went on. "Meanwhile, Oscar and I would like to make sure you are available in the fall. Do you have commitments for the summer?"

"I do, Mr. Rodgers," I said, happy to tell him about the Pittsburgh Light Opera and St. John Terrell's Music Circus.

"Good! It's important for you to work over the summer," said Mr. Rodgers. "Oscar and I will talk to your agent about setting some sort of interim personal agreement between you and Oscar and me, so we know we have you locked in for the fall. Then Harold Clurman can talk to you and hear you sing when he gets back from the west coast. Is all of this agreeable?"

I nodded. "Mr. Rodgers, I'd heard you wanted Julie Andrews to play the role of Suzy."

"We did, originally. But Julie will be in the new Moss Hart musical called *My Fair Lady."*

"I see. But how can you tell so much about me? I only sang one song this morning."

"Yes, and I'm grateful it wasn't *Rockabye Your Baby With A Dixie Melody*," Rodgers chuckled. My cheeks burned, but Mr. Rodgers didn't seem to notice. He became serious. "Ah, but what you sang was a tour-de-force, Pat. It took courage to even attempt such a song for us." I didn't feel courageous. My stomach was already telling me it was time to hiccup again.

Mr. Rodgers continued, "Oscar and I are a team, and both our antenna told us at the same moment—you can be a great star. We want to take credit for discovering you!" He smiled as he got to his feet and took my hand. "Goodbye, Patricia. We'll be seeing you soon."

I don't remember saying goodbye to Richard Rodgers, but I almost kissed a startled office assistant on the way out. I called Rick from a corner phone booth. There was no answer. Letting myself into our apartment, I found my husband sitting on the living room sofa with our cocker spaniel, George. I babbled out the details of my meeting with Richard Rodgers. "Oh, Rick! It's the thrill of a life-time!"

"Pat, I'm so proud of you. And happy for you." He stood and kissed me on the cheek before I could blurt out more details. His eyes looked misty.

"Excuse me," he said. "I have to take George to the vet. I think he has a cold."

scene xii: Spring 1955, Enter problems and Dr. Eugene Braun, New York City

Journal, May 18, 1955: Something is wrong with Rick. He plays piano all the time. He doesn't talk to me. I'm popping out of my skin over Rodgers and Hammerstein —thought he would be, too. What's wrong? Maybe we can go to a movie. Something has to cheer him up.

"Rick, guess who is in my new dancing class?" No answer. "Rick! Grace Kelly!"

"Oh? That new actress in *Mogambo* with Clark Gable?"

"Yep. And she hangs her mink on a peg right next to my storm coat during class!"

"That's nice, honey." He hadn't heard me.

"And when I told her she should lock her valuable fur coat in our instructor's office, so it wouldn't get stolen, she said, 'Oh, don't worry, Pat—I have another one.'"

Not even my anecdote about the soon-to-be Princess of Monaco made Rick smile.

Journal, May 20, 1955: Rick is depressed. We called the counseling center at Marble Collegiate Church. Dr. Peale has set up this place for combined spiritual-psychological help. We have an appointment Tuesday at 9AM.

Journal, May 24, 1955: Feel better. Rick and I talked to the assistant minister together, then each separately with him. He wants us to do some psychological tests. Talking helped Rick, I think.

Journal, May 27, 1955: Wow, ink blot tests and all! Took nearly two hours. A nice, lady psychologist, thorough and caring. Pretty intense.

(Later) Yippee! I get to be June Allyson! Will play her role (Minerva) in Best Foot Forward in Pittsburgh. I sing the Barrelhouse part in The Three B's. But that's not all! I play that show one week—then open as Bianca in Kiss Me Kate the next!

Journal, May 31,1955: Heard from Dr. Peale's clinic. We are to call a psychotherapist, Dr. Eugene Braun, to make an appointment. He works on a sliding scale for people sent to him by Marble Collegiate. It scares me. I'm confused. Wish I hadn't agreed to do the damn tests.

Journal, June 6, 1955: Dr. Braun is nice. He's Viennese. We talked about marriages. He says they are "arranged" for young people in Europe. Love doesn't guarantee a happy "union." (His word, not mine.) I told him Rick and I are partners in love and work. I clasped my hands together and said, "We're like this." Dr. Braun held his hands side by side, not touching, but moving in a straight line together. "Better like this," he said. Then he asked if I knew about something he called codependence. Hmmm. He also asked about sex. I knew he would, damn it. I told him Rick and I haven't had a problem until recently. He just nodded. Maddening as hell.

Journal, June 9, 1955: Dr B. asked if I think Rick is unhappy because I'm moving beyond him professionally. I said, no, that was only for now. I was crying. Why do I cry so much? He asked if I thought Rick was better off in Columbus than he is in New York. I said no, Rick loves NY. Dr. B. said that's not the point. I hate Dr. Braun! Rick and I belong together. It doesn't matter what city we're in—God, and my heart, and Rick's—know best, not any Dr. Eugene Braun. I'm not going back.

(Later) I had a long talk with Jet MacDonald. What a good pal since the Oldsmobile tour! She's having her own problems. Her marriage is over. She's sad and angry, but she takes time to listen to my troubles. I have a lot to think about. I've decided to see Dr. Braun one more time.

Journal, June 13, 1955: (Rick's 31st birthday): Today I told Dr. B. I want to go back to Columbus with Rick. He asked do I want to give up all I've gained here and I said no, but I would if it meant Rick and I could be happy again. I love NY! I'm excited about the wonderful things that are happening! But I also love Rick. Dr. B. says Rick feels he can't make it in NY himself, and doesn't want to be "just a guy carrying around his wife's music." Oh God! Dr. B. says I must let go of Rick professionally. He says Rick will not be the piano virtuoso I always thought he'd be, and can I live with that? Of course I can. Can Rick? Why hasn't he been able to talk to me about his feelings? I spew mine out all the time. I'm sobbing on this page—damn my ducts!

Journal, June 17, 1955: I'm 26 today. Rick and I went to The Tattler for dinner. At home we talked about my session with Dr. B. We cried, both of us. We made love, for the first time since—?

scene xiii; Summer 1955, Enter Harold Clurman, Doylestown, PA

Journal, June 20, 1955: I leave for Lambertville, New Jersey, to play Me and Juliet at St. John Terrell's Music Circus today. Still worried about Rick, but I'll be close to NY. We'll see each other. He'll continue with Dr. Braun, and Dr. Braun says I should call him any time I want or need to.

Me and Juliet, one of Rodgers and Hammerstein's minor successes, was a backstage love story. Jeanie was my first straight romantic role. I'd played theater-in-the-round before, at The Stadium Theater at Ohio State, but the intimacy of the venue proved to be disconcerting during love scenes. In the round, the audience is not the "Big, Black Giant" beyond the footlights of a traditional proscenium stage that Oscar Hammerstein wrote about. The front row is barely a few feet away, plainly visible to the actors onstage. My leading man in *Me and Juliet* took his part seriously. He shoved his tongue down my throat during our stage kisses.

"Ron, what the heck did you do that for?"

"Sorry, Pat,...I got carried away." From then on, I kept my mouth tightly clamped during love scenes. Ron must have felt like he was hitting a brick wall. I'm sure it looked pretty silly to the up-close audience that spotted it, too, but I didn't care. I'm not a prude. But I resented my leading man's attempts to exploit me as a woman.

After our final Lambertville Music Circus bows on the night of July 3rd, a bus waited to whisk us to Asbury Park. We opened the next night in The Neptune Music Circus, with only a brief afternoon run-through to acclimate ourselves to a different stage. It was there that the stage manager told me people were coming from New York to see me. "They ask for Rodgers and Hammerstein's new star—the one they discovered for *Pipe Dream,"* Bruce said.

I remember little about Asbury Park. I drove the blue Chevy back and forth to New York often to see Rick. We closed *Me and Juliet* on July 10th, and I was due in Pittsburgh on the 12th to begin rehearsals for *Best Foot Forward.* I wanted to see as much of my husband as possible.

Journal, July 7, 1955: Our fourth wedding anniversary! Drove into New York after the show last night to be with Rick. A lovely night and day together—treated ourselves to Eggs Benedict at Rumpelmeyer's, walked through the park—a sweet time. I had to leave at 3:30 to drive back to Asbury Park. Rick says he's busy and happy. That makes me happy. I wish he could be with me! But it's not fair for him to be sitting around while I rehearse and perform. I'll soon be in New York in a hit show. We'll have every day and night to spend together.

Journal, July 12, 1955: Pittsburgh. Huge theater! A stadium, outfitted with a stage at one end for the summer season, open air. Hot under the sun for rehearsals. We rehearsed underneath the bleachers for part of the day. Heads turned when I opened my mouth to sing "What Do You Think I Am?" I'm just so loud. They're used to light, operetta-type voices here.

Alice Pearce is my roommate. Gus introduced us so we could share this apartment. She is famous! She was in On The Town (both Broadway and movie) and has been at The Blue Angel tons of times. Her husband is a musician-songwriter, too. He wrote "It's a Big Wide Wonderful World." How many times have I sung that? Alice said she would tell John (Rox). She's playing "The Blind Date" in Best Foot Forward, the Nancy Walker part—she plays all these "ugly-girl" roles and she is soul-beautiful.

Journal, July 17, 1955: Rehearsing onstage under the hot sun all day, wearing bathing suits or shorts. I'm copper-colored. I didn't

know I could get this dark—me, old " freckle-and-peel." Neile Adams (she sings the "Boogie-Woogie" part in The Three B's) has some stage makeup left from "Kismet." She's loaning me some dark pancake. My makeup from "Juliet" is too pale. Neile talks about her boyfriend constantly, an actor named Steve McQueen. They're getting married soon. We're all meeting for drinks at Downey's when we get back to NYC. Combined tech/dress rehearsal tonight—will be a late night. We open tomorrow eve. Have the day off to rest.

Best Foot Forward—I sang the "Barrel-house" part of the "Three B's."

"Let's go to an air-conditioned movie this afternoon, room-mate!" Alice and I sat at the worn, laminate-topped table in the kitchenette of our apartment. "I hear Charlton Heston is in the new one about Andrew Jackson, and he wears *tights!*"

I laughed. "Then by all means, let's go see Charlton in tights, Allie!" I sipped my iced coffee laced with a dollop of chocolate ice cream.

"That's a dickens of a breakfast, Patty."

"It's all I can down in this heat."

Journal, July 19, 1955: We're a smash! What a great time! I begin rehearsing Kiss Me Kate at 10 AM. Alice is sleeping in.

Journal, July 21, 1955: I'm zapped— hot days rehearsing, then playing at night—phew. Forgot lyrics to Always True To You In My Fashion at rehearsal. The director took me aside to ask what's wrong. My old bugaboo, nervous fatigue.

Journal, July 25, 1955: Have gone in early every night to rehearse "Always True—" onstage by myself. I know it cold now, though "cold" isn't an apropos word. Best Foot Forward closed. Alice went back to NY and I miss her like crazy. She'll call Rick for me. Have to take a nap, we open tonight. So long, 'Minerva'—hello, 'Bianca'!

Next AM, July 26th: Great opening! A big laugh when I entered as Bianca. I don't know why. I'll ask the director. (Later) He says it's because I stomped downstage in the beautiful Elizabethan gown to say my first Shakespearean line. He says to leave it in, it's funny. I'm embarrassed to tell him it wasn't planned! I'm learning a lot—

When I went from Pittsburgh back to Lambertville, to rehearse for *Wish You Were Here,* Gus called. "Pat, Harold Clurman, the director for *Pipe Dream,* is back in New York. Rodgers and Hammerstein know you can't get into the city to meet him while you're rehearsing, so they're sending Clurman out to you. You'll be picked up in a limousine at the theater at five-thirty tomorrow afternoon. John Fearnley will be in the limo with Clurman. And Rick."

"*Rick?* My husband?"

Bianca in Kiss Me Kate, *Pittsburgh Light Opera, 1955. The laugh on my entrance was unexpected.*

"Yes. I've already spoken to him. He'll ride out with them to play for you. Thank God you don't have the same last name! They don't have to know he's your *husband*." There was that dirty word for Gus again. He assumed everyone shared his prejudice. What was it? Did all young actresses have to appear to be succulent virgins? I let it pass. I was happy Rick would be with me. Gus continued, "You're all going to Oscar Hammerstein's farm in Doylestown, right across the river. His housekeeper will have dinner waiting for you there. Then you'll sing and read for Clurman. Oscar just finished a new draft of the first scene, and they'll bring it with them."

It was a little past five when the limousine pulled up outside the Music Circus the next day. Harold Clurman was a short, heavy-set man with a thick, prominent nose and narrow, close-together eyes, looking more like a Russian prime minister than a famous director.

John Fearnley winked as we shook hands. "Hello, Patricia! I hope we haven't disrupted your rehearsal." John loved our private joke about my first audition for him. Rick leaned across from a jump seat and kissed me on the cheek casually, as if I were a friend he'd accompanied before. He squeezed my arm gently, and my skin tingled. *Keep it professional,* Gus had said.

The limo drove to the beautiful Doylestown farm that was Oscar Hammerstein's country retreat. *Like Tara!* I thought. We sat down together to a simple meal, chicken, vegetables and rice pilaf, served to us on the screened-in porch of the beautiful house. Black cattle grazed in a pasture not far away, their rhythmic chewing mirroring the beat-beat in my chest. I barely remember the dinner conversation, except that it centered around Harold Clurman, his life and his successes. Rick sat across the table from me, his eyes smiling when they caught mine.

Finally I spoke up. "Mr. Clurman, thank you for coming all this way to meet me." No answer. Clurman never spoke to me directly or included me in the dinner table conversation. *Rodgers and Hammerstein must have filled him in on my background*, I thought. *Or maybe he's hard of hearing.* John Fearnley's warm smile made me feel relaxed and comfortable.

When he'd eaten a dessert of fresh peach pie a la mode, Harold Clurman stood. "I'm ready to hear her sing," he announced. He looked as if he were about to belch, glancing at me as a lab assistant might at something growing in a Petri dish. *I hope that peach pie agreed with him,* I thought. We all adjourned to the French provincial living room, where Clurman and John Fearnley sat on a beautiful, floral-upholstered sofa. I stood by Rick at the piano and sang *I Had Myself a True Love*. Harold Clurman didn't crack a smile, or a frown, or anything else resembling a facial expression. He just stared at me, his face registering no emotion at all. He turned to John. "Does she have a script?" John handed one to me.

"Tell her to read the opening scene," Clurman said to John.

In Suzy's *Pipe Dream* entrance scene she has cut her hand, and appears on Doc's doorstep, a defensive waif seeking medical attention. Her first song, *Everybody's Got a Home But Me*, reveals her inner fears and weariness, as well as her dreams. I read the lyric as part of the scene. John read the role of Doc. We finished to silence. John's face was touched with emotion, telling me I'd read well.

"That was a cold reading, Harold," he said to Clurman. "Patricia has not laid eyes on this scene prior to this evening. The character is just a part of her."

Harold Clurman stared at me. He stood, pulling a piece of paper from his pocket. He walked to the desk, picked up the phone, and dialed.

"Rodgers? This girl won't play Suzy."

I smiled at John, thinking I was overhearing a joke. He looked stunned. So did Rick.

"OK, Dick, I won't argue about it," Clurman said into the phone. "Let me put it this way: You and Oscar decide if you want this girl for Suzy, or me to direct." He hung up.

The flush started at my toes and rose, a signal that I was going to vomit or cry. Rick grabbed my hand. Clurman thanked the housekeeper who had prepared our dinner, and waved for us all to follow him to the limousine. Nothing was said by anyone during the drive from the Hammerstein farm back to Lambertville, and I gulped down the gorge that kept rising in my throat. I said as cheerful a goodbye as I could muster when the driver dropped me in front of the Lambertville Inn. Rick called me later, when he arrived back at our New York apartment.

"Pat, honey, it wasn't you. Your singing and reading were fine. Clurman wants to pick the leading lady for *Pipe Dream* himself, and I think Rodgers and Hammerstein oversold you to him. There's a power struggle going on, and you got caught in the middle."

"It was so cruel, Rick, the way he did it—as if I wasn't even there!"

"Nobody said a word on the way back to Manhattan. I think Fearnley was as stunned as you and I. Clurman hummed under his breath—off-key, by the way—for the whole trip. I kept thinking, this jerk is going to direct a *musical?* All we could do was listen to him, sour notes and all."

When Rick hung up, I repeated "up-again-old-heart-I-refuse-to-cry" over and over into the soft down of the Lambertville Inn pillow, and finally fell into exhausted sleep.

scene xiv: End of summer 1955, Enter Judy Tyler and disappointment

"Pat, it's not over," Gus said. "They go into rehearsal in a month, and they haven't found anyone yet. Suzy is a difficult role. I know the talent in this town. I don't know anyone else who can play her. They're auditioning people out of deference to Clurman, but Rodgers and Hammerstein are getting angry."

Journal, August 27, 1955: Gus wants to know if I'll go to the new music tent in Saginaw, Michigan, to finish out their season with Wish You Were Here. Might as well. I've been playing the role for two weeks here in Lambertville. Won't have to learn anything new. Rick says "go!"—it's just another eight days—after Labor Day we'll be together again.

In Michigan, I stayed in a pretty bed-and-breakfast in the little town of Clio. On the morning of our opening, I walked down the main street, looking for the town drugstore. A familiar car appeared, moving slowly, its driver craning to find an address. It was Momma, driving Grandma Daisy's old Packard Clipper.

"Mom!" I yelled. An elderly couple stopped on the sidewalk and stared. Momma pulled to the curb, beaming. We hugged and hugged. I don't think I'd ever been so happy to see anyone.

"You get this near to Ohio, you're going to have to put up with me!" she laughed.

"Near? How long a drive to get here? Five hours?"

"Six." We hugged again, beginning a week of total joy for both of us. She slept in the extra bed in my room. We giggled like school-girls, and pigged out on butterscotch sundaes together.

"They're not as good as Graeter's!" we declared. Graeter's was a family-owned ice cream store in Cincinnati. I grew up on their sundaes. That little, one-family ice cream store is now an international corporation, shipping to customers all over the world, thanks to Oprah Winfrey. Oprah discovered the special-recipe ice cream on a trip to Cincinnati, and touted the confection to her TV audience.

Momma charmed the cast and crew in Saginaw. She sat with me in my dressing room while I made up, and watched every performance. The nights were nippy, and she worried that I'd be chilled in the bathing beauty contest that ended the show.

"When Rodgers and Hammerstein call you to rehearse for *Pipe Dream*," she said, "You don't want to have a cold!"

When the show closed, Momma drove me to the Detroit airport for my New York flight, then continued on to Cincinnati. It was September 7th, with *Pipe Dream* scheduled to start rehearsals on September 20th. I was disappointed to learn that Henry Fonda had withdrawn from playing Doc. He decided he wasn't up to a singing role. Rex Harrison, another straight actor wary of doing a musical, summoned up his courage and took the plunge that same season, creating a whole new style for musical theater leading men in *My Fair Lady*. William Johnson, who'd replaced Alfred Drake in *Kismet* and played Billy Bigelow in the London production of *Carousel,* was signed to replace Fonda as Doc.

On Friday of the week I returned from Michigan, Gus called.

"They've found somebody else for Suzy, Pat." I sat down. He continued, "She was in Hollywood until recently with her husband, Colin Romoff—the pianist and coach? They rejected her there, but Clurman said, 'That's the Suzy I want!' and Dick and Oscar capitulated. Clurman was determined to cast the role himself. He wore them down. This girl has never done theater, except for a four-week summer run in *Annie Get Your Gun*, only TV."

"What's her name, Gus?" The words were like sticky dough against the roof of my mouth. "Judy Tyler," he said. It'd been only three months since Rodgers and Hammerstein said, "That's 'Suzy'!" when I sang for them at the Winter Garden Theater.

"You have to make a decision, Pat. Rodgers and Hammerstein want you in the show. Oscar will write a small part in for you, and they want you to stand by for Suzy." My heart dropped and rolled around in my stomach. I wanted to stick pins in Harold Clurman's effigy.

"What do you think I should do, Gus?"

"Patty, hundreds of young women would kill to be in your shoes. Rodgers and Hammerstein care about you. John Fearnley says they're disappointed that you won't be 'Suzy.'"

"Then why won't I be? God, Gus, what does this Clurman guy have on them?"

"Patty, he's the hottest dramatic director in town. They're breaking new ground with *Pipe Dream*. They want someone besides George Abbott or Josh Logan to direct."

"There's something twisted inside the man, I swear. Okay, he's done wonderful things in theater. But it'll be hard for me to be around him."

"He'll be gone after the show opens. You'll be with Rodgers and Hammerstein. Who knows what their next show will be? Or what might happen when this one is on its feet? Don't cut off your nose to spite your face!"

"That sounds like something my Ohio grandma would have said."

"Well, maybe it's Grandma Daisy speaking through me. It's common sense, Pat."

Journal, September 9th—no it's the 10th—it's 4 AM. Rick is asleep. We talked almost all night. Of course I'll do Pipe Dream. I must grow up. Gus is right, it's a privilege. But so bittersweet! Well, I'll be doing a Broadway show from the start, anyway. A Rodgers and Hammerstein show, at that. Could it be the next Carousel or South Pacific? Where's my faith that it's all for the best? Up again, old heart!

scene xv: Autumn 1955, Enter Pipe Dream and John Steinbeck, New York, New Haven, and Boston

Journal, Sept. 16, 1955: Bought a new dress to wear for the first day of Pipe Dream rehearsals—pale green wool. Also have been vocalizing like crazy. That'll show 'em!

The stage of the Barrymore Theater was set up with three rows of chairs for a first read-through of the script. Someone clapped me on the shoulder.

"Hello, there," Harold Clurman said. "How are you this morning, Patricia? Isn't this a beautiful day? I love autumn in New York! Oops! Did Dick Rodgers write that song?" He laughed at his joke. It was more than he had said to me during the four hours I'd spent with him at Oscar Hammerstein's Pennsylvania farm. My ever-vigilant stomach urged me to throw up.

Mr. Rodgers was talking to distinguished-looking arranger Robert Russell Bennett. Rodgers, dapper in a charcoal gray suit, white shirt and striped tie, waved from across the stage. Oscar Hammerstein, comfortable-looking in a tweed jacket, came over to say "hello." He crossed his arms and looked down from his six-feet-plus with a gentle smile. "Dick and I are pleased you're here, Pat," he said.

Judy Tyler was a small, black-haired girl with flawless ivory skin, a prominent widow's peak, and what seemed to be endless energy. *She's pretty, damn it.* I'd looked forward to seeing warts on her nose. Bill Johnson was manly and handsome, looking as "Doc" should, with a rugged beard. Titian-haired, larger-than-life Helen Traubel, the opera star, sat on a stool next to the piano.

What inspired casting! I thought. Helen Traubel, famous for intense Wagnerian roles at the Met, had a couple of years earlier allowed the world to enjoy her jovial personality in films, TV, and supper clubs. Her laugh was so contagious that Jimmy Durante declared: "I'd hire dat woman anytime, just to sit in my audience!" Miss Traubel had a run-in with Rudolf Bing, the director of the Metropolitan Opera, over what he considered her undignified extra-Met activities, so she resigned from the Opera. Guts. I liked guts.

It was earlier that summer, prior to my encounter with Harold Clurman, that Miss Traubel had been signed to play Steinbeck's *Cannery Row* madam, Fauna. I had called Alice Pearce with the news.

"Allie! Did you hear about Helen Traubel?"

"Henry Fonda, Helen Traubel, and Patricia Wilson," Allie said. "*Pipe Dream* sounds like a blockbuster to me!"

From my back row seat of the chairs onstage, I watched *Cannery Row's* raffish characters spill into the theater. Mike Kellin was cast as big-hearted, dim-witted Hazel. John Steinbeck, in his novel, had his character of Hazel explain his feminine name: "My mother had eight children in seven years—she got confused!" Mike was a serious actor with rubber features. Every dopey thing Hazel thought registered on his face. When I got to know him a little better, after a week or two of rehearsals, I mentioned my observation to Mike. He grinned.

"Well, that's interesting," he said. "Do you know what I call you, as I watch you during rehearsals? I call you 'Patty-With-The-Lived-In-Face.'" That meant my feelings had to be showing. I resolved to look less grim when I was around Harold Clurman.

A tall actor with scruffy beard-stubble, Warren Kemmerling, grabbed our company hairdresser up in his arms. "Ernie!" he boomed, whirling the little man off his feet.

"Ooo—oo—oo! Warren, baby!" squealed Ernie. They kissed full on the lips. Ernie fanned himself, rolling his eyes. "Mercy! That man!" he cooed. Warren Kemmerling, a steeplejack-turned-actor, was to stand by for Bill Johnson as Doc.

I marked my script for my lines as Harriet, one of the girls in Fauna's brothel. I would be onstage in every scene set in the Bear Flag Café, the gin mill/brothel of *Cannery Row*.

The man sitting in the third row of theater seats was John Steinbeck I thought his remarkable face was what the term "craggy" was created for, seeming as if all the characters he'd written registered there. Mr. Steinbeck, in his early fifties, had suffered a recent stroke. The side of his mouth drooped, slurring his speech, and a cane was propped between his knees. His disability only made him as fascinating as any movie star had been to me as a teenager. I kept sneaking glances at him, and decided if I was there for no other reason, it was an honor and thrill to meet this great man.

Journal, September 26, 1955: Dare I dig up the theme I wrote on Of Mice and Men in Lit class and show it to John Steinbeck? No. Presumptuous. Have read Cannery Row and Sweet Thursday over and over—what marvelous characters! Can't wait to see them come to life onstage. I'm glad I dropped my pride and stayed on. Wish Rick could be a fly on the wall to enjoy this experience with me.

A solemn Oscar Hammerstein gathered the cast together on the second day of rehearsal.

"Dick Rodgers and I want you to know before it hits the news: Dick had cancer surgery this morning. A tumor was discovered in his jaw during a dental exam last week." None of us uttered a sound. Mr. Hammerstein, shaken himself by the news, continued, "He's expected to make a full recovery. And he said for me to tell you—REHEARSE!"

Harold Clurman clapped his hands like a nursery-school teacher. "Let's go, actors," he said, smiling happily. *Could one lose one's Equity card for punching a director?* I wondered.

This was a star-crossed week. On Friday, September 30th, Mike Kellin returned from our lunch break, his rubber face solemn. "Did everyone hear about James Dean?" The young New York actor, a fast-rising Hollywood star, was a friend to several in our company, including John Steinbeck. Dean played the troubled younger son in the film version of Steinbeck's *East of Eden.*

Mike Kellin's eyes filled with tears. "Jimmy cracked up in his Porsche in California a few hours ago. He was killed instantly."

Journal, September 30, 1955: Midnight. Difficult to rehearse today. We managed a rough musical run-through. I can only tell you, Journal, —and Rick—that Judy Tyler can't sing worth a damn, except for a few good low notes. Sour grapes? I guess so. She got the job, I didn't. Anyway, what she lacks in voice she makes up for in self-confidence. I could use some of her chutzpah. Alvin Colt (costumer) says I'm too quiet, sitting in the back row without saying much. Mr. H. says Mr. R. is coming back next week. They got the cancer in time. He says he misses Mr. Rodgers's editorial mind.

Richard Rodgers returned to rehearsals five days after his cancer surgery. He sat in an onstage chair, away from Harold Clurman, holding a big handkerchief to his chin. He commented without self-consciousness through the handkerchief, only sometimes containing the drooling aftermath of the surgery. His mind and energy were focused on the task of molding this new piece of work. I realized what Oscar Hammerstein meant when he spoke of his partner's editorial mind. And I teared up with admiration for Mr. Rodgers's courage.

Harold Clurman laughed at all of Rodgers's remarks, glancing at him for approval each time he offered direction.

"That little bully is the most *obsequious* person I've ever known!" I said to Rick over supper that night at home.

"Obsequious? W—e—ll! Nice big word, English major," Rick teased.

"One of the cast calls him the ass-kisser. Would you rather I'd have said that?"

"No, I prefer obsequious. It's sad, isn't it?"

"Yes, if it weren't so horrifying. A successful man with a great reputation. Why is he so unsure of himself?"

"Maybe he's not so successful in all areas of his life," Rick said. My husband was wise.

Oscar Hammerstein always stood in the back of the theater, listening intently to his libretto and lyrics, only critiquing his own work. John Steinbeck continued to sit in the third row, mostly scowling, this man of formidable words speaking nary a one. It wasn't just the effect of the stroke. John Steinbeck was allowed *no* creative input into *Pipe Dream.* Only professional courtesy allowed him to be present during rehearsals and out-of-town tryouts.

We were in Boston, and I was at my place in the wings of Boston's Shubert Theater. It was my job to watch Judy Tyler rehearse script changes written overnight and given us each morning. I peeked around the side curtain to see if John Steinbeck was in his usual, third-row seat. Before I could register disappointment at his absence, I realized he was standing next to me, braced against his cane. I nodded an uncomfortable, shy "hello." He nodded back. We stood watching Judy rehearse a scene with Helen Traubel.

"Thmpth," John Steinbeck said. I went into alert mode. If John Steinbeck had something to say, I'd be all ears. I turned to look at him.

"That girl can't open in New York! That girl ith *not* the character I wrote!" said Steinbeck, the slurred speech of his stroke, as well as his dismay, very apparent. He nodded towards the stage. "Thuthy ithn't tough!! The girl ith like a wounded kitten! That'th the point—why Doc fallth in love with her! *You* are the girl I wrote!"

"Harold Clurman didn't see me as Suzy, Mr. Steinbeck. He thought—"

Steinbeck exploded. "I don't give a damn what Clurman thought! He didn't write the character, *I* did! He'th been wrong all along. Did you know he wath rehearthing another play at night in New York, and working on *Pipe Dream* in the daytime? He'th throwing *Pipe Dream* away!"

I thought he'd cry. Me, too. "Can't you do something, Mr. Steinbeck?"

"No, they know how I feel. They'll go down the drain before they admit they were wrong."

"I'm —uh—well, I'm a little stunned here, Mr. Steinbeck—"

"It'th the truth, Pat." Steinbeck's voice and demeanor softened. "You and I both got a bum deal. Dick and Othcar raved about you! You were their new find! Then Clurman took over, and brought the wrong girl in. I've theen you rehearth—*you are Thuthy!* You'll open in New York, if I have anything to thay!" His sad face got even sadder. "It won't happen, kid. You got thcrewed. Me, too."

He shook his head. "Call me John." He shuffled off with his cane.

"I will, Mr. Steinbeck!"

Pipe Dream tryouts took us to New Haven for a short week, then to Boston for a month. There, most of the cast stayed at an apartment hotel across Boston Common from the Ritz Carlton, where the stars and producers were ensconced. I spoke with Rick, at home in New York, every night. I missed snuggling close to him, falling asleep with his arm around me.

"I like the walk through the Common, Rick. The leaves are changing. We've begun understudy rehearsals, finally, on Wednesday and Saturday mornings, before the matinees."

"How does everyone stack up?"

"Great. Warren Kemmerling is a really good actor. He's gay, but you'd never know it onstage. We've learned our parts cold."

"Well, I knew *you* would. It's nice to hear everyone else is a pro, too."

Warren Kemmerling, I thought, *for a gay man, could certainly play straight well.* I made this comment to Joe Leon, an actor from the cast who had volunteered to help coach us privately in the Doc/Suzy scenes.

"Warren *gay*? Hardly, my dear," Joe laughed. I recalled what I'd witnessed between Warren and our company hairdresser.

"That's how secure Warren is as a man," Joe said. "He and Ernie knew each other from *Me and Juliet.* Take my word for it, Pat. Warren is anything but gay." Something inside of me was relieved.

As we understudies rehearsed, Helen Traubel, Judy Tyler, and Bill Johnson, the three stars, played out the *Pipe Dream* saga. We opened in Boston on November 1, 1955. The Boston critics saw possibilities in the piece, as had the New Haven press, given that Rodgers and Hammerstein had a month to hone the production before the New York opening. The sets were called "handsome." Alvin Colt's costumes were "weatherworn whimsy." All agreed the score and lyrics were quintessential Rodgers and Hammerstein, therefore memorable, particularly the love ballad, *All At Once You Love Her*, and a duet sung by Fauna and Suzy, *Suzy Is A Good Thing*.

The problem, according to several of the reviewers, was that the primary story, the love story, wasn't coming across the footlights. The delicate love match between Suzy and Doc, promoted enthusiastically by the ragamuffin citizens of Cannery Row, wasn't believable, and didn't involve the audience. One critic said that Judy Tyler couldn't act. Another beat around the bush, saying *"the acting on the part of some of the cast prevents the story from being realized."* Still another said Judy couldn't sing, but had *"the inner determination of a policewoman."* Almost all commented on Judy's good looks, and Bill Johnson's undeniable capability as a Broadway leading man.

Warren Kemmerling wasn't one to mince words. "The problem with the story? No man in his right mind would fall in love with Suzy the way Judy plays her," he growled. "It'd be like sleeping with a bucket of nails. I'd rather go back to climbing steeples." Judy complained that she had no dancing in the show. "I'm a dancer," she said, executing a pirouette. "They need to add choreography for me!"

Watching Suzy's scenes from the wings every night was how I learned the blocking, the stage movement. I knew Helen Traubel would need me to be letter-perfect if I went on with her. And I liked being backstage.

"Charlie," I said to our stage manager, "It may sound silly, but I feel close to God when I'm here!" Momma and I had talked about it. To her, unfolding scenes in the golden light bathing the stage was a spiritual experience.

"Beyond the lights are *people*, Patty, other souls waiting to be touched," she had said, her face shining. I shared Momma's thoughts with Charlie Atkin.

"Oh, I know exactly how she felt, Pat. There's nothing like the magic of theater. It's got to do with human beings communicating with each other—somehow God approves. I'll bet you feel it when you're out there!" He nodded towards the stage.

"I'll tell you a secret, Charlie. I say a prayer every time I'm waiting to make an entrance: 'Let your Light shine through me.' Mom taught it to me." Charlie put his arm around my shoulder. But he looked grim when he approached me the next night.

"It's hard for me to say this, honey. You've got to stop watching Judy from the wings. She says not to worry about going on for her. She's healthy as a horse, and plans to stay that way." I knew Charlie was carrying the message he'd been ordered to carry, and after that I stayed in my dressing room until I was needed onstage for my scenes as Harriet.

In one of those scenes, the Cannery Row citizens stage a ball, its theme "L-O-V-E." They prevail upon Doc and Suzy to create a mock wedding ceremony for the ball's grand finale. Their simple-minded scheme is to get a love match going between Doc and Suzy by allowing the lead characters to act it out. The Bear Flag girls, bedecked in skimpy bridesmaid's costumes made from the brothel's curtains, attend the bride. As Harriet, I had a line during the mock ceremony, "Oh-h-h!—it's so BEA-U-TI-FUL!" I padded my part, and did what women do at weddings. I cried. I wailed the line, sobbing on the last syllable. I snuffled and blew my nose into my lace-curtain sleeve.

Choreographer Boris Runanin had staged the scene.

"Bravo, young lady! I love your invention," he said. It received a huge laugh opening night in Boston, and even Harold Clurman said, "Leave it in!"

In every performance thereafter, the other Bear Flag girls began to weep and wail along with me. The girls were not mean or competitive. They just thought whores crying at a wedding was a funny idea, so they all joined in. The comic moment I'd created for myself was soon dissipated. Even my line, "O-h-h!—it's so BE-A-U-TI-FUL!" was lost in the noise of collective weeping. No one stopped them, and I don't know why. It probably wasn't important to anyone but me. What was one lost laugh, when everything was lost in the messy landscape of the show?

Life Magazine photographed **Cannery Row's** *mock wedding: I'm ready to break into tears, on the end (R.)*

The rest of the cast began drifting into understudy rehearsals. Warren said in his half-growl, "They're not coming to see me, Pat. They've all heard what happened to you. They think they've signed on to a lunatic asylum, and they come to see sanity."

Journal, November 10, 1955: Homesick! I want to sit on Rick's lap! This is ridiculous. Am I working with amateurs? Is everyone afraid to speak up to Harold Clurman? Everyone sees how this isn't working. It's awful for Helen Traubel—she's floundering. The show depends on her. I'm glad I have Warren Kemmerling to talk to.

Warren began waiting for me after the performance every night, to walk with me across Boston Common. We commiserated in our frustration with the show. The experienced actors in the company were putting together skillful characterizations, working by and among themselves, but Helen Traubel hadn't a clue how to proceed with her role. She relied on her hearty laugh and robust personality to carry her performance. And her sumptuous voice, though the irony was that it was her only asset that was underused. The simplest melodies were hers to own, but Richard Rodgers wrote nothing approaching the potential of her magnificent voice for *Pipe Dream*. Perhaps he wanted to underplay her operatic background, so that her transition from opera diva to musical comedy star would be complete. But no one worked with her on her role of Fauna, so vital to the success of *Pipe Dream*. I never saw our director in a private discussion with Helen. Often he was offstage with a leggy dancer, giving her the benefit of his Group Theater wisdom. But never did I see him offer Helen Traubel definitive direction or technique.

Richard Rodgers looked grim, and I mentioned it to Mr. Hammerstein. He said, "Dick is a worrier! And don't forget, he's been through a lot with his health."

Warren Kemmerling and I became close friends. He might have welcomed intimacy in the beginning, but respected my marriage and my determination to make it work. One cold November night, as we zipped across the Common, he took the scarf around my neck and pulled me close to his chest. I was comforted by his strength and warmth, and for a defining moment, I leaned into his heartbeat. We were both lonely. Warren was recently divorced. He traveled with his dog, Pulie, for company. I was apart from my husband, and we were suffering difficulties in our marriage. Rick and I couldn't share the intensity of what was happening in the painful creation of the all-involving world called *Pipe Dream,* as Warren and I did. There is a classic joke-line that describes such scenarios in theatrical circles: "I loved you, baby! But the show closed!"

Journal, November 18, 1955: May have avoided disaster tonight. I know I couldn't handle an affair. I'm as lonely as I've ever been, but I don't think bed-hopping solves anything for anyone, married or otherwise. Could I love Warren? He's warm and intelligent. I wish I still thought he was gay.

scene xvi: Autumn 1955-Summer 1956, Broadway, New York City

Journal, November 30, 1955: Pipe Dream opened on Broadway tonight, at the Shubert Theater. We have the largest advance sale in theatrical history!

But even though it ran on its advance for seven months, *Pipe Dream* was the only Rodgers and Hammerstein musical ever to lose money for its backers. The reviews following our opening were lukewarm. Brooks Atkinson of the *New York Times* called the show "sweet, pleasant, and enjoyable." Walter Kerr of the *Herald Tribune* commented on Oscar Hammerstein's penchant for social discourse in referring to the first act song called *The Tide Pool,* Oscar's metaphor for diverse humanity. McClain of the *Journal American* confessed to being a Steinbeck/*Cannery Row* aficionado, and expressed disappointment that his first joy at hearing of the project morphed into a great letdown. He complimented the "pleasing score," then commented, *Boy meets girl, sure, but who cares? The love interest, Judy Tyler, is an attractive young girl with an acceptable voice, period.* "Letdown" was to be a comment I heard in reference to *Pipe Dream* often, though never as poignantly as when I heard it expressed by John Steinbeck during our backstage conversation in Boston.

Helen Traubel was over-tired on opening night. Her natural heartiness that generally served her character of Fauna seemed forced. She paid a dear price with the critics. Bill Johnson came off well, most reviewer comments being of the "rugged, good baritone" variety. Judy received some nice notices as a "bright, young newcomer," and all made mention of her good looks. Director Harold Clurman made a clean getaway. His name was not mentioned in the reviews.

Rick went with me to *Pipe Dream's* opening night party at Sardi's. I wore a grape-colored taffeta Dior cocktail dress with a portrait neckline, cinched waist, and full skirt. It wasn't new. I had bought it in Columbus years earlier, discounted, of course, and had it altered. Judy came to our table.

"Hi, kid," she said. "Nice dress. Very classy." I thanked her, and introduced her to Rick. She gave him a disarming kiss on the cheek.

"Listen, kids, I heard your story with this show. I'm sorry, but it was 'kismet,' you know. I didn't care about doing this turkey like you did, Pat. I just wanted to shove it to Hollywood. Now that I've done that, it's all yours."

Warren came over to meet Rick. "Your wife should be playing Suzy," he said.

"From what Judy Tyler just told her, she will be."

"I wouldn't count on it."

Rick watched Warren walk away. "I thought you said that guy was gay. Is something going on between you two?"

"No, Rick. At first I thought he *was* gay. I was mistaken. We work well together. We're friends. That's it."

Rick nodded. "I don't think that's the way Warren feels about it."

Pipe Dream played out its advance sale of seven months, but audiences never took to the show. Hit-makers Rodgers and Hammerstein had created a major Broadway disappointment. During our run I began acting studies with Uta Hagen, and resumed therapy sessions with Dr. Braun. Rick and I enjoyed a quiet Christmas together, having an excuse, my eight performances a week, not to rush to our families in Ohio. John Steinbeck gave us a keepsake gift, a silver liquor bottle tag engraved, "A little gin, a little bourbon, a little red wine." It was a recipe prized by *Cannery Row*'s denizens.

My mother visited after the holidays and attended an understudy rehearsal. Warren Kemmerling said to her, "I'm in love with your daughter, Mrs. Wilson."

Mom didn't bat an eye. "You two would probably make beautiful music together," she said.

My friend Jet MacDonald, from the Oldsmobile tour, came to see a Wednesday matinee. "My, Bill Johnson is good in that role of Doc! Handsome, too. Is he married?" Her divorce from her husband was final.

"No, he's not married, Jet. Come backstage with me and meet him!" Her fair skin grew pink.

"No, no," she laughed. "I just think he seems special. He has a great career ahead of him." Jet was right. Bill was the only member of the *Pipe Dream* family to be nominated for a Tony.

I headed for Bill's dressing room. "My friend Jet saw the show this afternoon, Bill. She's a fan of yours. I think you should meet her."

"Then why don't I take the two of you to dinner at Sardi's after the matinee on Saturday?"

Jet and Bill were married four weeks later, before another Saturday matinee early in 1956, at The Waldorf-Astoria. Ray Walston, then playing the Applegate/Devil role in *Damn Yankees* (and later, television's "My Favorite Martian") was Bill Johnson's best man. I stood up for Jet.

"Remember what I told you once?" Jet asked before the ceremony. "When I suggested Gus Schirmer should be your agent, and you said you wanted to do something for me someday? Well, consider it done."

Helen Traubel lost all enthusiasm for playing Fauna. During the cast recording of the show, she asked to dub in her high notes "at a later time." She began forgetting lines and lyrics during performances. The beautiful duet she sang with Judy, *Suzy Is A Good Thing,* reveals how a loving Fauna attempts to build Suzy's self-esteem.

Fauna says, "Now, Suzy, repeat these things after me!" Suzy sits at the older woman's feet. Fauna sings a series of uplifting affirmations, beginning with, "Suzy is a good thing—this I know is true!" The affirmations are repeated by Suzy, reflecting her growing self-confidence. It's a lovely scene, quintessential Oscar Hammerstein. When Helen began forgetting the lyrics, she covered by singing operatic tones in her glorious voice. It exasperated Judy, who was supposed to repeat the words Helen sang. One night, after several instances of Helen's forgetfulness, an impatient Judy mocked her onstage, repeating Helen's nonsense syllables in a strident pseudo-mezzo-soprano voice. I raced to the wings. Charlie Atkin looked up from his stage manager's podium, shaking his head.

It was hard to take sides. Helen's forgetfulness put Judy's performance in jeopardy. I've worked with actors who have forgotten their lines. It's a difficult situation. On the other hand, Helen was distressed by the fact that she'd gotten no direction or support with her role. She was an extraordinary artist deserving of respect and consideration.

Helen missed many performances after that humiliating incident. Ruth Kobart ably subbed for her, but eventually Helen was replaced by Nancy Andrews, a brassy, vivacious comedienne with a Broadway following. Nancy's performance was vastly different from opera star Helen's, but she was a fun and convincing Fauna.

I was fond of Helen Traubel, and I think she was of me. We discovered we were both Geminis, her June birthday a day ahead of mine. She had left the company before those dates rolled around, so I called to wish her a happy birthday.

"And back at you!" she boomed. I was glad to hear her sounding rested and happier, but she turned wistful. "I could have been a good Fauna—I know it, Pat."

"You *were* a good Fauna, Helen," I said. I meant it. But I didn't add that she might have been, with direction and support, a brilliant Fauna. Possibly rescuing *Pipe Dream.*

On the night of June 26th, the last Tuesday of our run, Ruth Kobart was waiting for me as I got off the Broadway bus.

"You're late, honey! Judy is sick! You're playing Suzy tonight! Hurry!" We ran to the Shubert Alley stage door. Colin Romoff had called the theater to say Judy had laryngitis, and had sent me a telegram saying, "GO!" signed, "Judy and Colin." Ruth called Rick while I got into makeup and Suzy's first costume. Exact duplicates of the Suzy wardrobe had been made for me at the beginning of the run. This was to be the only time I wore them. Rick located Gus Schirmer, who was having dinner at Sardi's with actress Audrey Christie. Everyone rushed to the theater. The cast, especially Bill Johnson, reacted and adapted to a new interpretation of the scenes during the performance. Conductor Salvatore Dell'Isola watched me closely, allowing me to sing Suzy's songs my way. I belted the high note in *Everybody's Got A Home But Me,* and held it, letting the melody build to the lyric "Won't there ever be a home for me, some –where!" Holding that note, then almost whispering the last phrase—"Ev-rybod-y's got a home but me"—emphasized the poignancy of the song. The orchestra applauded along with the audience at the finish. Gus stood at the curtain calls, weeping, leading the audience in a standing ovation. The cast then applauded me, thus validating what my knowin' had always told me: I could succeed in the Broadway theater.

The next day Judy was back in her dressing room, to play out our last few days. She wasn't prone to laryngitis. She and Colin had deliberately arranged the night for me. I thanked her, for she had relinquished her record of no missed performances for the run. A package lay on my dressing table. It was a copy of *Sweet Thursday* inscribed: "To Pat from her understudy, John Steinbeck." There was a crude drawing that looked like a pig with wings next to the inscription. In parentheses, Mr. Steinbeck added: ("That's like Pegasus.")

It took a few years before I understood the inscription. Then John Steinbeck and I, in London at the same time, spoke about the

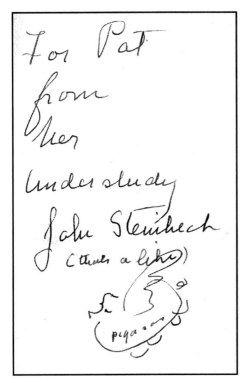

One fabulous memory from my fabulous life.

cherished copy of *Sweet Thursday* he'd given me. "But," I confessed, "I don't quite understand the drawing of Pegasus!"

"Don't you remember the myth, Pat? Pegasus was a golden-winged horse." Mr. Steinbeck, along with his speech, had thankfully recovered from his stroke. "A fellow captured Pegasus," he continued, "and tried to ride him into Heaven. The gods wouldn't let the fellow in. They knocked him off the golden horse's back."

John Steinbeck had to say no more.

scene xvii: Flash-forward to Early 1957, Tragic Epilogue to a Pipe Dream

A year after *Pipe Dream* closed, Bill ('Doc') and my friend Jet MacDonald Johnson became parents of a baby girl they named Julie. Bill joyfully moved his family to a country home in Flemington, New Jersey.

At four on a wintry morning. Rick answered our phone.

"Oh, God, no!" I heard him say. I braced myself.

"It's Jet, Pat—Bill Johnson just died." I took the first train that morning to Flemington. Bill had complained of chest pains the night before. Jet drove him to the hospital, where he died within an hour. He was forty-three. *Bill had Jet and Julie, if only for a short while,* I thought.

A few months later, in early July, I walked into the Sacramento Music Circus in California to begin rehearsals for *South Pacific*. Co-producer Howard Young was waiting for me.

"Pat, sit down, honey. There's been a terrible accident. Judy Tyler was killed."

Judy, *Pipe Dream's* Suzy, the nemesis of my young ambition, had achieved her dream of Hollywood stardom, filming the female lead opposite Elvis Presley in *Jailhouse Rock*. Divorced from musician Colin Romoff, to whom she was married during our run of *Pipe Dream*, Judy had remarried a young actor. She and her new husband were both killed in a Wyoming crossroads collision. Judy was twenty-six.

I talked to Helen Traubel at her home in Santa Monica. She was having a difficult time with the deaths of her young co-stars. "Pat, the two of them! I wish I could see you! Could you come to Santa Monica when you close in Sacramento?"

I planned to go. I wanted to see her. But I was called back east. I never saw Helen Traubel again.

scene xviii: Flash-forward to Early 2006, Monterey, California

Journal, *January 19, 2006: After all these years, I've visited Cannery Row. I've lived in California for thirty-odd years and have never before made the trip. I took off on a drive yesterday and ended up today in Monterey! The dogs were along for the ride, snoozing in the backseat. By San Luis Obispo it was getting dark, and I had to find a motel that would take my couple of critter-pals in along with me. Early this AM we pressed on up the beautiful coast highway. Big Sur, Carmel, Monterey. A magnificent, unplanned trip.*

Impressed that much of the real Cannery Row has been preserved. The "Doc" biological lab is still intact, as is the Monterey Canning Company, from the '20s and '30s. Even tourist shops are installed in original buildings.

The next day I traveled inland to Salinas, the town of Steinbeck's birth. There I visited The Steinbeck Center, where among the many exhibits is a replica of one of the sets from *Pipe Dream,* the old boiler pipe where the character of Suzy sets up housekeeping to move out of the Bear Flag Café. She adorns the pipe with fluffy pillows, café curtains, and candlelight. There is a loop of the cast album constantly running, and a cast picture, all of us frozen in time. Bill Johnson, Helen Traubel, Judy Tyler, Ruth Kobart, Warren Kemmerling. *And was that really me?* Still young and vital in the picture. The exhibit narrative explains that *Pipe Dream* was a disappointment for John Steinbeck. I felt sad for him, and for my young self, all over again. Richard Rodgers was quoted before his death, saying the failure of *Pipe Dream* was his fault, for it was he who insisted on casting Helen Traubel in the role of Fauna. Even that quote made me sad, for I condemned a different culprit for *Pipe Dream*'s murder.

Humbling to look at this display, I thought. Humbling to realize I'd known John Steinbeck. But sad that he saw his quirky, brilliant *Cannery Row* family destroyed on the stage. And sadder still that two other legendary men, Richard Rodgers and Oscar Hammerstein, became impotent at the wrong moment in theatrical history, allowing the debacle to happen.

ACT TWO

BIG-TIME TRAINING GROUNDS

"We will draw the curtain and show you the picture."
…William Shakespeare

scene i: Summer 1956, After Pipe Dream's close, Wallingford, Connecticut

From the fertile ground of Broadway's Golden Age grew an abundant crop of summer theaters, the "straw-hat circuit." Audiences across the country loved the informality of converted barns and movie theaters, open-air stadiums, and tents (theaters-in-the-round), that offered prime Broadway fare from Memorial Day to Labor Day. Star or name performers were not used or needed, and "the straw hat circuit" afforded rich opportunities for aspiring young actors to be seen in leading roles.

Journal, July 2, 1956: Richard Rodgers has recommended me to The Oakdale Theater in Connecticut to play Julie in Carousel. I love the role, but it terrifies me. I'm not sure my soprano voice is developed enough to do justice to If I Loved You. I'm a belter!

"I'll be the judge of your soprano voice, Pat." Richard Rodgers was imperious. *"You are Julie."* I was thrilled at the prospect of playing the role, for I loved *Carousel*. Its mystical aspects touched something deep inside me. The bench scene in Act One, the scene in which small-town Julie agrees to meet carnival barker Billy Bigelow, jeopardizing her reputation and her mill-worker job, mesmerized me. The musical underscoring, the dialogue, half-spoken, half-sung, Julie led by the star-crossed attraction she feels, Billy blustering against it, each singing *If I Loved You* to express inner feelings—if there is better theater anywhere, lead me to it.

Yet when I once told Richard Rodgers I thought *Carousel* was brilliant, his face puckered.

"Oh, boy, I wish you'd been around on opening night to tell me that," he said. "I watched the critics and thought we were dead in the water!"

Journal, July 10, 1956: I know Carousel is adapted from the French play Liliom, but everything about it—the "heaven" scenes with The Starkeeper, Billy coming back to help his daughter, the cosmic things—are so Oscar Hammerstein.

Even though I revered Oscar Hammerstein, I knew from first-hand observation that he was a "mere mortal man." I'd walked into the theater in Boston early one *Pipe Dream* matinee day. There,

72

behind the backdrop, was Mr. Hammerstein in an embrace with a beautiful showgirl. I'd heard dressing-room gossip that the girl had bewitched Oscar. But I'd also heard the Hammerstein marriage was a love-match. I decided that whatever it was I'd stumbled upon was an aberration, a by-product of the old theatrical bugaboo, out-of-town stress.

Of the two men, Richard Rodgers seemed the more complex, and was reputedly a womanizer. I personally never saw that propensity acted out, and he was never anything but professional with me. Perhaps it was his bout with cancer, or his frustration that *Pipe Dream* refused to gel, but his mind was not then on infidelity. I read later in biographies that he was an alcoholic, but his drinking is also something I never witnessed, although *Pipe Dream* was certainly enough to drive anyone to drink. No dirt here. I adored these gentlemen, Richard Rodgers and Oscar Hammerstein.

Journal, July 14, 1956: (Wallingford, CT): Mr. Rodgers was right! I am Julie. I connect with this role in all ways. And what a beautiful score! A wonderful company, too.

Walter Farrell and I were Carousel's Billy and Julie in 1956. Something magical happened.

There was never any doubt about handsome operatic baritone Walter Farrell's voice as Billy Bigelow, and as Richard Rodgers had predicted, my soprano began to pour out of me, seeming as if Julie sang through me. We were all confident as we approached dress rehearsal, the night before opening.

Carousel's director was a young Theater Arts professor from Brandeis University, Aaron Frankel. Very astute, with integrity for the work and the whole, Aaron transcended ego. When the sets appeared for dress rehearsal, they were cumbersome, primary-colored, dismayingly ugly, as if a demonic kindergartener had splashed papier mache and poster paint over the stage. Aaron ordered everything removed. For sets he used the unadorned modular blocks of varying heights we'd rehearsed with, now refreshed with a coat of white paint. During between-scene blackouts the blocks were shifted to create new patterns. All props, save one, were eliminated. Picnic baskets for the clambake scene, the bright gingham tablecloths for Nettie's restaurant, the knives Billy and Jigger carried: all gone. The sole remaining prop was the silver star Billy steals from Heaven to bring to his daughter. His daughter is frightened, but Julie finds the star, and knows Billy is there.

So for our opening night we had nothing but *Carousel,* ourselves, and God. During the final scene, the ensemble of actor-singers moved up the aisles and through the audience singing a reprise of *You'll Never Walk Alone.* Actor Walter Farrell, as Billy's returned spirit, spoke the last line of the play: "I loved you, Julie! Remember that I loved you!" and I stood to sing the last notes of Oscar's beautiful *You'll Never Walk Alone.* The lights came down, Julie's face in a lone pin-spot. The audience knows what Julie knows: Billy has been with her, on a last visit from Heaven.

During the black-out, I stayed in place on a modular block at stage left. Walter took his position on an identical modular at stage right. We stood rock-still while the lights came up center stage and the other cast members took their bows. The lights dimmed to blackout again while the stage cleared. A spotlight picked up on Walter/Billy. He stepped down and moved across the stage to me/Julie. He raised his arms and lifted me down. Embracing one last time, we moved to center stage to take our bows together. There was no applause.

Walter and I stood for a full thirty seconds in embarrassed confusion. Finally, from the back of the theater, came the sound of a choking sob. Then another, and another, building to a roar that sounded like a train. The audience got to its feet. They cheered, but it was more like a Hallelujah chorus.

My friend Alice Pearce was in the audience.

"Was that you sobbing, Allie?"

"It was everybody out there, honey! That performance was more than a stage production—there were angels flapping around everywhere in that theater!"

On our day off, I went to New York to be with Rick. When I returned, a cab picked me up at the Wallingford train station to take me directly to the theater for that night's performance.

"Oh, the Oakdale Theater," said the cab driver as he pulled away from the station. "I can't stop thinkin' about a play my wife and I saw there last week. We hadn't been gettin' along so well, you know, me and my wife, but this play we saw—boy, it changed our way of lookin' at things. It was some powerful story! And there was this girl—her voice sent shivers up and down my spine!" He glanced in the rear view mirror. "Oh, dear Lord! It's *you*!!" He swerved to a stop at the side of the road and turned to offer his hand across the seat. "Ma'am, thank you," he said. "That was beautiful! My wife and I will be talkin' about it the rest of our lives."

That is what theater is all about. Communication on the deepest level. I silently thanked Richard Rodgers for believing in me. To this day I think playing Julie in *Carousel* at The Oakdale Music Theater is the best work I've ever done.

I never played her again.

scene ii: Summer, 1956, Enter South Pacific, New York and Florida

Journal, July 30, 1956: Home. Hard to see Carousel end. I'm still awed by what happened. But good to be with Rick. He's moody again. I wish he could have seen Carousel! Such a spiritual happening.

"Pat, I'm looking for a job," Rick said, soon after I returned to New York.

"What kind of job, Rick?" He'd been playing pit piano in an upstate New York theater that summer, but was disenchanted with the work.

"Well, something solid. Something outside of show business. Music is a hobby for me now."

"It should be easy for you to find a job, Rick. You were smart to get a business degree. But are you sure?"

"It's the best thing to do. By the way, I've stopped seeing Dr. Braun."

Two important revelations, both lost amidst the bustle of the 1956 summer.

Journal, August 5, 1956: On a plane for Florida. I'm playing Nellie Forbush in "South Pacific" at last! At the Starlight Theater in Jacksonville. We open in four days—good that Rick and I have worked on the music since forever. I know it well.

I'd auditioned for director Ed Greenberg earlier that spring, to play Annie Oakley in *Annie Get Your Gun,* but his production conflicted with *Carousel* at The Oakdale.

"Ed likes you, Pat. He'll use you in something else," advised manager Gus Schirmer. Yeah, show biz talk, said my cynical edge. But after *Carousel* closed, Ed had a last-minute opportunity to direct *South Pacific* at the Starlight in Jacksonville. Remembering my audition, he called Gus to see if I was available, as well as if I was a quick study. I was both. At last I'd play the role of Nellie Forbush.

A South American baritone was cast as Emile DeBeque, *South Pacific's* leading male character, the French plantation owner with whom Nellie falls in love. The Latin actor swaggered through rehearsals, bragging about his arguable celebrity from a television coffee commercial, boring everyone. He pinched cheeks and swatted buttocks of college-girl-apprentices, perhaps feeling the need to fulfill the stereotype of Latin Lover. He'd mastered the art of suggestive eyebrow raising, and that was about all.

Nellie - SOUTH PACIFIC - 1956

Playing Nellie Forbush in South Pacific at last! Pop said there wasn't a dry seat in the house.

Opening night, with the huge stadium packed, just after I'd finished singing *I'm Gonna Wash That Man Right Outta My Hair*, the stage lights abruptly failed. The song ended with Nellie, blinded by shampoo suds, bumping into an amused Emile. There I was, close up to Latin-Lover-Man. We stayed in place. The blackout made it dangerous to move around.

The Starlight Theater in Jacksonville, Florida, was set in an open-air stadium, inspiring a sports-rooting mentality. The crowd impatiently stomped and hooted during the blackout, while Latin-Lover-Man grabbed at my breasts.

"Hey!" I yelled, jumping back. He snickered in the dark.

A pin spot relit itself and landed on my face. Everything around was still pitch black. Director Ed Greenburg yelled from the wings, "Sing, for God's sake, Pat! Sing!" Because the orchestra pit was in front of me, I could see musicians fumbling with their music. They couldn't read orchestrations until the instrument lights were restored. I walked to what would have been the footlights.

"Well, folks," I said in Nellie's Arkansas accent, "Since we've only got one spot goin' here, it looks like you're stuck with me for a while." I babbled on, all about my life as Nellie from Little Rock, and how I was falling for this foreign fella I'd met. When the instrumental lights flickered on, I started singing *I'm In Love With A Wonderful Guy*. The orchestra caught up with me. Eventually the lights all flashed back on, and the audience whooped and hollered while I took exaggerated bows and pranced around the stage. Ed Greenberg stood in the wings, grinning. Latin-Lover-Man was planted upstage, arms folded, having moved nary an inch during the blackout.

When the scene ended I expressed my off-stage fury to Latin Lover-Man. "Keep your hands off me, senor! I have a very large husband!"

"Perhaps, dearie, but very small breasts," Latin-Lover-Man snorted, stalking away.

The next morning's papers reviewed the blackout's impromptu performance first, calling Nellie and me "winning." Latin-Lover-Man as Emile was "stiff, awkward," and worse. Even I felt sorry for the dolt, he took such a critical lambasting.

During the next night's performance, my co-star looked at me with a completely blank expression at the end of the song *Cockeyed*

Optimist. He had the first line after the song, but didn't deliver it. Hoping to help him recover, I said the line, then as Nellie, I answered myself, and waited for Emile to pick up on his next line. Nothing from the glassy-eyed senor. Silencio.

"Hey, Emile!" I said. "We're never gonna get together if y'all don't talk to me!" The audience laughed and applauded.

"I am going to *k—i—i—ll* you!" Latin-Lover-Man hissed under his breath. Then finally, as Emile, he resumed his lines from the scene: "I am older than you, Nellie! If we have children—"

We played it through, the beautiful love scene between Nellie Forbush and Emile DeBeque. The music soared and the lights dimmed. I broke away from Latin-Lover-Man and sprinted to my dressing room. There was an urgent knock at the door. Ed Greenberg was accompanied by a large, pimply-faced stagehand, who wore such a frightened expression I knew there was something wrong.

"Pat, lock this door and don't open it! Jimmy will stand guard. Security has called the police."

"Good Lord, Eddie, what happened?"

"He has a knife. He swears he's going to kill you."

"You're kidding, Ed. I was just trying to keep the show going."

"I know that, and you know that, but this guy is crazy! Stay here. I'm going to talk to him."

Now it was my turn to worry about Ed. But when the offended Latin-Lover-Man was told his career would be ruined if he carried out his threat, and all would be forgiven if he peacefully continued with the show, he calmed himself. Ed explained that I was just a zany American girl, and knew nothing of good taste and manners, like the infinitely more refined Latin American ladies Lover-Man knew. Couldn't he, as the big person everyone recognized him to be, find it in his magnanimous heart to forgive me and go on with the performance?

With the wide-eyed cast and crew watching, Latin-Lover–Man strode dramatically to my dressing room, bent into a deep bow, and kissed my hand. As he raised himself from the bow, he glanced at my breasts, the ones he had groped during the black-out the night before. He smugged a smile as he turned on his heel, muttering something in his native language.

"I wish I understood Spanish!" I said to Ed Greenberg.

"Yeah," Ed said, "Mine's not so good either." He shook his head. "It doesn't make sense, but I think he said something about thimbles!"

Journal, August 12, 1956: I'm already booked to play Nellie again this summer, at The Brandywine Music Box in Delaware. I leave in nine days. Thank God it will be with a different actor playing Emile.

Mom and Pop came to Delaware to see *South Pacific.* Pop, solemn, took me by the shoulders.

"Pat, you've developed as an *actress.* Nellie's emotional soliloquy on the beach, when she thinks Emile may be dead? It couldn't have been played any better, and don't accuse me of bias!"

Playing Ensign Nellie was safer without "Latin Lover Man."

"Really, Poppa?" He laughed as we said it together, "There wasn't a dry seat in the house!"

Journal, August 24, 1956: Had a chance to talk with Mom alone before the matinee. I told her Rick's and my marriage is suffering. I'm away from home too much. "But how else could you pay rent and eat?" she asked. A good question.

Ten days after I closed with *South Pacific* in Delaware, the actress playing Nellie Forbush in The Westbury Music Circus production of *South Pacific* became ill the day after their opening. The producers needed someone who knew the role to step in that night and finish out their season. Gus called me in the morning, I was on a train to Westbury in Long Island by noon, rehearsed with the cast at two, and went on that night.

Journal, September 5, 1956: What a privilege to play Nellie again, with this company. Juanita Hall is playing Bloody Mary. She won a Tony award originating the role on Broadway. She says such kind things—(even that I remind her of my idol, the original Nellie, Mary Martin!)

Best of all, I don't have to leave Rick and home. I can commute. But nights are getting cool for Wash That Man Right Outta My Hair! Brrr! Asked the prop guy to rig up a little warmer water in the shower scene.

The straw hat season was over for another year when Westbury's *South Pacific* closed at the end of September.

scene iii: Autumn 1956, Enter Carol Burnett, Jean and Walter Kerr, and Leroy Anderson, Back in New York City

Journal, October 2, 1956: Working again, doing another industrial show (like The Mighty O!) in the Waldorf Astoria Hotel ballroom. Sing a duet with a nice gal named Carol Burnett—a parody of Gershwin's old song S'Wonderful. We sing "S'Fi-ber-glass! S'Wonderful!" Imagine! Industrial show writers have no shame. Carol is a GREAT gal, fun to work with.

Sometime during that New York autumn, I attended a party in Gus Schirmer's townhouse on East 62nd Street.

"Come over! I made chicken-in-aspic to die for," Gus said. "And I have a new edition of *'Stolen Moments'* to screen!" Gus always had a reel of film clips to show his guests, outtakes of film stars in musical numbers. These snippets of film, often with missteps or errors of some kind, were intended for the cutting room floor, but magically found their way into Gus's hands. He called his reels of film clips *Stolen Moments.*

When we were invited to Gus's for a party, Rick and I knew we might be at the piano for most of the evening. We didn't mind. We owed Gus a great deal.

At Gus's party that autumn, I met Peggy Cass and her husband, Carl Fisher. Peggy was a brash, funny redhead. Carl, her husband, was the company manager for George Abbott productions. That evening, Peggy pulled a chair up close to the piano.

"Gus tells me he calls you up in the middle of the night so you can sing to him." It was true. My phone would ring at any hour.

"I need to hear you sing," Gus would say. "Did I wake you up? Were you making babies?" I knew open-hearted, sentimental Gus must have been hurt by someone. He called the morning after I'd met Peggy Cass and her husband.

"Peggy wants to recommend you to Jean and Walter Kerr. They need someone to sing the score for a new musical they've written, *Goldilocks,* for potential backers. Leroy Anderson wrote the music. He composed *'Sleigh Ride'* and *'Syncopated Clock.'* I think you should do it. They're good people to know."

Walter Kerr was the theater critic for the *New York Herald Tribune.* (Later for *The New York Times.)* His wife, Jean, had written books based on their family life, including *Please Don't Eat the Daisies.* That book became a movie starring Doris Day, then a television series with another of Gus's clients, Pat Crowley.

The phone rang again, an hour after Gus called.

"Patricia? This is Walter Kerr. I just wanted to say 'hello' and to thank you for agreeing to sing our auditions. Peggy Cass says you'll more than do our material justice. I'm going to put my wife on to talk to you."

"Hi, Pat!" Jean was less formal than Walter. "Could you come out to our place in Larchmont tomorrow to go over the score with Leroy? I'll meet you at the train station, and feed you lunch when you get here."

I'd never met nicer people than the Kerrs and Leroy Anderson. Nor had I ever seen such a beautiful home as the Kerrs'. It was like a comfortable version of an English castle, with a two-story living-room, its tall windows overlooking Long Island sound. A mahogany staircase, down which I could envision an actress like Joan Crawford or Bette Davis sweeping in a sable-trimmed gown, led to a balcony full of nooks and crannies and doors. Periodically, the face of a small boy would poke through the banister. The Kerr family included five sons.

After lunch in a big country-comfortable kitchen, Leroy Anderson and I went to the piano in the living room. I was nervous. This man was an icon in American music, and a tall, imposing figure. I told Mr. Anderson my ear usually picked things up faster than I could read music. He nodded. Truth to tell, I was a lousy sight-reader. We went through a ballad called *My Last Spring.*

"Patricia," said Leroy Anderson, "I hear the rhythms of this song through your interpretation!" He played a gentle, rocking introduction. "You've inspired me!" What a kind man. My nervousness dissipated, and we became a working team. We continued to an upbeat song, *If I Can't Take It With Me,* and a novelty, *Who's Been Sitting In My Chair?* Mr. Kerr spoke up. "We've written this show for Mary Martin. You'll be singing it for her next week, if that's okay."

"You mean you want me to sing this score for Mary Martin in person?" Everyone laughed.

"Yes, and her manager—her husband, Richard Halliday."

Stunned as I felt at the prospect, I took the score home, thankful I was a quick study and had Rick to help. This was Friday, and Leroy Anderson and the Kerrs and I were to meet Mary Martin on Tuesday morning.

Tuesday dawned cold, windy, and sleeting, nary a cab in sight. My umbrella was turned inside out and my hair soaking wet by the time I got to the bus stop at Broadway and 85th Street. There wasn't much opportunity to repair on the bus ride to 57th Street and the Nola Studios.

How did Mary Martin manage to look so pristine? She was tiny, groomed, adorable—and sitting right under my nose. I faced her, with the *Goldilocks* music on a stand in front of me. My hair hung limp from the inclement March morning.

"Miss Martin, I feel like a drowned rat! And I don't think I've ever been so nervous in my life!"

"Oh, pish tosh," said the icon of the musical theater. "Don't be nervous! And don't let Richard intimidate you!" She nodded to her manager/husband, Richard Halliday, on the opposite side of the room, talking to Walter and Jean Kerr. "He can be a real sourpuss." She got that right. Richard Halliday was a real sourpuss.

The audition went well. Mary Martin smiled and applauded and thanked me for my time. As I've said before, class always tells. Miss Martin turned the show down, which I know was a great disappointment for the Kerrs and Leroy Anderson. Mary Martin chose to do a new Rodgers and Hammerstein musical instead. One called *The Sound Of Music.*

Goldilocks was auditioned several more times for potential financial backers. I recorded the original score for the Kerrs, with Leroy Anderson accompanying me on piano, early in 1957. After singing the score live for Roger Stevens and Robert Whitehead at The Producers Theater, I was dismissed from the room while they discussed a possible replacement for Mary Martin. Roger Stevens had nodded towards me, asking, "Why not Pat?" I was thrilled by the overheard suggestion, but even I knew I wasn't established enough to play the lead. The Kerrs and Leroy Anderson needed a name to sell tickets. The Producers Theater presented *Goldilocks* with actress Elaine Stritch in the lead. Since the show was developed for Mary Martin to play the role, its score was considerably altered to feature the talents of the very different Elaine Stritch. Even so, it was not a success.

Thirty-three years later, in 1990, while having dinner at Joe Allen's in New York with theatrical agent Andrew Zerman, Andrew handed me a tape. "It's a bootlegged copy of your *Goldilocks* recording with Leroy Anderson, Pat."

"Where in the world did you get this, Andy?"

"Every musical comedy buff in New York has a copy of this," he said.

A different version of *Stolen Moments.*

Flash forward to a journal entry of February, 2006: *Leroy Anderson's son, Kurt, just called. He wants to include some of my Goldilocks recordings from 1957 in a special edition DVD about his father's amazing career, to be shown on PBS. I gave my blessing.*

scene iv: 1957-1959, Enter the Club Star, New York, Dallas, and the rest of the country

"I can't get a job because I don't have a stinking degree!" Rick never shouted, and George the cocker spaniel began to tremble.

"What are you saying, Rick? You graduated in Business Administration! I had a party for you—I gave you that ID bracelet!" I pointed to the silver circlet he wore every day.

"Yeah, well, you didn't go to any graduation ceremony, did you? I flunked out! *I didn't graduate.*" He paced around our living room. "Then we were married, and I had a good job at WBNS-TV. I thought a degree didn't matter. Who knew I'd need a *damn* degree to get a *damn* job in *damn* New York?"

It was January. Heavy snow assaulted our living room window. Neighboring Riverside Drive was windy and cold, but my first instinct was to run outside.

"Rick, we've been married for six years! You didn't have to keep anything from me." Rick sat on the sofa, silent. "So, okay, so what! It can be fixed. Go back to school! You can still get your degree."

"It'll take me two years to get a degree in New York, Pat. I've already checked it out."

"Well, then go back to Ohio State and pick up that last quarter. We have lots of friends you could stay with."

Rick put his head in his hands. "It's more serious than that. I faked that I was in classes for my whole last year. I was busy with our school shows, that was what was important. I have at least a year to go, even at Ohio State. I'm so sorry, Pat."

It wasn't the no-degree-no-decent-job dilemma. It was the betrayal, mostly of himself.

Journal, January 7, 1957: I'm trying to sort stuff out. It boils down to one thing: I'm scared. What happens if I get sick and can't work? What if we have a baby? I'm 28 this year. I can't go on working forever. This business isn't one that will let me. I've been lucky. But even now is a dry spell—nothing to audition for. Could I get a job? Non-show biz? Here come the tears. I've thought trust was the best thing we had going. Rick shouldn't have kept this from me.

Was I making a mountain out of a molehill? I was resentful, but I was also aware of the guilt Rick must have carried. I went to see Dr. Braun.

"You and your husband were married very young, Patricia. Let me ask you something important: might there be other things about Rick you don't know?"

Journal, March 18, 1957: Nothing written here for too long. I've spent this whole winter walking. I met Jet for lunch today. Told her about Rick. She said, "You could have a baby, like Bill and I did. How would Rick take care of a family?" I wonder, too.

Summer auditions start soon. Producer Charles Meeker comes in from Dallas next week. I'd love to play the Dallas State Fair Musicals. Or do I just want to get away?

Journal, March 25, 1957: Finally met and sang for Charles Meeker. He books the Statler Hilton in Dallas as well as the State Fair Musicals, and wants me to open in that hotel's elegant Empire Room on April 4th— only ten days away! He says just stand up and sing, but I need a 45-minute act. This takes my mind off my troubles.

"Well, my dear, you're an official chanteuse!" Gus was laughing. Chanteuse was what singers at the top of their game were called in the '50s, singers who performed in posh rooms like the New York Plaza's Persian Room, and the elegant Maisonette at The St. Regis Hotel. Such entertainers had to hold an audience for up to an hour with their solo acts.

"Goody, I always wanted to be one of them chantoozies, Gus. Okay! Let's get to workin' on me!"

"Stop!" Gus laughed. He liked my hick act. "We have to find you something special to wear for opening night, when the critics will be there. Dallas is a sophisticated town, you know. The Empire Room is very exclusive." I wished he'd kept his comments to himself. I didn't need to be intimidated. He located a designer willing to design a gown for me, for cost and credit. Gus added, "And I also called the William Morris Agency." That alarmed me. I knew he had sold his contract with Shirley Jones to the Morris Agency.

"I know *bupkes* about supper clubs, Pat. This is a big opportunity. You'll be an immediate headliner at the top of the circuit, making at least a thousand a week. Let's not fool around." Gus was being discreet. He knew all was not well with Rick and me. "I talked to Kenny Welch. He's done a lot for Carol Burnett. He'll organize your act, write special material, and go to Dallas with you for your opening." Kenny was not just a writer and arranger, but also a great accompanist.

Kenny and I settled down for nine days of hard work, and on April 2nd, invited friends to a run-through of our new show. From the opening song, a rousing, double-time arrangement of Jule Styne's *Just In Time*, the act played brilliantly, but my mind was on Rick, who had chosen not to attend the run-through. The opening night designer gown wasn't finished in time to make the run-through a dress rehearsal, and was delivered to me in a garment bag as I waited for a taxi to the airport the next day. I hurried it into the cab, along with a caseful of arrangements for a 20-piece orchestra, on which the ink was still wet. I heard those arrangements for the first time in a rehearsal the next day, the day of my opening.

After boarding our flight for Dallas, Ken and I both promptly fell asleep. We were awakened by the captain telling passengers to fasten seat belts, since we were heading into a thunderstorm. The plane swooped and bumped for twenty minutes. Kenny turned green and took out a barf bag. I consumed a Baby Ruth bar. Sweets were always my answer to stress, and airplanes were the only place my stomach didn't bother me.

The captain's reassuring voice came over the loudspeaker again. "Folks, we may have to divert a few miles here. There's bad weather around Dallas. Memphis is making room for us to land. We'll sit things out there." Crackle, crackle from the loudspeaker, then, "They just evacuated Love Field?" The pilot had missed turning off a switch, and we passengers heard what we weren't supposed to. Love Field in Dallas, where we had been headed, was being hit by a tornado. We landed for a few hours in Memphis, then flew into Dallas late that night. Ken and I were exhausted, emotionally and physically. *We should turn around and go home*, I thought. It was a good knowin'.

Opening night was a convergence of nervous fatigue, unfamiliar material, and that too-good-to-be-true-bargain gown. The thing hadn't been given a trial run. Its soft mauve, flowing chiffon cape caught on a music stand as I strode grandly onto the stage. Nearly garroted, I was stopped short. The trumpet player freed me to proceed to the microphone as I realized, too late, *"Dear God! I'm starring in a nightmare! I must look like a purple Superman with a beaded bosom in this get-up!"* It was all downhill from there.

"EVEN MICKEY MANTLE KNEW THE BUSH LEAGUES!" screamed the headline of the review of my new act in the *Dallas Morning News*. It criticized my material, my gown, my lack of poise, even Gus Schirmer. Gus was called a Svengali, trying to pawn an amateur off on sophisticated Dallas audiences. It was such a disastrous opening that The American Guild of Variety Artists called and offered to fight for my full salary. They assumed I'd be fired. So did I.

Why did it happen? With years of performing under my belt, including club work, I *wasn't* an amateur. Heartsick over my faltering marriage and Rick's seeming indifference to this milestone in my professional life, I was carrying an underlying depression. The sounds I heard coming from the orchestra at rehearsal were nothing like Kenny's piano accompaniment, but I didn't have the demanding nature to request additional rehearsal time before the opening.

If I'd had my way, I'd have snuck out of Dallas like a kicked pup, but Charles Meeker was a different kind of boss. He didn't fire me, but kept me on, actually paying me to work on my act while headlining in the prestigious Empire Room for the next two weeks. I couldn't let Charles down. I worked hard by day, and during performances engaged audiences by reading the worst of my horrific reviews, and tearing up expensive orchestrations. "See this loser?" Rip, rip. "Out it goes!" I cut the chiffon cape from my Superman dress, picked most of the hideous beading from the bosom, and wore it as a straight, simple sheath. When I cashed my first week's paycheck I blew it all on two stunning gowns: a black Halston and a white-sequined Ceil Chapman. One by one the critics came back. They re-wrote their reviews into glowing reversals of the originals. Sid Epstein, a prominent agent from the William Morris office, appeared on closing night. He beamed. "Great, Pat! Welcome to our roster of supper club stars!"

I called Gus to tell him, "I'm an official chantoozie, Gus. I think angels must have kept Sid Epstein away until I worked out the kinks."

"Well, at least one did," Gus said, "and his name is Charlie Meeker."

Charles and I had dinner before I left Dallas. I thanked him, and apologized for letting him down in the beginning. "It's not about how it began, Pat. It's about the journey you took and how you acquitted yourself," he said to me. Thank you, Charlie. A life-lesson from a wise mentor. My mantra, "Up, again, old heart!" had served me well. When I returned to New York, Dr. Braun agreed.

"You grew up, Patricia," he said. "You respected yourself enough to fight for your career."

"I want to fight for my marriage, too, Dr. Braun."

"Ahhhh," Dr. Braun became very European. "But that takes two, Patricia. That takes two."

scene v: 1957-1958, New York

Journal, April 25, 1957: The other shoe has dropped. Rick wants to separate. He says he needs time apart, and wants me to leave our apartment so he won't have to move the Steinway. I don't want to be in our place anyway, damn him. But he wants to keep George! (Later: I'm cooled down.) Makes sense, I guess. I travel so much. George has never known a home except W. 87th and Riverside Drive Park. But I'll miss him. Can't believe this is happening.

Journal, May 2, 1957: I've rented an apartment in The Wilshire House, at 134 W. 58th. Lots of show people in the building, a switchboard and doorman. Haven't been able to eat. Gus says, "This will make a difference! Rick has held you back!" That made me angry, but I kept quiet. Jet said something strange, "Thank God the veil has lifted!"

"But Jet," I said, "I didn't break up our marriage. Rick did!"

"Then he lifted the veil for you. Someday you'll understand."

Journal, May 18, 1957: I'm like a blubbering child, at 28 next month. Please, old heart! Up again! I'm in such pain. My heart isn't listening. Sometimes I think it has stopped beating.

scene vi: Late 1957-Early 1958, Enter "Charlie",Kansas City, Winnipeg, Canada

Journal, June 19, 1957: Working in The Starlight Roof at the Chase Hotel in St. Louis. It helps take my mind off Rick. What went wrong? Ken and his wife Mitzie are with me. I'm sure they're worried about me. I've lost 12 pounds.

Journal, July 16, 1957: Things are snowballing. The Chase Hotel manager has contracted me for three return appearances in The Chase Club, the largest, most exclusive room in St. L. Only big name stars play there. As word of the agreement gets around, I'm booked for six months in advance: The Shamrock in Houston, the Statler in Detroit, the Drake in Chicago, the Ritz Carlton in Montreal.

Thus I was launched to the top of the supper club circuit. Today young singers tour and play amphitheaters and sports arenas like New York's Madison Square Garden. In the 1950s, singers

An important re-do after the disastrous Dallas opening. No more nightmare gowns!

at the top of their game played supper clubs. The gowns with sequins and bugle beads of my day have given way to black leather bustiers and thigh-high boots, but one thing about touring life remains the same: it is grueling and lonely.

Journal, November 27, 1957: Kansas City. No word from Rick. Not even a phone call for seven months.

My Kansas City booking was a popular night spot, a high-class dive run by some not-so-high–class guys. I was spoiled by the beautiful hotel clubs I'd been working, and hated the job. Passing through the lobby of my hotel on Thanksgiving Eve, headed for the club, I spotted two of the most adorable pups I'd ever seen. They were toy Yorkshire terriers, ten weeks old, weighing less than two pounds apiece. Their owner explained that she bred the little dogs, and had brought the puppies to the hotel to meet a potential buyer. One of the puppies love-attacked my outstretched hand, tugging at my coat sleeve. He rolled onto his back, exposing a fat pink belly. Adorable. My heart lifted.

The lady sighed. "Well, I've waited as long as I can. My buyer hasn't shown up. I have to get home." I always carried a hundred dollar bill tucked in my bra in those days, my "lucky hundred," and I offered it to her.

Yorkshire terrier Charlie, my entourage.

"I'd like to buy this pup," I said, allowing the tiny black-and-tan ball of fluff to lick makeup from my cheeks.

"Oh, I'm sorry! These dogs have champion pedigrees," said the lady-seller. "They're three hundred dollars apiece."

"Oh, I see." I sat the pup back on the lobby floor. He scrambled across the marble and wrestled his brother into a Yorkie strangle-hold. "Thank you for letting me play with him. I'm sorry your buyer didn't show. Good luck." I turned away. I wasn't negotiating, as you do with a used car salesman. I had no more to offer.

"Oh, miss!" The lady-seller called after me. "Take him," she said, handing over the tiny, bright-eyed fuzz-ball. "Have a Merry Christmas!"

The little dog had to be smuggled into the club in my large, flat-bottomed purse. Looking at me with button-bright eyes, he sighed, nestled in next to the makeup kit and hair dryer as if he knew he belonged there, and fell asleep. The club owners be damned, my new friend was going with me. He was a gift from God that lonely holiday, my salvation and companion. "Your name is 'Charlie'," I told him, "After a good friend of mine."

When I'd say, "Show time, Charlie! Hit it!" he'd run and jump into the purse. For the next year, Charlie rode in the purse on airplanes, into the best hotels in the country, and even once, in an emergency, across the border into Canada. That was, admittedly, a real smuggling job, but he never gave himself or me away, and I did it without apology. I called Charlie my entourage, and he saved my life.

Journal, December 23, 1957: Home in Cincinnati for Christmas. Charlie has won everyone's heart! A nice warm time. Eases the pain of this holiday without Rick. He's dropped off the face of the earth.

The William Morris Agency called on Christmas Eve. Emergency. I was to report to the Cork Club in Houston, to open on Christmas night. I left my family early Christmas morning. Ten days later, the engagement over, I planned to return to Cincinnati for a belated holiday celebration. But the Morris Agency reached me on my closing night in Houston.

Journal, January 4, 1958: Another emergency! (Hope all of 1958 isn't going to be this hectic.) Lena Horne is ill, and cancelled out of a club engagement in Winnipeg. The agency has booked me on a flight from Houston-to-Minneapolis-to-Winnipeg to replace her. Charlie is with me. No time to leave him anywhere—I must put him in my purse and smuggle him into Canada!

On a bitter-cold Sunday afternoon, I arrived in Winnipeg. The airport customs official was a small, colorless man with a brush of insipid blond moustache and deep-seated suspicions of a stateside singer arriving with nothing but a verbal contract to play a Canadian nightclub.

"You say you have a job here, but you don't have a contract to prove it."

"Arrangements were made over the phone by my agency with the owner of the club. I'm an emergency replacement for Lena Horne."

"Well, I've heard of Lena Horne. I never heard of you." He eyed my borrowed mink coat, then my purse. Charlie flip-flopped in the bottom of the bag, thudding against the side. I made a show of shifting my weight and stamping my foot against the floor.

"Ouch...cramp in my leg from sitting on the plane."

"Well, if I can reach the owner of the club to confirm your employment, I'll let you go through." It was Sunday. The club was closed. "What's in this luggage, Miss?"

"My evening gowns. The ones I sing in."

He opened the bag, and, stone-faced, lifted out each gown and inspected it, running ink-stained fingers over chiffons and silks. *Something weird here,* I thought.

"And this case?"

"Music. Orchestrations. It's heavy!" A play for sympathy-camaraderie.

"Please just sit over there, miss. This'll take a while."

The border fellow wasn't kidding. He thumbed through the orchestrations. He gave each gown another once-over, running his fingers over the fabrics. *Creepy.* There I sat, Charlie in my purse, for three hours. Had it been in today's world of travel, my purse would have been ransacked as well. Then, a lady's handbag was sacrosanct. A small electric heater blasted out dry hot air, and it was uncomfortably warm in the small room. Again, Charlie flopped over in the bottom of the purse with a noisy sigh. I stood, making what I thought was a similar noise by stomping my foot. "Ow-oo! Leg went to sleep again!" I smiled at the grim-faced customs agent. *Boy, that moustache of his never moves.*

"I'll have to charge you duty on your dresses and music."

"How much?"

"Oh, I think three hundred American dollars will cover it." I gulped, reaching for the checkbook in my purse. A small, warm tongue licked my hand. I dried it on my skirt before Mr. Moustache caught sight of Charlie's saliva.

"All right," said my captor. "I guess you are who you say you are. You're to leave Canada in exactly one month." I corralled a cab driver from in front of the airport to gather up my bags, and left quickly, pup-in-purse.

The hotel room phone rang the next afternoon, as I prepared to attend orchestra rehearsal. A gruff voice said, "Miss Wilson? We're sending a car to pick you up. Don't try to get a cab." Charlie hopped in my purse. He would, as usual, wait for me in the dressing room, and I prayed it would be warm. I grabbed my mink coat, which a friend had insisted I borrow to advertise her cousin's fur salon. *Ah, the "perks" of a glamorous profession.* I wished I felt comfortable in the damn coat. I didn't. It always felt borrowed.

Appearing at my door was Joe, a polite, handsome young man, looking more like a college football star than the gangster I assumed he was. I'd had by then enough experience with nightclubs in major American cities to know many of them were mob-owned and run. Joe escorted me to a warm Cadillac, helped me into the car, stowed my gowns and orchestrations in the copious trunk, and unloaded them for me when we got to the club. I rehearsed with the band, half of which was missing because of the weather. Joe stood to one side, listening intently. The club owner, Del Martino, appeared about an hour before scheduled showtime. He looked as I imagined he would. Warm Italian eyes that had seen a lot, set in a face that looked as if it had been hammered a lot, like that of a pro boxer.

"Welcome to our place, Miss Wilson. Sorry our town is so cold."

"I'm worried about an audience. Are there any reservations?"

"Well, no," said Mr. Martino. "There probably won't be, until it warms up."

In my second-best and warmest gown, I performed the first set of songs in my act for an audience consisting of the club owner and five of his friends. The cold was paralyzing. There weren't even waiters in the club, save the two attending Mr. Martino and his buddies. The engagement should have been cancelled. The group was polite, trying to be attentive, but when I finished the upbeat part of my act, heading into ballads and a dramatic piece, I stopped the orchestra.

"Look," I said to Mr. Martino and his friends, "isn't this ridiculous? You gentlemen don't want to hear my act. You don't care whether I'm good or not, only if I bring people into the club. I can't do that with no reviewers here, no audience. Maybe Lena Horne could, but I can't. Why don't we call it a draw? I'll go back home to Ohio and see my folks." I thanked the half-orchestra, and walked off. *Aha, Patricia, learning to be a diva at last!*

A voice broke the silence from the table of men. "Did you catch that broad? Boys, that's *class!*"

Journal, January 6, 1958: Guess I'm OK after my grand exit from the stage. Mr. Martino asked me to stand by for the weeks of my contract, in case the weather warms and customers return.

Although I didn't sing another note in Winnipeg, I was paid in full. Delicacies were sent to my hotel, not just for me, but for Charlie. Joe drove me wherever I wanted to go, and to and from the club each night. I reported for duty, just to make sure no customer ventured in from the cold. I was never treated as a trophy for Mr. Martino and his friends again.

Gentlemanly Joe was highly intelligent, sensitive, and college-educated. A mobster stereotype is what I'd expected, but I was amazed to find he liked Emerson and Steinbeck as much as I. We shared deep discussions about Life— what it was about, why we were here, what Greater Force put us on our life-paths. We laughed

93

together about my arrival in Canada's customs office with Charlie in my purse.

"There was something fishy about that customs guy. Do you think he pocketed my three hundred? I was so relieved that he didn't discover Charlie, I handed it over without a peep!" Joe scratched the little dog's ear.

"I'm glad," Joe said, "I might have missed knowing this terrific fellow."

Crying openly, I told Joe about my failed marriage. He nodded, non-judgmental. "I blame myself, or my career. Rick and I left our home in Ohio mostly because of me."

"Well, from what I know about Ohio," Joe said, "it's a nice place. But don't be so hard on yourself. Your husband could have said no. You had to go with it, your Destiny, I mean. Something swept you along."

Joe was wise, and he and I were swept along, I into the first affair of my life. Even long separated from a missing husband, I felt guilty. But the affair was warm and lusty and sweet, and damn, it was cold that winter in Winnipeg.

"I didn't know my Dad and uncles were 'connected'," Joe said about his childhood. "They were businessmen, for all I knew. My mom was a great Italian mom, my sister a sweet kid my brothers and I protected. I look back, and it was pretty typical, except that I was taught early on I'd be part of the family 'business'."

"I don't see how it's 'destiny' to do what you do around here, Joe. You're an awfully smart guy to be a chauffeur for lady singers. But I guess it beats killing people."

Joe laughed. "I was sent here as a kind of apprentice. My home is in Toronto. And I asked to be your chauffeur. What about you, Pat? Your family?" I told him about my background, *The Touring Wilsons*, Poppa, and my mother.

"Then you can't help but be who you are, just like me. But show business is a lousy life for a woman."

I don't know if Joe's philosophy of fatedness was learned in classrooms, or if he developed it to spare himself doubts about his life. There was something about him that touched my heart, for I don't think his was a destiny he wanted.

Not once did we discuss a future together. We both knew it wasn't a possibility. I carry the feeling of quiet joy and inevitability of those weeks, even today. Joe didn't follow me on my travels after our Canadian romance, though sometimes, in my loneliness, I wished he had. But I received yellow roses on every special occasion for the next several years. They were always signed in the same way: "Love, J." I never questioned how he kept up with my whereabouts.

Joe gave me a phone number when I left Canada. "Call this number any time, for any reason, for anything you need." It was the last time I spoke with him. Several weeks after my return to New York, I received a check from the Canadian government. The amount was for three hundred dollars, a full refund of the duty I'd paid the customs officer/twerp upon my arrival in Winnipeg.

scene vii: February, 1958, Back in New York City

Dr. Braun spoke in sincere, measured tones. "Rick had problems to work out, Pat. Sometimes counseling reveals things that must be addressed, if not together, then apart. I'm sure he's all right. Tell me how *you* are," he asked.

"Well, I'm learning to live an independent life the hard way! I've never thought of myself as particularly independent."

"And why is that, Patricia?"

"I guess because my father was so controlling. He ran everything." I blew my nose.

"I understand he didn't want you to marry Rick."

"He walked me down the aisle in front of Rick's family and a church full of people, and when the minister asked, 'Who gives this woman in marriage?' Pop said, 'Her *mother* does!'"

"What made him so controlling, in your opinion?"

"Oh, undoubtedly *his* mother, my grandmother Henrietta. I never knew her, but I've heard stories. She must have been a pistol. Henrietta wanted to be on the stage, and shoved her husband and kids—Pop and my aunt Lois — on with her. My father hated his childhood, touring and performing. He told me all he wanted was to live in one house in one place, and go to school with kids he'd known all his life."

"So your father tried to create the stability for his family that he didn't have as a child."

"Yes, and a part of me understood." I paused. "We've never talked about my family before, Dr. Braun. Does this mean I'm in analysis?"

"I believe therapy could help you through this transition in your life. Call it *supportive* therapy, if you like. It can be with me, or anyone you feel comfortable with..."

Several of my friends were "on the couch," as we called it in the '50s. I'd done a lot of reading about the human psyche while I traveled. I was intrigued by Karen Horney, Carl Rodgers, Sigmund Freud. Carl Jung was my favorite, for his work included the mystical. How could one be fully human without taking an Invisible Force into account? I'd read about the sign that hung over the door to Jung's home: Bidden or unbidden, God is present.

That night I wrote in my journal: *I hardly noticed the kindness in Dr. Braun's eyes before today! I've always found his Viennese accent off-putting. Now he makes me feel safe, like an older, wiser friend. God knows I need a friend.*

scene viii: A week Later, Enter The Touring Wilsons, Dr. Braun's office, New York City

The carved mahogany desk gleamed in the soft lamplight of Dr. Braun's office. I sat opposite him, stiff in a soft leather chair.

"Tell me more about your family, Patricia," Dr. Braun said. "It will help me know you better. We began speaking of your father."

"Yes. I should begin with *his* birth. That will tell you a lot. When my grandmother Henrietta knew she had a newborn son, she said, 'Good! We need a boy in the act! His name is Ross Howard, and we'll bill him as Little Master Howard!'"

"So your grandmother thought of herself as the center of a theatrical universe, and her family as her supporting players."

"Exactly," I said. "She barely slowed down for Poppa's birth. She was onstage, on a showboat, starring as Juliet—yes, Juliet, fifteen and virginal!—just hours before her labor began. She hid her pregnant belly behind the scenery!" Dr. Braun and I both smiled, but we both knew it wasn't funny. "While she was in labor, the showboat started chugging downriver. She didn't make it ashore for Poppa's birth. She said, 'I'm from Sullivan, Illinois. Write that down as his birthplace!'"

"Control," Dr. Braun said.

"In spades," I said. Talking became easier. For the next hour, across the gleaming mahogany desk, I told Dr. Braun about my grandparents and *The Touring Wilsons.*

Grandmother Henrietta was the second youngest of five girls. She worked for her father, who owned *The Progress*, the daily news-paper in Sullivan, Illinois. Great-grandfather Eli was a rigid, upper-middle-class Methodist, a father of his times with one difference: he raised and educated his daughters as if they were sons. He expected

Not Edna Ferber's fictitious "Cotton Blossom," but the "Eisenbarth/ Henderson Floating Theater," my father's home for the first years of his life.

them to work. Henrietta was bored by the newspaper business, and joined the Sullivan Drama Club. Four feet eleven inches tall, wearing a size two-and-a-half AA shoe, she was fiercely beautiful, with an hour-glass figure and dark brown hair and eyes (reflecting the family's French and Cherokee heritage.) Avidly following her burgeoning career (as well as her hour-glass figure) were numerous Illinois suitors. Among them was the new typesetter employed by her father's newspaper, John Ross Wilson.

John Ross was a handsome, calm-tempered Scot imported from Tuscola, Illinois, to work for the *Progress*. He was bewitched by his employer's daughter, and Henrietta, recognizing a good leading man when she saw one, found it easy to entice him into joining her in the Drama Club.

"I fell in love with Henrietta at first sight!" John Ross proclaimed. It must have been true, for he tolerated her tempestuous nature throughout their courtship and marriage. Henrietta, from all accounts, was manipulative to the extreme, her dramatic fainting spells a favored ploy.

"My sweet girl is so delicate!" John Ross would say, when told Henrietta had swooned yet another time. "Lean over her, will you? Tell her I'll be there in a minute!"

Henrietta extracted a promise from John Ross: "You'll never ask me to settle down! You'll allow me to spend my life on the stage!" John Ross agreed, but was promptly fired when Henrietta's father heard of their pending marriage. They married in 1893, leaving her family and steady employment on *The Sullivan Progress* to join a professional repertory company.

They became a family of four, *The Touring Wilsons*. John and Henrietta's children were pushed into stage careers, ready or not. My grandfather, aside from playing everything from leading men to villains, was Chief Marketing Officer for the group, writing the publicity brochure touting the Wilsons as *"Versatile, Dramatic People!"* Henrietta is pictured as a demure girl, in character as *"Rebecca of Sunnybrook Farm,"* from the 1890s' play, but the copy states that her skills included playing *"Juveniles, Ingénues, Boy Parts,"* and performing a singing specialty. Several pictures show her as the character Topsy, in blackface and pigtails, in the melodrama *Uncle Tom's Cabin*. It was the early 1900s. Political correctness was three-quarters of a century in the future.

Paternal grandmother Henrietta,
better known as Hell-On-Wheels.

Paternal grandfather John Ross,
a forbearing Scotsman.

"Little Master Howard," my father, at age three, is pictured in the acting company brochure as a small, very sad-faced boy. Next to him is a picture of my aunt, a coquettish five year-old known as "La Petite Lois," beloved for her *"strong emotional child parts."* At the margin of the brochure, beside a group picture of the four Wilsons, is the underlined declaration: *"Splendid wardrobe and not afraid to wear it!"* Then the bottom line of the page proclaims, *"NOT THE BEST ON EARTH, BUT WE CAN DELIVER THE GOODS!"*

Dr. Braun interrupted with his soft laugh. "Your grandfather John Ross had a sense of humor, Patricia."

"He did. He probably needed one." I continued the story.

The Wilsons *en tour* played every state of the union but California and most of Canada, and they played it all: repertory companies, stock shows, "tab" shows (mini-musicals) as well as "the waters"— showboats. On land, The Wilsons lived in the railway cars on which they traveled. When on the waters of the Ohio or Mississippi Rivers, they occupied living quarters behind the showboat stages. A Chinese chef, Sam Lee, traveled with the troupe. In those

Grandfather John Ross Wilson showed a sense of humor when he designed the family publicity brochure in 1900. My father (back row, center picture) wore long curls.

times, restaurants, hotels, and boarding houses barred actors, signs posted everywhere: NO DOGS OR ACTORS ALLOWED. On a frigid night, stranded in a small Indiana town, Henrietta and her children couldn't find a room. She had plenty of money for lodgings, for she always carried cash in an embroidered velvet bag around her neck. Still, they were turned away from every hotel and boarding house. Finally, a landlady at the edge of town took them in, and they fell into warm beds and exhausted sleep. The next morning Henrietta learned she and her children had spent the night in the town brothel. The kind landlady who sheltered them was the madam. Henrietta drew herself up. "So what if she *is* a madam!" she declared. "That woman is the only true Christian in this town!"

In the popular play, *Uncle Tom's Cabin*, Poppa's sister Lois played the dying Little Eva, who was hauled up to Heaven—the "fly" space above the stage—on a rope for every performance. One matinee day, Lois broke out with chicken pox just before curtain-time. Henrietta put her to bed, and made four-year old Poppa play the matinee as Little Eva. She shoved her son, kicking and yelling, into his sister's lace bloomers and frilly nightshirt. He already sported long golden curls, for Henrietta had never allowed his hair to be cut.

"Pox on the pox! The show must go on!" Henrietta declared. Poppa was Little Eva until Lois recovered. I told Dr. Braun I didn't think Poppa ever recovered.

Mostly, my father played Little Willie in the

Poppa, in long curls and top hat, and his sister, my Aunt Lois. At least she enjoyed being a performer!

tragic classic, *East Lynne*. In that play Little Willie is abandoned by his mother, Isobel, and lies dying when Isobel, fraught with remorse, returns to his bedside. It was a great moment for Henrietta/Isobel to emote over my father on his stage deathbed. As the curtain slowly descended, she flung herself, sobbing, across his frail body.

One night Poppa heard a small boy's voice from the audience: "No wonder he died, lady—you fell on him."

"Even Poppa smiled telling that story, Dr. Braun, and he didn't smile very often," I said. "He suffered a lot from his childhood, and I haven't even told you the saddest part yet." Dr. Braun's eyebrows lifted.

"In 1909, John Ross and Henrietta toured without their children. My father and his sister, who'd done most of their schooling with Henrietta on tour, were left in a Catholic boarding school in Chicago for a taste of formal education. They were outsiders, Protestants in a Catholic school. And Poppa was the only boy in an all-girls' school."

The doctor's eyes darkened, and I went on.

"Audiences across the country loved attending touring stage plays, but actors were sometimes attacked offstage. Hauled off, tarred and feathered, beaten, strapped and straddled to a rail and carried out of town. Armed guards were hired to patrol at night, protecting the sleeping quarters of the actors. Then the players could rest without fear of being raided in their beds. My father told me of recurring nightmares about such incidents as a boy. They lasted long into his adulthood.

On the thirteenth of May, 1909, Poppa and Aunt Lois were finishing their term at the Chicago convent school. John Ross stood backstage in a theater in Laurens, South Carolina, awaiting his entrance as the sheriff in the play, *The Klansman.* The property boy with the show handed him the "prop" gun, supposedly loaded with blank cartridges, to be used in the upcoming scene. But the gun had been used the night before by the patrolling guards. It was loaded with live bullets, and was somehow carelessly left on the property table in the wings. The guards were probably drunk. The gun accidentally discharged, and the bullet struck John Ross in the abdomen. He staggered to Henrietta. 'I've been shot, 'Etta,' he said, 'but don't worry. It doesn't hurt.' He collapsed, and died the next day. He was forty-three."

"A tragedy—for everyone, Patricia," Dr. Braun said.

"Yes. Newspapers everywhere carried the story. Most claimed my grandfather was shot by another actor onstage, during a scene, and that melodramatic version of the story was perpetuated by Grandmother Henrietta herself. She undoubtedly felt if one had to lose one's husband in such horrific fashion, the incident might as well be utilized for maximum publicity value. Poppa was thirteen. The headmistress of the school took him into the graveyard of the church. The graves were in a garden surrounded by lilac bushes in May bloom.

"'Ross Howard, your father has been killed. You must say prayers on these graves,' the nun told him. She pushed him to his knees and stood behind him. Poppa told me he was unable to utter a sound. He was sickened by the sweet lilac-smell surrounding him, and puked all over the first grave.'"

Dr. Braun blinked.

"I can't even imagine the devastation to Poppa and Aunt Lois at the death of their father. John Ross's solid Scottish sensibility, the loving, stable anchor he was for his family, was gone. A few months later, Grandmother Henrietta told my father she could no longer take care of both him and Lois. His voice hadn't changed, but she told him he was now a man, on his own in the world. He found a job as an office boy, and a boarding house room in Decatur, Illinois. He told me the story of his fourteenth birthday. 'I had no money for food that day,' he said. 'I'd spent my entire week's salary on a tutor. I needed to catch up in my studies. I was alone in my room with my stomach growling when the mail arrived. There was a

Poppa joined the army to get out of show business.

birthday card from Lois with a five-dollar bill inside. It was the best birthday I ever had!' My father struggled to survive, Dr. Braun."

"Did he never act again, Patricia?"

"He returned briefly to The Wilson Stock Company, to Henrietta and Lois, when he was seventeen. He was by then a young leading man, dapper and handsome, but he thought of acting only as another means to an end. He'd earn money to further his education. He found he still hated it, though, and joined the army just to get away. But it was during this return to the theatrical life he deplored, ironically, that he met my mother."

Dr, Braun stopped me. "Patricia, your father had a very difficult childhood. How did that affect you?"

"How was I affected? He became Henrietta as a parent. I never knew my grandfather, John Ross. But if it weren't for my maternal grandfather, my Grandad Ben, I would have grown up thinking all men were tyrants, emotional abusers like Poppa."

"Is Rick more like your father or your grandfather Ben?"

"Definitely Grandad Ben!" The sobs came. "I guess I'll never understand why my father did what he did to my mother. Or why Rick abandoned our marriage."

"Rick will tell you why in time. He's done you a loving favor, Pat. What is it you feel your father did to your mother?" Dr. Braun asked, as kindly as Grandad Ben.

"What did he do? He stole her soul!"

The doctor looked at his watch. The maddening therapeutic moment had arrived, the moment when emotions are supposedly suspended until the next session.

"Ahhh. Then I'd like you to tell me about your mother next," Dr. Braun said.

scene ix: 1957, Enter Momma's story, Several days later, New York City

"My mother's talent was transcendental, Dr. Braun."

"Transcendental?"

"Her talent transcended an entertainer's ordinary skill in communicating with an audience. It was mystical, like an invisible cord of love hung between Momma and her audiences. But from the moment she married Poppa, her career was over."

"How did your parents meet?"

"Remember I said Poppa returned to acting one more time? To earn money for his education? He was booked into West Mansfield, Ohio, with The Wilson Stock Company in the summer of 1913. The company needed a pianist, and auditioned local musicians for the job. A gorgeous fifteen-year old kid with auburn hair walked onstage— West Mansfield's musical prodigy, Beatrice Ruth Baughman."

"And she was to become your mother."

"Yes. My father told me he was bedazzled from the moment he set eyes on her."

Dr. Braun nodded.

"They were just kids, and Poppa had to move on with his show,

Momma, Beatrice Baughman Wilson, in 1918. She lit up the stage.

but they stayed in touch for twelve years after their first meeting. Pop enlisted in the army in 1918, then continued with his education. Momma went to The Cincinnati College of Music on a scholarship. When she graduated she signed on with Redpath Chautauqua."

Chautauqua, I explained to European Dr. Braun, was an American entertainment form unique to that era. From 1900 to the late 1920s, films were a silent novelty, television unknown, vaudeville too secular and bawdy for many audiences. Chautauqua filled the gap. High quality musical artists and entertainers, offering suitable fare for the entire family, comprised its troupes. They toured small towns and rural areas as well as larger cities, and were generally welcomed and sanctioned by local church groups. William Jennings Bryan, the famous orator, headlined one of Momma's tours. Renowned actors between stage engagements appeared to recite monologues from plays. One was Cornelia Otis Skinner, hailed in her time as the "American Sarah Bernhardt." Momma watched Skinner closely.

"I can do that," she said. "I can do monologues. I have ideas for characters." She developed insightful sketches by observing people she encountered in her travels.

"Audiences across the country fell in love with my mother, Dr. Braun. They loved seeing themselves reflected in her characters. She made them laugh, then cry in the next moment. She was a major star for her era. Her stardom—even some of her reviews—are chronicled in The Library of Congress. They say things like, 'She not only stopped the show, she *was* the show!' They talk about her 'unqualified ability' as an interpretive reader. I believe it. She mesmerized audiences."

"Then you saw her perform?"

I nodded. "During World War Two, while Poppa was in Europe with the Ninth Infantry division. She hadn't worked in years, but the USO asked her to come out of retirement to entertain servicemen. How could Poppa object?"

"And that's when you were able to watch her onstage."

"Yes. I was twelve at the beginning of the war. Poppa was called up right away. It wasn't long after he left that she agreed to work for the USO. I'd sit in her audiences, awe-struck, like everyone else. She was older then, in her forties, heavier. She didn't think she'd have any appeal for young servicemen and women, but her work touched everyone. Few have the gift to be great. My mother did."

"And that has had a profound effect on your life, hasn't it?"

"Yes. When she became my father's wife, the mother of his children, their marriage and family life couldn't echo a whisper of the childhood my father hated!"

"Why do you think she married your father?"

"Grandma Daisy told me Momma felt she was getting older. She'd loved her career, but she was twenty-seven, a spinster in those days. She wanted a family, and had been through a broken engagement. She never forgot my father, and wrote him in Fort Madison, Iowa, where he'd finally escaped show business, working as the sales manager of The Schaeffer Pen Company. Momma told him she was going to pass through his town on her way to a booking in Kansas City. Would he want to meet her? He did, and they were married a month later, in Chicago."

I took a sip of water from the glass next to me on Dr. Braun's carved mahogany desk. I didn't want to cry, but hot tears slipped down my cheeks. "Momma probably thought she knew what she was signing on for. I'm sure she'd loved my father from the time they met as teenagers. But her talent and creativity were sacrificed. She didn't realize how much they were the soul of her. You can't throw away your soul." I blew my nose. "Poppa became a tyrant, Momma a drudge. Grandma Daisy said, 'My daughter's light is hidden under a bushel!'"

"Your grandmother had a colorful way of expressing herself."

"Yes. She once told me Momma had walked through the woods and picked up the crooked stick!"

Sadness eased with Dr. Braun's gentle laugh. "But did you feel your father was a crooked stick, Patricia?"

"No, I knew he loved her, and all of us. But I did worry about my mother's light being hidden. I thought, what if I had a light? I wasn't sure I had one, but if I did, I didn't want it under a bushel. I spent my childhood vowing such a terrible thing would never happen to me."

"And it didn't."

"No. Momma and Grandma Daisy saw to that."

"Did they push you on the stage, like stage mothers?"

"No, but they let it happen. They supported me. They thought my voice might give me the opportunity to be an independent woman."

"So in spite of your father's wishes to maintain a family life apart from show business, your light was released from under the bushel."

"Yes, early on. My first performance was the Christmas I was three, for a charity show."

I imitated my mother for Dr. Braun. "'It's a benefit, Ross, a one-time thing! It's for orphans—the poor tykes have no one at Christmas!'" I smiled. "How's that for manipulation, Dr. B.? That's how she and Grandma Daisy kept me singing throughout my childhood. Then they'd take me to movies and stage shows to watch other singers, like Judy Garland! Oh, I loved her! I'd sit on the porch steps every evening, singing her songs. My brother David teased me. 'Warn the neighbors!' he'd say. 'She's baying at the moon again!'"

"And your father?"

"He was preoccupied with business, and Momma would teach me songs my father liked from their era, like *I Don't Care,* Eva Tanguay's song from vaudeville. One song she taught me he'd sung himself as a young man. It was pretty lusty, but he couldn't resist hearing me sing it!

An-na, from India-na, she's just as playful as a baby grand pi-a-na!

She ain't so nifty, she weighs two-fifty!

But a big fat mom-ma now and then

Is relished by the best of men!

I rolled my eyes and clapped my hands like Eddie Cantor. Dr. Braun laughed.

"Your father was older. How did he happen to be in the service?"

"He was in the army in 1918, and stayed in the Reserves between wars. He was a Captain when Pearl Harbor happened, and they called him up immediately. His business, The Wilson Advertising Agency in Cincinnati, shut down for the duration. They trained him at Fort Bragg and sent him overseas, through North Africa, Sicily, Italy, the Normandy invasion, then most of Europe, until Germany surrendered. He was gone for three and a half years, and awarded a Bronze Star for valor. I was proud of him."

"Rightly so. But those were important years for you to be without your father. You must have changed. You were a young woman by the time he returned."

"Yes, sixteen. And he'd changed, too. The war mellowed him."

"By then you were a professional singer."

I was fourteen, thinking maybe I was Rita Hayworth.

"I was. I sang with local bands and on the radio. My professional name was 'Rusty Wilson,' because of my hair."

"And your mother incorporated you into her USO act?"

"When I was about thirteen, sitting in her USO audience in Fort Thomas, Kentucky. I was dressed in the school clothes I'd worn that day, a pink sweater and grey plaid skirt. Saddle shoes and anklets, of course. My slip hung about two inches too long. Mom called me onstage and played the introduction to a Betty Hutton song I practiced singing in front of my mirror.

"Did you bring down the house, Patricia?"

"I did. And after that raucous opening, I sang '*My Buddy.*' Remember that sentimental bromide? As my father used to say, there wasn't a dry seat in the house when I finished. I'd learned how to turn from laughter to tears, from the best show-woman in the world."

Now Dr. Braun didn't laugh.

"And you'd pleased your mother."

"Yes. That was what mattered most of all."

"Why did you go to college instead of New York or Hollywood when you graduated from high school?"

"Oh, I wanted to go to Hollywood. I loved the movies. I enrolled myself in The Pasadena Playhouse. But Pop was back from the war by then, and he wouldn't pay my tuition to The Playhouse. He said I wasn't pretty enough to be a movie star. Also he didn't want me tying up with some 'ham actor,' he said. So I went to Ohio State because David was there, and I was able to live with Grandma Daisy in Columbus. I got my own Columbus radio show while I was still a freshman. When they opened the television outlet for CBS a couple of years later, WBNS-TV, I was all over the tube singing, too, and became the spokeslady for The Ohio Fuel Gas Company. My brother used to say they couldn't shut me up!"

Dr. Braun smiled. "You were quite the local celebrity."

"Yes. And I was over eighteen. My father couldn't do anything about it. But I also finished college, so he got what he wanted."

"And your mother? Did she get what she wanted after the war?"

I heard my own voice grow quiet. "She never set foot on the stage again."

"So you kept busy living out her career for her."

"Do you think that's what I've done, what I'm doing?"

"Perhaps. But I definitely think you wanted something else, beyond show business."

"I did."

"So you fell in love with Rick."

"Oh, God, yes, Dr. Braun! I fell in love with Rick! What happened to Rick and me? Please tell me! What happened to us?"

The hot, unwanted tears began to fall again.

scene x: Spring 1958, Everywhere, then back to New York City

Journal, February 6, 1958: On the road again. I'm at The Shamrock Hotel in Houston until late April. I miss talking to Dr. Braun, and I haven't heard from Rick. I bless my Yorkie pal Charlie—he keeps me company. And sane.

After my disastrous debut in Dallas the year before, I now seemed to be able to do no wrong.

New Orleans: *Almond-eyed Patricia Wilson knocks off a melodic soufflé in a pleasing voice and looks extremely good while doing it—gives impression she sings not just for you, not for herself, but for posterity…*

Houston: *fresh!…a real find…*

Kansas City: *…easy on the eyes and a real crowd-pleaser..*

Washington, DC: *…an attractive redhead whose face has the planes of true beauty, and as girl singers go she is one of the most tal-*

ented around.... ...a marvelous comedienne as well, she is strictly class...

Chicago: *...one of the most attractive and vivacious young singing stars today is Patricia Wilson, appearing at the Drake Camellia House.*

While I was playing the Lotus Club in Washington, I decided it was time to call my old ally, Warren Kemmerling, who had tempted me with an affair when we worked together in *Pipe Dream.* I wanted to tell him Rick and I had separated. Before making the call, I picked up a Washington paper to read while I fortified myself with morning coffee. There was an announcement in Walter Winchell's column of Warren's marriage the day before. *Talk about kismet,* I thought.I didn't know his new wife, but I silently wished them well, and wondered what might have happened had I called Warren a year earlier, when Rick and I first separated.

Gus phoned while I was playing a month-long engagement at the Ritz Carlton Hotel in Montreal. "How's the act going?" he asked casually.

"It's come together, Gus. Audiences like it."

"Well, that's good," Gus said. His dramatic pause told me something eventful was forthcoming. "You're opening at the St. Regis Maisonette in New York on May 8th!" The St. Regis was, along with The Persian Room in The Plaza and The Empire Room at The Waldorf, the epitome of prestigious supper clubs.

I had one engagement to work before the New York opening, a return to The Chase Club in St. Louis. Comedian Dick Shawn was the headliner. I had a lot of respect for Dick. He was an incomparable, well-seasoned, acting comedian, far beyond the run-of-the-mill—should I say *gin*-mill?—comics of the day. Dick's material was tasteful, his timing masterful. I confided to him that I had trepidations about opening my supper club act in New York.

"Your orchestrations and material are top-grade, Pat, and you're one of the best singers in the business," Dick said. I was attracted to Dick Shawn, and it was obvious he liked me. He helped me hone small bits of between-song patter. He was married, though, and what was it with affairs? Like peanuts, once you've had one, you can't stop? No, I decided. Affairs weren't for me. I wasn't cut out to be a bed-hopper, married or single.

Gus Schirmer's mother, Florence Owen, was manager of the famous Elizabeth Arden Red Door Store on New York's Fifth Avenue. Mrs. Owen sought out gowns for me from the Arden collection at bargain prices for my St. Regis debut. They were originals, by Arden's exclusive designer, Count Sarmi, so they were hardly bargains. But I was a size eight then, so the samples worn by the Arden models and discounted after showings were a perfect fit. One we chose was salmon-colored beaded satin with a full skirt of deeper salmon organza and a voluminous matching stole. There were only two of this dress made, the sample and one made for Zsa Zsa Gabor. The second gown was another sample, a strapless daffodil-yellow chiffon sheath, with flowing panels reaching from the top of the bodice to the hemline.

"I think you should change your hair, Patricia," said the refined Mrs. Owen. "Let me bring in one of our stylists to have a look-see."

This is how the experts made me look for The Maisonette. I liked the old me better.

"Mother is right," Gus told me. "You're not playing Nellie Forbush from Little Rock now." I'd been wearing my hair pulled back in a French twist, cut short in the front with wispy, gamine-type bangs, a hair-do that evolved from doing *South Pacific*. The song, *I'm Gonna Wash That Man Right Outta My Hair*, during which Nellie shampoos her hair onstage, had only a short intermission following. There was no offstage time for a re-do. Mary Martin spent the entire Broadway run with something like a girl's "butch" cut. I didn't want to cut my hair that short, so

I swept it back and up, a la Audrey Hepburn. On the club floor, it made me look very young, and it was the decision of the "experts" that I should look more sophisticated for my Maisonette debut. With Mrs. Owen supervising, the Arden staff trimmed and permed my hair to short fluff. At last I passed muster with the experts, and, with much help from a top-notch public relations person, Betty Lee Hunt, I was a success in my New York opening.

REDHEAD SCORES AT ST. REGIS! was a headline in the *New York Mirror*. The ensuing article says, "*Wilson is impressive, poised and interesting to watch——*"

Louis Sobol, *Daily News*: "*A delightful and highly talented newcomer receives a rousing welcome—has what it takes to achieve stardom—not only a splendid singing voice, but a great showman personality and originality in her material.*"

Even *Variety*, the show business trade paper known for its tough reviews, liked my act: "*Patricia Wilson has come a long way—she evidences longtime grooming, and eclipses, on basic merit, some of the glam babes booked into this class bistro. A tall, lissome girl with a neo-comedy pan, she knows her way around upbeat tunes as well as ballads.*" The critic singled out a slowed-down version of *Rhythm*, calling it "*...a minor classic in arrangement and rendition.*"

On opening night I received a telegram I still have: "*We will be thinking of you and it won't be the first time. Best of luck and love, Dick Rodgers and Oscar Hammerstein.*"

One of the most enjoyable aspects of the month-long St. Regis engagement was seeing and hearing from New York and Ohio friends. The St. Regis put a beautiful suite at my disposal, and I entertained there every night after my shows. My brother David and his wife, Wanda, arrived from Cincinnati, and happened to be there on the same night as Viennese Dr. Braun.

"I was disappointed that you didn't sing '*Anna from Indiana!*'" Dr. Braun laughed. Later David told me how much he'd enjoyed speaking with the doctor from Vienna.

"He's helped me through a rough time, Davey."

"He said he came to support you because you'd decided not to turn your back on success!"

From Dr. Braun, I recognized that as high praise.

scene xi: June 1958, Re-enter Rick, New York City

My month-long engagement at The St. Regis Maisonette had ended a few days earlier. The voice on the phone made my heart leap.

"Pat, it's Rick." I wasn't sure what I felt. Relief? Anger?

"Rick! I've tried to reach you!"

"I know. No one knew where I was. I was traveling, then my father died and I went back to Ohio."

"Oh, your father! I'm so sorry."

"Yes. Dad left his house to the three of us, to my sister and you and me, since you haven't divorced me yet. I have a favor to ask. I'd like my sister to have the house. She took care of Dad for the last couple of years."

"Of course she should have it, Rick."

"Good. I have papers for you to sign. And there's something else I'd like to talk to you about. It's our birthday week. Can I take you to dinner?"

Was it possible? Did Rick want to reconcile?

"Yes, I'd like that! It *is* our birthday week. I can't believe I'll be twenty-nine on Tuesday!"

"And I'm thirty-four tomorrow," Rick said. "How does steak sound? Gallagher's at seven on Saturday?"

"All right. See you then."

After the shock of hearing from him passed, I felt very little. I sat for a while, quiet, then called Dr. Braun and left a message to tell him I'd heard from Rick.

Certain my marriage was over, I dressed up to meet my husband for our birthday celebration, just the same.

"You look beautiful, Pat. That yellow silk is perfect with your hair and eyes."

"Thanks, Rick. You're looking well yourself."

Gallagher's wasn't a very romantic restaurant, its austere white tablecloths and bright overhead lights not offering much in the way of atmosphere. We ordered steaks and red wine.

"Thanks for doing this for my sister." Rick handed me an envelope of legal papers to be signed and notarized, releasing my claim to his father's house. I folded them into my purse.

"How's George?" I asked. I took a bite of steak.

"He's in Ohio now," Rick said. "He loves having a yard. I hear you have another dog?"

"Yes! Charlie. He keeps me from being lonely while I'm on the road."

"I didn't think you'd be lonely."

"It's a lonely life, Rick, touring."

Silence. *This isn't going well.*

Rick finally spoke, "I need to tell you something, Pat. I should have told you a long time ago. I'll feel better if you know."

"You don't have to tell me anything, Rick."

"Yes, I do. Call it an early birthday present. It's important that you not blame yourself for our break-up. It wasn't your fault." He cleared his throat. "Remember how we told each other we were virgins when we married?"

"Of course."

"Well, it wasn't true in my case. It's something else I didn't tell you the truth about, something besides not graduating, I mean."

"Oh, so what, Rick! Whoever she was, she's yesterday's mashed potatoes now!" Rick smiled, then grew serious again.

"No, you don't understand. I *was* a virgin. With *women*. But I'd had a long affair before I met you." His soft eyes darkened. "With a man."

I knew I didn't want to hear it. "A *man?* But Rick, that's impossible! How could we——?"

"Because I cared about you. I thought it wouldn't matter. But it does. I should have told you." Rick's face was agonized. I grasped his hands across the table.

"Oh, God, Rick, we were so young. Neither of us knew *who* we were!" I pressed his hand against my cheek. "How excruciating for you, telling me! You didn't have to!"

"I wouldn't have hurt you for the world. I loved you, Pat, I always will. I thought it would work. But I can't guarantee I'd be faithful. You deserve better than that!"

My roiling stomach needed warmth, comfort. Gulping my glass of wine like a Soho barmaid, it didn't matter to me who in Gallagher's Steak House might be watching. *Let the whole damn family of Shuberts look, for all I care!*

Yellow dress, red wine, confession. Our birthday celebration. A heavy menu.

Journal, June 14, 1958: I need to talk to Dr. Braun. I called and left a message. Has he always known about Rick? Will he tell me if he has? How could Rick be so passionate with me? I wish I weren't so dumb. Could I talk to David? No. Not fair to put my brother on the spot. I have so many questions. I'm glad I saw Dr. B. so recently.

Journal, June 16, 1958: I haven't heard from Dr. Braun. Is he on vacation?

Journal, June 17, 1958: I'm 29. Too upset to celebrate. Charlie is nibbling doggie-treats. Left another message for Dr. Braun. I wish I'd hear from him!

The next day, a certified special delivery letter arrived from an attorney's office, informing me of the sudden death of Dr. Eugene Braun. My confidential files were at their office, sealed, said the letter, and I could have them delivered to another therapist of my choosing. I sat down and wept, with Charlie in my arms, licking the tears from my cheeks.

scene xii: Later that summer, 1958, Dallas, Texas

"Get out of your funk, Pat!" Gus was adamant. "You're going to Dallas again. Charles Meeker wants you to play missionary Sarah Brown in *Guys and Dolls* at The State Fair Musical Theater. Johnnie Ray will be your leading man, in the role of Sky Masterson. Alan King and Janis Paige, the second leads as Nathan and Adelaide. Pat Rooney will be repeating his Broadway role."

Johnnie Ray's recording, *The Little White Cloud That Cried*, catapulted him into stardom, then a later recording, *Cry*, made him an international favorite. Women swooned when he stood bent-kneed and pigeon-toed, snapping his fingers, belting out songs in his emotional voice. His onstage demeanor was that of a little kid, so he was offbeat casting for macho gangster Sky Masterson, played onscreen by Marlon Brando. Johnnie was gay. He traveled with a male companion, and those were years when it was impossible to be out-of-the-closet and maintain a career. I learned later of the elaborate public relations effort it took to hide his homosexuality from the public. Johnnie was also handicapped, completely dependent on a hearing aid. To me, he seemed a lost person with a giant heart.

During my brief sojourn in *The Pajama Game* three years prior, its star, Janis Paige, had warmly welcomed me, whispering a friendly "Hi!" during the musical number, *I'm Not At All In Love* on my first night. I admired her as a great performer and a free spirit. In the finale of *The Pajama Game,* in which the girls wore pajama tops and the guys pajama bottoms, I stood behind Miss Paige. When she bent over for her bow, I marveled that anyone would go onstage wearing so little.

In Dallas, Janis, who seemed not to remember we had met, took an instant dislike to me. Everything about my performance was wrong in her estimation, especially the scene leading up to our duet, *Marry The Man Today.* I never got Sarah Brown right in her view. When we were assigned a shared dressing room, I expected that she'd complain to the management. She was a star performer, entitled to her own dressing room, and brilliant in her role as Adelaide, which afforded her a great amount of respect. I thought Janis was the best Adelaide I'd ever seen, on a par with Vivian Blaine, who originated the role on Broadway. For whatever her reasons, Janis suffered our dressing room arrangement, sharing in hostile silence.

On opening night, Janis found me saying my usual opening night prayer. "Oh swell," she said, "a missionary offstage as well as on!" George Schaefer, our director, commented, "I think Janis is going through a bad spell with a man, Pat." Well, hell's bells, so was I.

The Dallas critics concurred with my appreciation of Janis Paige's performance as Adelaide. They liked Johnnie Ray and his singing, but across the board agreed he was miscast as Sky.

I fared well : *".a dandy Sarah Brown...looks like Greer Garson might have as an ingenue...invests the part with much warmth and gaiety....comes out with the liveliest rendering of If I Were A Bell that*

117

*we have ever heard from any Sarah. I'll Know and I've Never Been
In Love Before are sung admirably. Put the lady together with Janis
Paige for Marry The Man Today and you have a double-headed
treat."*

In the *If I Were A Bell* scene, Johnnie's character, Sky, has taken
Sarah to Havana and gotten her drunk. The scene ends with Sky picking Sarah up when she passes out, carrying her offstage fireman-
style, slung over his shoulder. One night as Johnnie picked me up, he
whispered, "Damn, Pat! You just ejected my battery! I can't hear!"
Somehow my body had grazed the hearing aid under his jacket as he
shifted me to his shoulder, and the battery popped out. In the dark
during the scene change, we all got on our hands and knees to con-
duct a frantic search. Johnnie's road manager rushed to the dressing
room for a spare. "Eureka!" yelled the two stagehands who found the
device, and Johnnie's hearing aid was set right again.

Johnnie rented a large apartment with a big kitchen for his Dallas stay. I liked to cook, and soon a crowd of us began having meals
together at his place. I welcomed the chance to be busy, to be with
people, to not miss Rick as much as I did. I'd shop, or give Stan,
Johnnie's companion, a list to shop for me. One afternoon (we ate
early so we wouldn't be stuffed for showtime), Stan told me he was
going to the airport to pick up a friend of Johnnie's.

"Will there be enough food for an extra person?" he asked.

"Sure, it's spaghetti. Plenty for one more. I'll throw together a
salad while you're gone." An hour later Stan returned with Johnnie's
friend. My back was to the door as I ladled out marinara sauce.

"Dot, this is John's leading lady, Patricia Wilson." I turned, wiping tomato-splashed hands on my apron, to face Dorothy Kilgallen,
one of the most famous and powerful celebrities of the 1950s. She
was a syndicated newspaper columnist, rivaled in stature only by
Walter Winchell, and a regular panelist on the weekly television
show, *What's My Line.* She and her husband, Broadway producer
Richard Kolmar, *(Plain and Fancy)* hosted a popular daily New York
radio broadcast.

"Hi. So glad to meet you, Pat. Call me 'Dottie'."

Dorothy seemed enamored in a genuine girl-boy way of Johnnie. I understood his appeal, but it couldn't have been a secret to
Dorothy Kilgallen that Johnnie Ray was not sexually interested in

women. It didn't seem to matter. Dorothy's eyes shone like a school-girl's when she gazed at him. She was a total lady of the '50s, circumspect and feminine, but she giggled like a teenager when she was with Johnnie. My knowin' told me to be careful, for her wrath towards performers was legendary. A negative mention in her column could put one out of business. But she was kind to me, mentioning me in her column favorably many times.

Dorothy stayed in Dallas for ten days. She slopped around with the rest of us in bathing suit or shorts, never asking to be treated in a special way. When we all returned to New York, we continued going out as a group. We went to dinner, to Johnnie's apartment to screen a movie, or to a club—Peggy Lee at Basin Street East, Frank Sinatra at the Copacabana,—then back to Johnnie's place to make "Frank Sinatra eggs" (scrambled with onions sautéed in olive oil.) I didn't know whether I was a "beard" for Johnnie, or for Dorothy, and I didn't care. I was still numb from Rick's confession and the break-up of our marriage.

Journal, November 3, 1958: I miss Rick. I miss being married. Does he miss me? Except for our birthday dinner he hasn't tried to be in touch. Does he know Dr. Braun died? I still can't believe it—

I left our Dallas social group to go to Cincinnati that year for the holidays, but I knew Johnnie and I would see each other early in 1959. He was booked to play The London Palladium at the same time I was booked into The Colony Club in London's Berkeley Square.

"I hope your family can help you heal your heart while you're home," Johnnie said. "I care about you. I know you're going through a rough time." Johnnie knew little about my marriage, but he was sensitive to pain. I wanted to talk to him about homosexuality, or bisexuality, to tell him how it had now touched my life, to ask his advice. But I never dared. Things were different then, not even a lifetime ago.

Back in New York after seeing my family, before leaving for my London club engagement, I ran into pianist/arranger Colin Romoff. Colin had been married to actress Judy Tyler when I understudied her in *Pipe Dream*. I had an appreciation for his sensitivity and remarkable talent. He and I began working on new material for my London act. Of all the arrangements in my act, Colin liked the plain songs: *I Got Rhythm, Limehouse Blues*, and *I'm Old Fashioned*. He had little use for special material. "Maybe it's necessary for variety," he said, "but it's too cutesy for me." One day I took in a song I liked for him to arrange.

"Aww, what did you bring this turkey in for?" asked Colin. "It's just an old movie song." Then Colin molded *You Are My Lucky Star* into one of the most brilliant arrangements ever made for me. Beginning as a small–voiced ballad, modulating upward four times, it had thrilling movement and was exhilarating to sing. Seeming to have a life of its own, together that song and I soared, an important new element for my career at that point. The moral? Never sell "an old movie song" short.

scene xiii: Early 1959, London and Paris

Journal, March 10, 1959: Hello, London! Great to meet you! I know why Pop loved it here. Wonderful people. Many to visit. John Steinbeck stopping at The Dorchester. Shirley Jones in town making a film. I'm going to Johnnie Ray's opening at The Palladium. This Stratford Court Hotel isn't fancy, just cozy and charming. And it has a good gas grate, thank heavens. Cold here!

The Colony in Berkeley Square was an elegant supper club, looking like something out of a 1930s movie, complete with a winding staircase down which society and celebrity Londoners had made grand entrances for decades. They loved American entertainers. My picture was snapped all around London, shopping, dining, sight-seeing. Johnnie Ray and I were leaving The Colony together one night, after he'd seen my show. To accommodate the paparazzi awaiting us, he swept me into a mad embrace. Flashbulbs lit the cold night air.

"Thanks, sweetie," Johnnie said as we sped away in a cab. "I always have to look as if I like girls for that bunch." It would have been the perfect opportunity for me to talk to Johnnie about Rick, but I didn't.

Journal, March 16, 1958: I'm enjoying London, even with this heavy feeling around my heart. Will it ever go away?

Just before leaving New York for London, I'd met actress Tina Louise (Ginger on *Gilligan's Island*) at a party. "Gosh, that's a great scent—would you mind telling me what you're wearing?" Gorgeous Tina, tossing her gorgeous auburn hair, replied, "Oh, it's a blend of special oils I've had made for myself!" Then she winked, "I can't tell a lie. It's Estee Lauder's new bath oil. They carry it at Saks Fifth Avenue."

Thus a small bottle of Estee Lauder's new Youth Dew Bath Oil made its way with me to London long before it was popular. I met friends I kept for a lifetime at a London theater matinee because of that scent. A married couple seated next to me were from Suffolk, they said, in for a day of city shopping and theater-going.

"My wife and I are wondering, what is that delicious perfume you're wearing?" the man asked. I told them about the new Estee Lauder bath oil. Looking crestfallen he said, "Oh, I'm sure we can't get it here, not even at Harrod's. But thank you just the same."

Taking their address, I promised to send them a bottle when I returned to the states. "And please take this," I said, handing the shy wife the small vial of the bath oil I carried in my purse. William and his wife Jen and I left the theater together, chatting about the play. We passed a vendor selling early spring lilacs. William astonished the woman, buying every bough she had. Loading me with armloads of fragrant blooms to carry back to my room at the Stratford Court, he and Jen put me in a cab. Beautiful scents had brought diverse people together. William and Jen and I remained friends and pen-pals for many years.

When I closed in London, I went to Paris to play tourist. A young film executive I'd met with Shirley Jones called me at The Claridge Hotel in Paris. We'd known from comparing notes in London that his business engagements and my tourist-time in Paris would coincide. He took me to dinner at Elizabeth Taylor and her then-husband, Mike Todd's favorite restaurant on the Left Bank. The waiters regaled us with stories of Elizabeth and her producer husband. They brought us "their favorite vodka—you must drink it straight, and chase it with Cointreau!" A lethal combination.

The young man and I were happy to have company to enjoy the sights and sounds and scents of Paris together. We toured museums and parks, neighborhoods, Notre Dame, The Eiffel Tower. We shopped, picking up Limoges demitasse cups and plates as gifts for family and friends. He helped me select a Paris hat, a solid cap of green silk cabbage roses, in a small boutique. There was no sex involved. I never saw him again, though he later became an important movie executive in Hollywood. At the moment, we were friends enjoying an extraordinary place at an extraordinary time of the year. April in Paris. It *was* all it was cracked up to be.

But I was homesick. As I was preparing to leave Europe, I received a letter from my new British friends. It contained a review from *The Stage,* the British version of *Variety,* about an appearance I'd made on a London TV show. The *Stage* critic wrote:

"I'm going to stick my neck out and make a prophesy: Patricia Wilson will be a big star before the year 1959 is out. Here is a singer with style, polish and vitality, the closest thing to a second Judy Garland I have ever seen. We must see more of her."

Immediately I swung back to age ten, sitting on the front porch steps, enduring my brother's teasing, wondering if I could ever give people goose bumps like Judy Garland did with her singing. I wrote in my journal:

Journal, April 16, 1959: OK, old heart, up again! I'm now a divorcee, on the job market one more time, and I'll be 30 in a few weeks. Gus has abandoned me to the William Morris Agency and I'm furious with him. But could this reviewer in London be right? Is 1959 my year? I have a knowin'! A knowin', maybe. But also bravado. I was determined to *make* 1959 my year, and my upcoming thirties my decade.

ACT THREE

SCENES FROM BROADWAY'S GOLDEN AGE

"Arise, shine, for your light has come!"
…Isaiah 60.1

scene i: Spring, 1959, Enter Fiorello!, New York City

Journal, April 25, 1959: I clicked my ruby slippers——there's no place like home! Back in Manhattan, in my West 58th Street apartment.

Over coffee and the newspaper in my living room, with Charlie rescued from doggie- care and nestled close, I read an item in Walter Winchell's column: "George Abbott and producers Griffith and Prince must replace Eydie Gorme as the lead in their new musical, *Fiorello!* Eydie and husband Steve Lawrence have booked the stork."

"Hey, Charlie," I said, "If this is a good score for Eydie to sing, it's a good score for me." I called Colin Romoff.

"Yes," he said. "You're perfect for that role. Speak to your agent." That was the problem. I had no agent.

Should I swallow my pride and call Gus? I've wished many times that I had. Gus had turned my contract over to William Morris for clubs, but I was wary of them for Broadway, and now I was estranged from Gus. I didn't want to get lost in a large agency. I remembered an agent I'd met a couple of years earlier at a summer stock audition, Ray Smith, associated with Ashley/Steiner, a prestigious group for theater people.

"I'm handling someone else for that role," Ray said. "It wouldn't be ethical for me to submit two people." My search for representation continued. When my friend Colin invited me to a dinner party that night at his apartment, I accepted, deciding it might be a good opportunity to network. No leads on an agent, but I met an attractive, tall, and balding young attorney, Marty. The Harvard Law School graduate was shy and laid-back, a former football player, a native New Yorker who didn't seem like one.

"Colin tells me you're a great singer. You worked with Judy Tyler?"

"Yes. And you're an attorney. From a long line of attorneys?"

"No, everyone else had an honest profession," he laughed. "My mother was a schoolteacher, my father's in business."

"What kind of law do you practice?"

"The socially-conscious-not-much-money kind of law." I liked the twinkle in Marty's eye. We made a date for lunch for the upcoming week.

Journal, May 22, 1959: Ray Smith now wants to represent me for the new George Abbott show. His client is officially out-of-the-running. He set an audition for the same day as my lunch with Marty. I called Marty and left a message to cancel.

The role in *Fiorello!* was that of a secretary, so I wore a simple grey flannel skirt, white silk blouse, and pearls for the audition. After I sang, I was given a script and asked to study it offstage for a few minutes, the actor's dreaded "cold reading." It was an emotional scene, not typical for a musical comedy. The character blurts to her friend that she fears the man she loves may not return from war. I gave it my all. My tour-de-force audition ended with an abrupt "Thank you!" coming from the front. *Maybe Gus was right. I'll never work for this group again after the trouble I caused them leaving The Pajama Game for another show.*

Within a few hours I heard from Ray Smith.

"They're interested in you, Pat. They want to see you again on Tuesday."

It was the day before the Memorial Day weekend. I called Colin to book his time to play for the audition Tuesday. I knew along with his new wife, Sally, his friend Marty and two other friends, he had rented a house for the summer on Fire Island. They were all going to the island for the long weekend.

Marty called me that evening. "Sorry we missed lunch, but I had a thought. Why don't you come along for the weekend with all of us? The house has plenty of room. Colin says you two can decide what you'll sing on Tuesday while he cleans out the refrigerator."

Fire Island charmed me. From the ferry ride to the walks along the dunes, I loved the weekend. As a child of the Midwest, I'd never experienced the beauty of the blue-gray waves of the Atlantic, rolling up to sands of endless beach, or watched the tiny, busy birds that flitted close to the ocean's edge, pecking at washed up bits. I'd never experienced the invigorating scent of the sea that made my senses spin. Or seen cottages like I visited that weekend with my friends, basking sun-baked and sea-washed behind the dunes.

It was the cottage that presented the one problem of the enchanted weekend, yet it also gave me the most endearing memory of the holiday. Marty had exaggerated the amount of space in the house. Colin and Sally had a room, I had a room, but the three single men were left fending for themselves on couches. I overheard one of them complaining to Colin.

"Who does Pat think she's kidding? She'll be shacking up with Marty in a week. She might as well do it now and give us a break on space."

There was cold fury in Colin's voice. "Leave it alone. Pat's not like that."

"She's an actress, isn't she?"

"Yeah, but she's gotten ahead on her talent, not her back."

I doubt Colin knew I overheard his defense of me, but I've never forgotten.

On Tuesday, June 2nd, Colin and I were back again in front of the *Fiorello!* production team. We'd decided to contrast the *Lucky Star* audition of the prior week with a single, simple chorus of Irving Berlin's wistful waltz, *What'll I Do?* Colin was a masterful accompanist and a great showman. He understood shadings and contrast. When we finished, I recognized the kind of silence from the auditioners that meant they were thinking.

"Would you sing the song you did for us the other day again, Miss Wilson?" The voice was George Abbott's. Colin and I launched into *Lucky Star*, which had become my favorite audition piece. We finished to another perfunctory "Thank you!" from the front, and left the theater.

"Shot down, Colin!"

"I don't think so, Pat."

Ray Smith was on the phone within an hour with the words every actor the world over dreams of hearing: "You got the job!"

So my favorite audition piece was a "Lucky Star" for me after all. Lyricist Sheldon Harnick, who was present when I sang the song for director George Abbott, overheard Abbot say, "Good lord! Listen to the girl ride that song!" Years later, composer Stephen Sondheim commented on *Lucky Star* as well, in Gordon Hunt's book, *How To Audition:* "Pat Wilson's ….was the most elegant audition I've ever seen... such a perfected and polished piece—startling and satisfying."

"You got the job on your first audition, Pat," George Abbot later told me. "We of course liked your singing, and the truth in your reading. But there was something else that reached us."

That "something else" was The Light I always asked to shine through me. My mother, Anne Bancroft in *Two For the Seesaw,* Laurette Taylor in *The Glass Menagerie,* Julie Harris in *The Lark.* Laurence Olivier, in everything he did——I'd seen the mystical manifest in a few performers. I felt it when it manifested through me, for it was like switching into overdrive.

Journal, June 2, 1959: Is it mystical? All I know is ego gets out of the way and something larger takes its place. Even if I hadn't gotten the job today I think I'd have been satisfied. I was in overdrive.

At a Sunday night Actors' Fund benefit performance during the run of *Fiorello!,* I saw Richard Burton as King Arthur in *Camelot.* Burton was so stunning, some of us sat motionless in our seats long after the house lights came up. Actor Nathaniel Frey, a burly tough-guy, sobbed into his hands like a child at Burton's performance. We knew Richard Burton as the near-surly Welshman who hung out at Chinatown Charlie's between shows, and soon after, as the actor who left to make a film, *Cleopatra,* with Elizabeth Taylor in Rome. But at the *Camelot* Actors Fund benefit for his theatrical peers, Richard Burton was otherworldly.

Judy Garland's live Sunday night concert at Carnegie Hall, on April 23, 1961, has since become entertainment legend. It was a once-in-a-lifetime, cosmic event I also was privileged to attend. I met Judy Garland, my girlhood idol, at a party at Luchow's Restaurant following the concert. I shared with Judy what I'd felt watching her onstage that night, that she'd gathered and lifted her audience beyond anything earthly. Judy was solemn.

"Funny you'd say that, Patricia! I understand exactly what you mean. Something happens that connects us to an audience in a way we can't explain. Didn't someone once call it 'the silver cord'?" She broke into the Garland giggle. "But you still have to be good!" That was never a problem for Judy.

Journal, June 3, 1959: Ran into Hal Prince today on Broadway. He's bubbling! We begin Fiorello! rehearsals in September. The publicity office will announce my casting next week. Female lead! Time to call home and share the good news.

I called my brother David, to let him carry the message.

Journal, June 10, 1959: Gus phoned immediately after he read the press release about Fiorello! My old friend hasn't abandoned me! I feel as if a stone has been lifted from my heart.

The day the New York Times carried my picture and casting announcement, there was a knock on my apartment door. It was Warren Kemmerling. I didn't ask how he knew where I lived. I congratulated him on his marriage, and he congratulated me on my new job.

"I'm going to California," he said. "Maybe you'll end up there, too. After *Fiorello!*, I mean. There's a lot of work there. Theater isn't what it used to be, and I want to get a toe into TV and film." We wished each other luck. He turned as he walked down the hall to the elevator. "I'll always love you, you know." It would be thirteen years before I saw him again, and only then did I learn that he'd been offered a role in *Fiorello!* and turned it down.

Once Dr. Braun and I had discussed the possibility of a relationship with Warren.

"Do you think I could be happy with Warren, Dr. B.?"

"Perhaps, but in my opinion actors shouldn't marry other actors, Patricia. What happened to your mother? Your father, beneath all his pronouncements about hating show business, was nevertheless jealous of her professional success. He buried her talent."

"But isn't it possible for actors to be of support to each other?"

"They'll always compete subliminally," said Dr. Braun. "They'll never sincerely support each other, particularly if the wife is more successful than her husband."

Phoning Gus that night to tell him again how much his call had meant to me, I also told him Rick and I were divorced after two years of separation. I didn't elaborate.

"It's about time," Gus said.

scene ii: Summer, 1959, Fire Island, New York, and Cape Cod, MA

Colin and Sally invited me to Fire Island for the Fourth of July weekend. Marty was there. We spent long hours walking on the beach and talking. He told me of his personal tragedy, the death of his fiancée two years earlier. He said I was the first woman he was interested in dating since her death, but he wanted me to know that he still had many problems in dealing with the event. He was seeing a therapist. I told him that Rick and I had just ended our marriage, and I, too, wasn't ready for a close relationship. Marty and I decided we'd be good friends.

Journal. July 10, 1959: It seems all you have to do to get job offers on the summer circuit is to be announced as the lead in a new Broadway show! I only want to stay in New York, but the show must go on. I've had an offer I couldn't refuse.

David Holtzman, a prominent New York attorney who managed theater star Gertude Lawrence's affairs, loved theater so much that he started his own, The Cape Cod Melody Tent in Hyannis, Massachusetts. He called Gus to see if I'd do *Bells Are Ringing* for him in early August. I'd always wanted to play that tour-de-force Judy Holliday role, written for the star by Betty Comden, Adolph Green and Jule Styne. I accepted.

Charlie and I stayed in a charming bed-and-breakfast inn on the Cape, owned by two nurses from the local hospital. Those dear ladies welcomed me with loving attention, and fawned over Charlie. When they learned Marty was coming for a week, they fretted that they were booked up, with no room for him. Then they remembered a cabin in the woods behind the inn that they could fix up for his stay. Marty would have a real country vacation. Mom and Pop scheduled their annual Cape Cod trip for the same time.

Marty was delighted. He arranged to be away from his office for a week. He'd vacation, I'd play Ella Peterson in *Bells Are Ringing*. I knew ambitious Marty was interested in meeting David Holtzman and his equally prominent attorney sister, Fanny Holtzman.

Poor Marty. He met Ross Wilson instead.

"Mom, Pop, this is my friend, Marty."

"Your father's a Jew, I hear," Pop said. Marty was startled, and so was I.

"Yes, sir, he is. And my mother is Sicilian, a schoolteacher. I was raised as a Catholic."

Pop snorted. "I know all about Catholics," he said. "I was beaten by nuns in a Catholic boarding school. Sicily? I was there during the war. Filthiest place and people I ever saw!" We were in a small diner for a snack before the evening performance. Pop had ordered fried clams for everyone. The character of Archie Bunker in Norman Lear's sitcom *All In The Family* was years away, but someone must have been in the next booth that day, taking notes. I couldn't believe

Pop's mean, irresponsible behavior. I was devastated for Marty, shamed for my father.

"Pop, what is *wrong* with you? I'm getting Marty out of here before you and I come to blows. He already knows I have a damn fool for a father."

Before my performance that night I was so angry, I had to say my prayer several times. Had I been Catholic, it would have equaled twenty "Hail Marys." The show was nearly halfway through before I could fully focus.

Mom came to my dressing room during intermission. "I'm so sorry, Patty," she said. "Marty seems like a nice young man. But your father is worried that you'll start a rebound relationship, now that your marriage is over."

"And he thinks he can play Svengali by spouting out that vile stuff? Marty *is* nice, Mom, and we're just friends. He didn't deserve what Pop did to him. Please remind my father that I'm thirty years old! I don't want to see him after the show. Tell him he can brag about me back home, to his buddies in the Ku Klux Klan."

I knocked on Marty's cabin door after the performance. "Still awake? Can we talk?"

We didn't talk. We made love, compromising a beautiful friendship. I didn't yet understand myself well enough to know that anger at my father drove me into an intimacy with Marty, before either of us was ready for deep commitment.

scene iii: End of Summer, 1959, Cape Cod to Cincinnati

Journal, August 8, 1959: Can't believe this level of fatigue. Flu? Bought a humidifier to keep my throat moist. Sleeping.

Forewarning director Ernie Saracino that I wasn't feeling well, I went on that night, but fainted during intermission. An actress who knew the role of Ella Peterson had been imported from New York that morning and was watching from the audience. She stepped in and played out the performance and the next day's matinee and evening. I blessed her, for I slept for three solid days.

One of my nurse/landladies insisted I have lab tests done at the hospital where she worked. I indulged her, but feeling much better, finished the rest of the sold-out run of *Bells Are Ringing*. I returned home to New York, only a little tired.

"Pat, dear," wrote my landlady from Hyannis, "your lab tests are not normal. I've forwarded them to your doctor in New York." I had mononucleosis.

"Pat," Dr. Kingman said, "If you want to make rehearsals for *Fiorello!* you'll need bed rest for the next few weeks." In spite of my anger with my father, Charlie and I flew home to Cincinnati. In the pink flowered bedroom of the home where I'd spent the later years of my childhood, surrounded by memories and stuffed animals, I was enfolded in the care of my loving mother.

scene iv: September, 1959, Back in New York City

"Rehearsal theater? What rehearsal theater?" Hal Prince laughed. I'd run into Hal in Times Square. "We'll rehearse in the studios above Al and Dick's Steak House. Mr. Abbott thinks they're lucky!"

The superstition was an odd facet of personality for no-nonsense George Abbott. He'd attended military school as a boy. He wasted little time, and fewer words. In the early days of our rehearsals for *Fiorello!,* Bob Holiday, playing a law clerk, was directed by Mr. Abbott to walk across the stage.

"But what is my motivation for this move, Mr. Abbott?" method actor Bob asked.

"Your motivation is your job, Mr. Holiday!" George Abbot's answer has become legend in theatrical circles.

George Abbott was a formidable man. Already in his seventies when we began rehearsals, he worked harder than any of us youngsters, yet found time for tennis, golf, theater-going, and his favorite pastime, ballroom dancing at Roseland. "Mr. Abbott" is what everyone called George Abbott, from producers Griffith and Prince, to Jerome Weidman, co-author of the play, to all of us in the cast. If anyone uttered "George," heads turned to see who the upstart might be.

Warm, approachable Jerome Weidman was a friendly, smiling elf of a man. He was a prolific novelist, the author of *I Can Get It For You Wholesale* and other books, but *Fiorello!* was his first Broadway show. During rehearsals he sat with pencil poised above a legal pad making changes as he heard dialogue spoken aloud.

George Abbott was tough on actor Tom Bosley, cast as Fiorello LaGuardia, during rehearsals. Tom Bosley and I had met when we were in *Guys and Dolls* in Dallas, and we enjoyed a celebratory dinner together when we each contracted for *Fiorello!* Fiorello was a star-making role, a big break for my actor friend, who looked uncannily like LaGuardia onstage. But Tom's voice was an announcer's voice, deep and resonant. An avid Chicago Cubs fan, his boyhood goal was to be a sportscaster. The real-life LaGuardia's speech was high-pitched and fast-paced. The show opened with the character reading comics to children on the radio, as the real-life mayor had done during a New York newspaper strike. The proper portrayal of LaGuardia's voice was vital, the scene setting a tone of reality for the show. Tom eventually rose to the challenge, but was shy and tentative the first few days of rehearsal.

"*Tom*! Any idiot in Hollywood could do what I'm asking you to do!" barked Mr. Abbott. In addition to vocal differences, LaGuardia was a fast-moving dynamo, Tom Bosley more easy-going. George Abbott was emphatic, and actor Bosley turned pale. Tom's jaw set with determination, the back of his shirt a perpetual circle of perspiration. Visibly stung, attempting to make light of the director's criticism, Tom responded, "But I've never even been to Hollywood, Mr. Abbott!"

"Well, sir, you're working up to it," George Abbott said.

On the fourth day of rehearsals, Mr. Abbott took me aside. "We've rescheduled your rehearsals for this afternoon, Pat. Be at the Cort Theater after lunch. Please don't mention this to anyone." All morning I wondered why I was needed that afternoon. After lunch, as I walked down Seventh Avenue toward Forty-Eighth Street and the Cort, I was joined by Mr. Abbott and Jerry Weidman. Mr. Abbott accurately sensed my curiosity.

"We want you to read with different actors this afternoon, Pat. We're afraid Tom Bosley doesn't have the fire for Fiorello."

All afternoon I read Fiorello/Marie scenes with potential new LaGuardias. Each of the actors was talented; all were physically possible for the role. Two of them, Harvey Lembeck and Sorrell Booke (later of TV's *Dukes of Hazard* fame) eventually either understudied or played Fiorello. Though it was my job to read with these actors, the afternoon made me uneasy. I was sworn to secrecy, but Tom Bosley and I were friends as well as co-stars. Tom was the only one in the *Fiorello!* company who knew how ill I'd been weeks before rehearsals began. While recuperating in Cincinnati I received a letter from him, dated August 28, 1959.

"Dear Pat: *Coward*! Who do you think you are? Leaving me to face the anxiety of what is to come all by myself! Here I stay, chewing off what's left of some one-time-good-looking fingernails! Seriously, the important thing is that you feel better." Although he knew how close I came to having to give up playing Marie, Tom never gave me away.

Mr. Abbott and I walked from the Cort Theater together, back to the rehearsal studios. He sighed. I suspected his heart was heavy, too. "I hope I never have to see another short actor," he said.

"What will happen, Mr. Abbott?"

"I'm not sure. This is a group decision. Tom has made progress. We'll wait and see." Mr. Abbott didn't speak about it again, and as rehearsals progressed, Tom was superb. But I heard that another well-known actor was quietly standing by, ready to step into the role, until our New Haven opening.

Meanwhile, another criticism from Mr. Abbott cut deep, this time at *my* soul: "Miss Wilson! This is not a nightclub you're singing in —it's *theater*!" Oh, that stung. The remark negated my considerable theatrical experience, and shook the confidence I struggled for in my first Broadway leading role. I brooded about it for days, and withered from spontaneity in rehearsing. I finally spoke up.

"Mr. Abbott, please don't treat me as if I've never stepped on a stage!"

George Abbott rarely stopped to humor actors, but he put his arm around my shoulder. "Pat, do you remember a show I directed a while back, the musical version of *A Tree Grows In Brooklyn?* It was not a success."

"Of course I remember, Mr. Abbott."

"When you walked onstage to audition for *Fiorello!*, I wished I could've turned back the clock in time to cast you as the lead in that show. I believe you could have turned *A Tree Grows In Brooklyn* into a hit. Don't ever think I don't appreciate you and your talent. But don't ever sell a song like it's a piece of club material in a show of mine again!" Lessons. From a master.

Journal, September 30, 1959: Off and running! A week into rehearsal. A lot at stake for us all and we're working hard. You'd think I'd never worked in my life before. I'm scared and I withdraw. Hell, we're all scared and insecure, otherwise we wouldn't be actors! Bobby Fosse always said the same thing.

Marie's Law was a counterpoint duet I sang with Nat Frey in *Fiorello!'s* first act. Nat and I had much interaction throughout the show, which was further developed as Abbott watched the friendship between Nat and me grow during rehearsals. Nat reminded me of my brother David. Both were loveable teddy-bear guys with a soft under-belly, gruff shell-exterior, and impish sense of humor. Abbott cannily transferred Nat's and my affinity for one another in life to the stage.

I lay down 'Marie's Law' to Nat Frey.

Much of what is seen in *Fiorello!* as the loving, familial rapport between the characters of Marie and Morris is drawn from the relationship I had with my brother. And several years after *Fiorello!'s* Broadway run, David Wilson played the character of Morris in a Cincinnati production of the musical. He was brilliant.

There couldn't have been a more exciting actor to play the character Ben Marino in *Fiorello!* than Howard DaSilva. To perform scenes with Howard was a master class in acting. His credentials as an actor and director were impressive. They included

Group Theater and Clifford Odets's plays, *The Cradle Will Rock* and *Waiting For Lefty,* and the role of the villainous Jud in the original cast of *Oklahoma.* After forty films and two academy award nominations (for *Lost Weekend* and *Two* Years *Before the Mast)* Howard was blacklisted in Hollywood during the McCarthy era. Director George Abbott and producers Robert Griffith and Hal Prince thumbed their noses at the blacklist. *Fiorello!* re-opened Howard DaSilva's career as a major player.

Tom Bosley as Fiorello (L); me as Marie; Howard DaSilva as Ben Marino (R)—headed for a hit!

When our costumes appeared, signaling the end stages of our rehearsal labor, the nerves and insecurities of the actors surfaced. We were about to give birth to our baby in front of audiences, during out-of-town tryouts. My favorite costume, an ankle-length dress of peach-colored chiffon, was designed for a farewell party scene near the end of the first act. Fiorello has volunteered for service in World War I, and is leaving for duty. The scene was an emotional one, and unbeknownst to costume designer Jean Eckart, the dress she fashioned for me evoked emotions in me far beyond nerves and insecurities.

"It must have purple in it somewhere," Jean said, surveying her realized vision of Marie's party dress. "Purple is Marie's color." She deftly sashed the peach dress in lavender, matching the sash with lavender-dyed satin slippers. That same color combination had been the color scheme for my wedding to Rick, and the unique coupling of colors revived feelings of deep longing and sadness in me. Actors are trained to recall and utilize real-life emotions in the characters they play. The peach-and-lavender dress enabled me to carry those feelings into the scene. With the men costumed in khaki and army puttees, and all the women in pastel party dresses, Peter Gennaro had choreographed the gently nostalgic Bock/Harnick ballad, *Till Tomorrow* as a romantic, softly-lit waltz. I was staged to waltz with Morris (Nat) for a few moments before breaking into tears and blurting my dialogue:

In my favorite "Marie" costume: peach chiffon and lavender satin

"What if I never see Fiorello again?" The tears were real. A part of me remained sad that I might never see Rick again. Across the stage, Tom, as Fiorello, waltzed with beautiful Ellen Hanley as Thea, revealing in dialogue that Fiorello intends to propose to Thea when he returns from war. *Till Tomorrow* and the sentimental scene perfectly caught the nostalgia of the moment. Every night, for two years, the cast heard sniffles beyond the footlights. Saying goodbye to loved ones in that wartime was no more popular then than it has been in wartimes since. The scene connected, and still does, with audiences.

A quick change in the wings, from party dress to beige jumper, white crepe blouse, and violet-covered pillbox hat, hurried me into the first-act finale, a boat-dock scene depicting LaGuardia's triumphal return from war. This scene appeared in *Life* magazine in full-color: Fiorello (Bosley) at the foot of the gang-plank, proposing to Thea (Ellen Hanley) in front of torch-carrying Marie (me). Ah, sadness. Morris (Nat) wears a concerned expression, as he watches Marie struggling for composure. Fighting back tears. Beneath all those purple violets.

First act finale, welcoming Tom Bosley as Fiorello home from war. Ellen Hanley (L) as Thea, Bob Holiday as Neil, Nat Frey as Morris, me as Marie.

My first costume in the second act was a 1920s-style coat. The wardrobe mistress, Claire Dixon, literally took this coat off my back. A newly-added scene required a new costume. There was no time before the Philadelphia opening to construct wardrobe, so Claire took my long, 1950s camel-hair coat and, overnight, fashioned it into

Singin' my heart out about marrying the very next man.

a 1920's cocoon-wrap-around, which I wore for the next two years in the second act. Producer Bobby Griffith at first objected to the company buying a replacement coat for me, but Claire said, teasing, "We can't let the girl freeze, Bobby!"

My final costume was the sophisticated 1930s ankle-length black skirt and white crepe over-blouse, topped by a black felt cloche with a white bow, seen most often in pictures of Marie, worn during *I'll Marry The Very Next Man* and the proposal scene/finale of the show.

Journal, October 16, 1959: We're in New Haven. Open here tomorrow night. Getting used to these revolving sets is tough —particularly in the dark. But they keep the show moving. I hang onto prop furniture for dear life! Orchestra rehearsal this afternoon. Pat Stanley cried when I rehearsed Where Do I Go From Here? Technical /dress rehearsal tonight. We're invited to be out front to watch scenes when we're not onstage.

My dressing room was at stage left. Dog-pal Charlie, as always, curled up in my purse and slept while I made up and vocalized. I left him snoozing while I sat in the theater watching the crew light Howard DaSilva for *Politics and Poker*. Horrified, I watched as Charlie strolled onstage. He sniffed Howard's pant leg, then the tempting leg of the poker table. I was halfway down the aisle towards the stage when George Abbott exploded.

"WHOSE DOG IS THAT? GET THAT DOG OFF THE STAGE!"

Howard DaSilva scooped Charlie up and handed him to me in the wings. I locked my dressing room door, but after that night, Charlie was forever banned from the theater.

scene v: Autumn 1959, New Haven and Philadelphia

Journal, October 17, 1959: In my dressing room early. Deep breathing, vocalizing—not to mention praying! Pat Stanley says Gus is here from New York for the opening. Her ex-husband, Johnny Burke, too. We'll see them after the show at the party at Kaysey's Restaurant.

Pat Stanley, Johnny Burke (of the songwriting team of Burke and Van Heusen) and Gus and I celebrated together after the opening performance. Peggy Lee's recording of my first act song, *Where Do I Go From Here*, had just been released.

"That song will make you a star!" Gus enthused. "It's a perfect fit for you, emotionally and vocally." We sang it together, a lusty duet. Pat and Johnny Burke, who had written a hit or two himself (Bing Crosby's *Swingin' On A Star*, for one), were sweetly indulgent.

I'll Marry The Very Next Man., my big second act solo, had stopped the show that night. It was, for the moment, the "11 o'clock song," the last song in the show, but I confided to Gus that because it was a "book" song, advancing the show's story-line, it wasn't as strong a recording possibility as the very commercial *Where Do I Go From Here.* He agreed. I learned later that Mr. Abbott had committed Jerry Bock and Sheldon Harnick to writing a song like my audition piece, *You Are My Lucky Star*, for Marie. He turned down several versions, including one called *Marriage Is the Pulitzer Prize of Love,* before okaying *I'll Marry The Very Next Man.* Even though it stopped the show that opening night in New Haven, it wasn't mentioned in the New Haven reviews the next day, and the ballad was: *"....Miss Wilson has a fine voice, presenting what will surely be one of the top songs, Where Do I Go From Here? "*

The day after opening night in New Haven, George Abbott invited me to his hotel suite after rehearsal, "to discuss the character of Marie." *What a thrill to have Mr. Abbott's individual attention!* Was I naïve? Yes. Composer Jerry Bock overheard George Abbott's invitation.

"Watch yourself, Patty," Jerry whispered. I didn't get his meaning. Later, as I read Marie's lines in George Abbott's suite, I was surprised when the director put his arms around me and pulled me towards him. My first thought was, "Hey, wait a minute, this isn't part of the scene!" It dawned on me that we were no longer rehearsing. But this new scene made no sense. This leading man was past seventy. I was barely out of my twenties.

A confession: I'm a blurter and a compulsive truth-teller. Hardly a diplomat. Call it an alignment of stars at the moment of my birth, but there I was, a blurting truth-teller in an awkward moment. Not a good thing in show business. I had no feminine wiles. Lena Horne once confessed, "I always said the *right* things to the *wrong* people, and the *wrong* things to the *right* people." So it was with me.

"Oh, Mr. Abbott, I admire and respect you so much," I said, totally sincere. "You're a legend. I'm thrilled to be working with you." *Truly* sincere. "But you remind me of my grandfather!" The truth.

Smooth, Patricia.

"Well," said George Abbott, dropping his arms, "You can take the girl out of Ohio, but you can't take the Ohio out of the girl!"

Where Do I Go From Here? was cut from the show the next day. I found the courage to speak my mind.

"Mr. Abbott, that ballad sets up everything I do! It allows me to express Marie's feelings in a musical soliloquy. I think it's a mistake to cut it, honestly I do!"

"And I think I'll be the judge of that, Patricia," said George Abbott.

Lyricist Sheldon Harnick has assured me for the last forty years that *Where Do I Go From Here?* was cut for first-act pacing purposes. I'm sure he's right. It's yesterday's mashed potatoes now, but then I was convinced that all I'd heard about big, bad directors getting even with young actresses who withheld sexual favors had to be true.

When we were in Philadelphia, a new song, *Little Tin Box*, was put into the show for Howard DaSilva and the politicians. This song is lyricist Sheldon Harnick and composer Jerry Bock at their witty, intelligent best. It's timeless, a brilliant satire of corrupt politicians. (Try it on today's bunch.)

I'll Marry The Very Next Man was repositioned in the show. I sang it originally in a scene between Marie and Dora. I now entered after *Little Tin Box*, and played a brief scene with Howard in which I asked him, as Ben, to help Fiorello run for mayor of New York City. Howard and the politicians left the stage. A few expository bits of dialogue with Nat Frey led into *I'll Marry The Very Next Man*. It prepared the audience for the final scene of the show. Fiorello proposes marriage to the long-suffering Marie. He is "the very next man." The haunting orchestral refrain underscoring the proposal scene remains the melody of my cut ballad, *Where Do I Go From Here?*

We opened to enormous success in our second try-out town, Philadelphia, overshadowing another show in its pre-Broadway trial, *Saratoga,* which premiered the same week. I held my own with the critics, in spite of the loss of what I considered a major chunk of character revelation, as well as my favorite song.

I appealed to Howard DaSilva. "Gosh, Howard, I feel as if I'm not coming through without that ballad." Howard and I discovered in New Haven that we were both walkers. We walked before and after shows, and at critical moments in our lives, to clear our thoughts. We continued our walks together in Philadelphia, by now good friends. Howard agreed that losing the ballad created empty space in the character of Marie.

"Mr. Abbott doesn't understand women characters very well, only comedy women," Howard explained. (That was food for thought.) "Almost every line Marie speaks is exposition," he continued. "She moves the political story line, the boring stuff. She says little about herself, only in a couple of places, to Morris or Dora. Your part can't be played at face value, Pat. You have a lot of filling in to do. I have no doubt you can do it."

He continued. "Every time you're with Fiorello onstage, the efficient secretary saying your dry dialogue, your inner feelings for the man are a subtext. Don't try to *reveal* those feelings with some sappy gesture. They're there. With you, the audience knows."

"My fourth grade teacher once told the class everything I thought showed on my face. I was very embarrassed at the time."

"You see? But now it's not an embarrassment—it's an actor's gift."

After *Fiorello!* opened in New York, venerable actress Ruth Gordon and I became friends. We sat next to each other every

Sunday at the Actors Fund benefits. We began by saying "hello," and idly chatting. Tiny, straightforward Ruth startled me one night.

"I gotta tell ya, Patricia—yer the hah-dest workin' woman on Broadway. I nevah saw someone do so much with so little help." Ruth never lost her New England accent.

"I'm not sure what you mean, Ruth." I did, but I wanted to hear her say it.

"Well, what I mean is, ya carry the show on yer back, and ya get no payoff till it's almost too late. But ya fool 'em! Ya make it work for ya anyway. That finale scene? That's a great moment for ya!"

Thanks, Ruth. And thanks, Howard DaSilva.

Journal, October 28, 1959: Philadelphia: Still tiring easily, too much to go to Variety Club after the show with the cast. Boy, mononucleosis is a downer!

I ran into Harvey Lembeck, Tom Bosley's standby, on the way to rehearsal.

"Hey, Patricia," Harvey said. "The gang and I miss you hanging out at The Variety Club with us. We have a great time after shows. It's good to unwind."

"I know, Harvey," I said. "But I go back to the hotel to make a phone call every night." (There were no cell phones in 1959.)

"You must have a fella. Serious, huh? Getting married?"

I shrugged. I thought I was being non-committal. A few days later it was in Walter Winchell's column that I was engaged. I decided Harvey must have fed Winchell the story.

On our second Sunday in Philadelphia, a welcome day off, I decided not to go back to New York for the day, but to stay in my hotel room, reading the papers and resting. The phone rang.

"Pat, it's George."

"Oh, hello, Mr. Abbott. You didn't go back to New York?"

"No, I'm not much for running back and forth. Did you know they have a tea dance here in the hotel on Sunday afternoons? I wonder if you'd like to meet me downstairs to dance? They have a small orchestra. It's quite charming."

George Abbott's affinity for ballroom dancing was well-known. He often asked dancers from his shows to go to Roseland with him. But I was wary that day, for he'd made a pass at me in New Haven. It was only later that I learned I was nobody special. George Abbott, single at the time, made passes at a lot of women. Actress Maureen

Stapleton, who later had a ten-year romance with him, told me I'd "really missed out." She gave me a wicked wink. But that Sunday afternoon in Philadelphia, I was still the kid from Ohio, wary of involvement, wary of my own feelings.

"I'm a little tired, Mr. Abbott. I'm not sure I'd be good company," I hedged. But I knew my relationship with Abbott needed fence-mending. Perhaps he felt the same way. *Tea-dancing in a public place would be safe enough—perhaps he had wonderful news for me. Would my favorite song go back into the show?*

"You know what, Mr. Abbott? It does sound like fun. What time should I meet you?"

I called my social mentor, Gus Schirmer. We'd mended our friendship fences. "Gus, what should I wear to a Sunday afternoon tea dance in Philadelphia?"

"Oh!" Gus said, happy. "Wear the little black outfit with the jacket we bought you at Arden's. And don't forget the hat!" He told me the "buzz" in New York was that *Fiorello!* was coming into Broadway as a surefire hit.

The Elizabeth Arden outfit I wore that afternoon was a black wool cocktail sheath with a square neck trimmed in black satin. Its bolero jacket was black-and-rust wool plaid, also trimmed in black satin. I loved the counterpoint of satin on casual wool plaid. The hat that topped it was a small black satin cap with a half-veil. When I took off the jacket, the sheath dress with the little hat became a dressy cocktail outfit.

"Superior!" said Mr. Abbott as I walked towards him. Even in my three and a half inch spike heels he towered over me. We waltzed, fox-trotted, and rumbaed for the afternoon, Mr. Abbott was, hands-down, the best dancer I'd ever known. At one point, I sat down for a cup of tea. Unfazed, Mr. Abbott asked several other women in the room if they'd care to dance. I had a twenty minute breather, but George waltzed and rumbaed on.

"I hear you're engaged," said Mr. Abbott, when we resumed with a cha-cha.

"No, not really. I don't know how that got into Winchell's column."

"Well, I think it's good if you are. You're a nice girl. But very lonely, it seems to me."

"Maybe it's just the Marie in me, Mr. Abbott."

He smiled, engineering me into a deep dip.

"You should be happy. You're in a hit show, and you're very good in it."

"But what about *Where Do I Go From Here?* Is it going back in, Mr. Abbott?"

"No," he said. "The show is frozen, and will open in New York as it stands. We won't make any more changes. I'm sorry, Pat."

At least I knew.

scene vi: Autumn 1959, Enter a long run, Broadway

So *Fiorello!* opened, a major hit during Broadway's golden age. It ran for two years, 795 performances.

We recorded the cast album on a cold December Sunday shortly after our Broadway debut. The recording began at ten in the morning, running through the entire show, from the opening *On The Side Of The Angels* to the closing song, *I'll Marry The Very Next Man.* The proposal scene and finale were taken out of context and recorded early in the day, probably to get Tom Bosley home to rest for the upcoming week of performances.

For most of the day after Nat Frey and I finished *On The Side of the Angels* and *Marie's Law,* I waited outside the studio, chatting with Miles Kreuger, the young man writing the album liner notes. It was ten that night before we got to *I'll Marry The Very Next Man.* I didn't speak up for myself to say, "Hey! I'm getting tired! Is it more important to record the taps from the *Gentleman Jimmy* dance chorus, or *I'll Marry The Very Next Man*?" To me, my voice sounds strained and tired on the album, my performance pushed and unnatural. To my ears, to this day, I wasn't at my best. Yet I've received many accolades about the recording, both written and spoken. Twenty years after the fact, vocal coach Gene Casey told me he had pupils demanding they be made to sound like "Marie" on the *Fiorello!* album.

The Broadhurst, an intimate, mid-sized theater, had small dressing rooms. Tom's and mine were adjoining on stage level. There was a door to close for privacy, but we left it open at half-hour so we could chat while we put on makeup. When the time came to choose new paint colors for our adjoining rooms, Tom wanted yellow and I wanted soft blue. I was voted down good-naturedly and the rooms became a cheerful yellow. For my capitulation, I was awarded a key to Tom's locked, private phone.

Publicity appearances became a part of almost every non-matinee day. I was happy to do anything our publicity contact, Mary Bryant of the Jacobsen/Harmon office, asked of me. I showed up for benefits, luncheons, radio and TV broadcasts. Singing at public relations events, I pulled out a few tricks from supper club days. Rather than doing one of *my* songs from the show, or a quick chorus of *Till Tomorrow*, which was emerging as a popular favorite, I took a bell tone from the piano as a starting note and launched into *Home Again*, the rousing first-act finale song, sung by the whole cast in the show. It took my audiences by surprise when they heard lyricist Sheldon Harnick's opening line, "UNCLE SAM SAYS HE WANTS YOU!" being belted out by the leading lady. It always got a good laugh.

Many political figures attended *Fiorello!* Eleanor Roosevelt was in our audience one night, and came backstage to tell us all how much she enjoyed the show. John Lindsay, the Republican congressman from New York's "Silk Stockings" district, brought friends and guests to see us, and made many backstage appearances. John became mayor of New York in 1966, and was likened to Fiorello LaGuardia as a fusion politician.

Fiorello's widow, the real-life Marie, was often an honored guest. My heart beat a little faster when I knew she was around, but Marie was always complimentary.

"I just wish I could sing like you," she said. Then in her sixties, a small, energetic lady, Marie LaGuardia was a straight-shooter. She had earlier made it plain to George Abbott that she did *not* pine for Fiorello, as the character Marie did in the show, but enjoyed politics and being a part of his exciting life. Director Abbott explained to her it was artistic license: the audience sharing the secret of a secretary carrying a torch for her unsuspecting boss was the thread that made the passage of years possible onstage. It was the "through-line" of the plot, the glue holding the show together.

There was no question in my mind, Marie loved her man. The lady's eyes sparkled when she talked about her late husband, so I found Mr. Abbott's plot insightful, not off-base. He intuited beyond Marie LaGuardia's self-image, into her depths. Her main concern was that Fiorello be represented in a good and proper light, and she was happy with both Tom Bosley and the show.

The real-life Marie LaGuardia (second from L) visited Tom and adorable Pat Stanley and me. An eye-opening experience, but the camera caught Marie and Tom off-guard.

"Yes, Patricia, I have no problem here," she said one day in my dressing room. "Except for what to do with all the attention and money

*I'*m getting!" A good lady. A pleasure to have known you, an honor to have entered your soul, Marie LaGuardia.

During the presidential election of 1960 we were sought to help in campaigns. Most of us were mesmerized by young John F. Kennedy. Jackie Kennedy, patroness of the arts, was our heroine. We volunteered, sang at rallies, passed out pamphlets. Both the Kennedys and the Nixons came to see *Fiorello!* on separate occasions. The drama of tripping over secret servicemen enlivened any tedium we began to feel after what was, by then, a year-long run, since both political families visited the cast backstage after performances. Richard Nixon spotted an informal picture taken earlier with John and Jackie Kennedy.

"Did the winners like the show as much as the losers?" Mr. Nixon asked.

He sounded downright wistful.

Even before *Fiorello!* emerged as a hit, I realized that the momentum gained from playing the lead in a George Abbott show would help me in other areas of entertainment. As soon as agent Ray Smith called to tell me I'd won the part of Marie, I told him I wanted to find a good personal manager to augment his efforts, and to help guide my career to higher levels. Ray suggested George "Bullets" Durgom, a beloved character with access to everyone in show business due to his foremost client, Jackie Gleason.

Bullets and I met at Colin Romoff's apartment. As I sang a few songs, Bullets closed his eyes and nodded his head, smiling. Instant rapport.

"I feel lucky that you fell into my lap, Pat. There'll be a lot of film and television work for you from here on," Bullets said. "As soon as they run out of New Yorkers who remember LaGuardia, your show will close. I give it six months." So said all the pundits, including agent Ray Smith when he told me the producers wanted me to sign a two-year contract. "Don't worry about being tied down," said Ray, "It won't come close to running for two years!" They didn't reckon on the genius of George Abbott.

Bullets refused a percentage of my *Fiorello!* earnings, saying, "No, you got the job before we met. That would be chicken of me." Here was a man with integrity. I couldn't resist kissing the bald dome for which this lovable character had been named. The dear man blushed, but the kiss sealed our contract, and Bullets became my manager.

So when *Fiorello!* opened as a major hit, I had esteemed manager Bullets Durgom to move my career along, but a two-year contract to keep me in place. "Don't worry," said Bullets. "There's plenty we can do while you're working. We'll get you a recording contract, for one thing." He introduced me to his new partner, the former manager of a New York City radio station, a young man breaking in as a talent representative.

"One of the first things we'll do for you is take care of your house seats, Patricia. They can be a nuisance," said the new assistant to my manager. As one of the stars of the show, I was allotted four, fourth row center seats per performance. When friends, guests or professional contacts called to ask if I could help them get seats, I'd call my manager's office, specify a date, and arrange for guests to pick up the allotted seats at the box office.

There was a small problem, however. My house seats were never available. Someone else had always managed to call for them just before I or my friends. When I became wiser in the ways of Broadway, I discovered that prime seats for hit shows could be sold at premium prices. One major star's fiancé lived for two years on her house seats. I told you I was naïve.

Early in the *Fiorello!* run, shortly after escorting me to Sardi's on *Fiorello!'s* opening night, Bullets disappeared. It was rumored that his marriage ended, leaving him despondent. He left the new assistant to run the New York office, and didn't turn up until months later in California. After our initially warm manager/client beginning, I never saw Bullets again.

How is a major hit such as *Fiorello!* absent from the Golden Age of Broadway retrospectives that play on public broadcasting stations? Those retrospectives show film clips of shows contemporary with *Fiorello!: Camelot, My Fair Lady, Gypsy, Sound of Music.* So why is *Fiorello!* not represented? The show won many awards, including the Drama Critics Circle Award for best musical, a Pulitzer Prize, and Tonys for Tom and George Abbott.

The film clips used on present-day retrospectives are about ninety percent taken from Ed Sullivan's *Toast of the Town* Sunday night variety show on television. There is one clip of Tom Bosley performing a short sequence from *Fiorello!* on a 1960's Tony Awards show that has remained, but Ed Sullivan, *Toast of the Town*'s producer/host, ran complete scenes, including dialogue, from hit Broadway shows as soon as they opened. Sullivan had p-o-w-e-r, with a capital "P," when it came to bringing Broadway shows to a national audience. Many of the kinescopes and clips from his show have survived.

Early in the *Fiorello!* run, my manager's new assistant called with great news.

"Patricia, have I got a sweet deal for you!" he enthused. "Ed Sullivan wants Howard DaSilva and the politicians to perform *Little Tin Box* on his show, then continue with the scene following it—your entrance, your speech to Howard, and *I'll Marry The Very Next Man.* The whole shebang!"

"How terrific!"

"And that's not all! Ed will use you in three solo guest spots on *Toast Of The Town* throughout the season! How did you know Ed Sullivan in Columbus? He thinks highly of you. This and the recording deal we're working on will launch you nationally!"

What transpired after that phone conversation amazes me still today, forty-odd years later. The five Broadway veterans who played the politicians and sang *Little Tin Box* with Howard DaSilva, decided they were entitled to more than what was universally paid Broadway performers to appear on the Sullivan show. Hal Prince made a speech backstage to the cast members involved in the scene. If the men playing the politicians felt it was fair to hold out for more money, he would back them, even though it was an important moment for the exposure of *Fiorello!* to a national audience. The politicians remained adamant. The characterizations they had developed in *Little Tin Box* and *Politics and Poker* had contributed greatly to the success of the show, and they were going to capitalize on what they'd helped to build. In retrospect, I think everyone expected Ed Sullivan would capitulate, but he didn't. He threw the politicians' stance back in our collective faces, saying to hell with the whole negotiation. He wanted nothing to do with *Fiorello!* Or anyone connected with it. It was a hefty year for Broadway musicals. He didn't need us. To proceed with the deal, *I* would have given Ed Sullivan a weeks' salary.

Bullets's new assistant pleaded with the television icon on my behalf. And I wrote Sullivan a note asking him to reconsider, if not for the show, at least for my individual deal and the three guest appearances. He didn't respond. Our show didn't appear on the Sullivan show, and consequently, there's too little film history of *Fiorello!*

None of the three girls, Pat Stanley, Ellen Hanley, or I, was nominated that year for a Tony Award. I think we were all disappointed. Certainly I was, and I was particularly surprised that Pat Stanley was overlooked for "Best Musical Supporting Actress." She was perfect as Dora. But that award went to Patricia Neway for *The Sound of Music,* which dominated the 1960 Tonys. Mary Martin won "Best Actress in a Musical" for her portrayal of Maria von Trapp, beating out Ethel Merman for *Gypsy,* Carol Burnett for *Once Upon A Mattress,* Dolores Gray for *Destry,* and Eileen Herlie for *Take Me Along.* Oliver Smith won for best sets (*The Sound of Music.*) Mr. Abbott, however, won for best director, over both Vincent Donahue for *The Sound of Music* and Jerome Robbins for *Gypsy.* Jackie Gleason won "Best Actor in a Musical" for *Take Me Along,* and Tom Bosley won "Best Supporting or Featured Actor in a Musical" for *Fiorello!* A strange designation for Tom's role. As good as Jackie Gleason was in *Take Me Along,* Tom Bosley's Fiorello LaGuardia was the tour-de-force, the star male musical performance of the season.

Oh, well, it was a weird year at the Tony awards, I comforted myself. Didn't *Gypsy* get robbed? Ethel Merman, too? Then greater consolation than my own opinion arrived. The New York Drama Critics' Circle nominated me as "Best New Actress of The Broadway Season."

scene vii: June 1960, Enter Dispute and Dismay, Manhattan

"BROADWAY SEES A LONG BLACKOUT!" screamed the headlines of June 3, 1960. *Fiorello!* was in the seventh month of its run when a dispute between Actors Equity and the League of New York Theaters dissipated into what one side called a "strike" and the other a "lockout." Actors had stopped work only once before, forty-one years earlier in 1919, when performers sought recognition for the group formed in 1913 that evolved into Actors Equity. None of us in 1960 believed that a pending Equity work stoppage would come to pass. How could actors, always overjoyed to be working, leave their jobs to walk a picket line? How could producers in a fragile business allow it to happen? But happen it did.

Actors were asking for a higher minimum wage, improved working conditions, and the start-up of a pension fund, supported by equal contributions from actors and producers. On June 2, 1960, after The League of New York Theaters, which represented producers and theater owners, deadlocked with Equity in a meeting, Equity shut down the play, *The Tenth Man.* The union planned a phased operation, closing one production at a time. But battle lines were drawn, and The League immediately closed down all productions running on Broadway. Were we actors to be starved out, not just financially, but emotionally and psychologically? This was a component the press immediately recognized. Performing was as much nourishment to actors as financial recompense. Murray Kempton of the New York Post wrote that producers had since time immemorial exploited the deep-seated psychological need of actors to act. He quoted George Bernard Shaw, who once said that actors would sign anything to fulfill their need to perform. Columnist Max Lerner allowed an outsider to read Equity's contract with the League, and the outsider commented, "An electrician would laugh at this."

Jackie Gleason, at that time starring on Broadway in the hit musical *Take Me Along,* pleaded for unity between actors in an interview with the press:

"We gotta do something for those kids on the minimum ($100.00 a week). It's pretty tough to work for that kind of dough. Equity has asked for higher minimums and pensions and a few things like cleaning up washrooms and getting rid of vermin in the dressing rooms. So what did they offer us? One can of Drano and some rat poison."

Venerated actress Helen Hayes also made an impassioned plea for unity. Miss Hayes, like Jackie Gleason, was hardly in dire straits herself, but she quoted Dickens and Tiny Tim: "God bless us all— *each and every one!"* Helen Hayes had been an actress all her life and brought honor to our profession. "Remember," she told us, "we actors speak of *giving* a performance! We *give* —that is the key word!—not just our talents, but our very souls, when we step onstage. Think what that means! We give our souls! We must be able to nourish our bodies!" Eloquent words from a beautiful lady. The profession of my grandparents, parents, and now myself, was a noble one. Helen Hayes had deemed it so. And now Miss Hayes, without ambivalence, was pleading for unity.

The Equity meetings I attended during the "Broadway Blackout," as the press called it, taught me that not all Broadway casts had the same benefits as those of us in *Fiorello!* Griffith and Prince were the good guys of producers. They respected actors. Our dressing rooms were immaculate. I couldn't blame our producers for my two-year contract, a prison for an actor, allowing him (or her) no bargaining power whatsoever. My agent had gambled that *Fiorello!* would not run long, and I allowed myself to be carried by someone else's judgment. And secretly, at the time of contract negotiations, a two-year mandate to stay in one place was music to my ears. I was weary of touring. How could I blame Griffith and Prince for shrewdly locking in their leading lady, with the full cooperation of her compliant agent? But I worried for other of my actor friends as the blackout progressed.

Journal, June 6, 1960: I love my Fiorello! family. Some of them, like Beverly Dixon, have kids. What they have to live on doesn't go far in New York. But I love Hal and Bobby, too. And I love to work! Confusing to try to take a stand.

The press quickly veered to the side of the actors when some of the producers in the League made vitriolic, outrageous statements. Producer Arthur Cantor was widely quoted: "If a kid isn't out of the chorus and into leads or featured roles within three years, then he or she should leave the business, anyway." That same producer called a labor lawyer/negotiator for Actors' Equity a "wharf rat."

Such remarks infuriated the media. Ed Sullivan stated in his *Daily News* column, "I cast a lusty vote for the actors. I believe the New York Theater League is completely wrong in the stance they have taken." He chided self-avowed, crusading political liberals like producer/writers Paddy Chayefsky and Lillian Hellman, and producers Arthur Cantor and Herman Shumlin, for calling the Equity plan to begin a pension fund, with equal contributions to be made by actors and producers, a "holdup." These producers, Sullivan stated, "always cast a vote for social reform in their productions," but were now doing a total about-face when it came to voting against their pockets. I was too young then to know what a pension fund might mean, though I'd heard family stories about actors dying in poverty after devoting their lives to their craft. Ed Sullivan wrote that he'd rather see ensemble kids with decent wages and a pension fund for actors than producer David Merrick "in a new designer suit."

Without question the New York press succeeded in shaping public opinion to the Equity viewpoint. At the beginning of the dispute, New York City Mayor Robert Wagner asked The League of New York Theaters to accept a fact-finding board to study the issues. The League refused the mayor's request to open their books. The press was infuriated, and reported that The League had appealed to Congress the year before to repeal a ten-cent-per-ticket luxury tax on Broadway theater tickets. It argued for Congress to "restore the luxury-tax money to ticket-buyers, to keep culture alive, and the theater industry at work." Yet when Congress repealed the tax, ticket prices remained the same. Where, the press asked, was the ten-cents per ticket windfall, some $2,500,000 annually?

Actors hopefully and dutifully reported to stage doors every night and matinee afternoons at half-hour. We stood waiting until after curtain-time, ostensibly ready to perform should the stage doors swing open. Equity considered all productions closed down by The League a lockout rather than a strike, and subsidized us with ten dollars for each missed performance, the rich sum of eighty dollars a week.

After one of our wait-outs, Pat Stanley and I decided to go to Sardi's to splurge on a good dinner. We had just settled into one of the leather booths and exchanged small talk with Jimmy, the head waiter, when we heard a familiar voice.

"May I join you?" asked producer Hal Prince. He sat down, and for the next couple of hours the three of us talked, stuffed ourselves, and never mentioned our positions on opposite sides of the Broadway fence. Hal picked up the check.

Most felt the blackout/strike/lockout would go on through the summer season, until fall. The League reported to the mayor's office that it was Equity holding the strong hand, that actors had prepared far in advance of the shutdown with a "monstrous strike fund." They decried the sad breakdown of culture caused by the "actors' strike." They bewailed the loss of revenue to associated businesses, yet they continued to refuse requests to open their books to an independent settlement committee. That fact enraged the media. Finally intense pressure from the city, the press, and the community of restaurants, hotels, and shops being adversely affected became too much. The League of New York Theaters capitulated after eight days.

Journal, June 12, 1960: It's over, thank God! We're all so relieved it didn't go on and on!

Minimum wages were improved, and an Actors Equity/Producers Pension Plan began. But the cost? Far beyond dollars and cents, for the entire Broadway community paid a terrible price for the dispute.

Producer Robert S. "Bobby" Griffith had devoted his life to the theater, rising through the ranks from actor to stage manager to producer. He and his young protégé/partner, Hal Prince, had already produced *The Pajama Game, Damn Yankees,* and *Fiorello!* One evening, as actors milled around the stage door hoping word of a settlement would arrive, Bobby suddenly appeared in our midst. He had bolted from his dinner at Sardi's to run across the street and stand on a chair on the sidewalk in front of the Broadhurst. Tears waiting to pour down his face, he talked passionately to us about his love for the theater, and of how horrified he was at seeing all of us, with what he knew was our shared passion, threatening what we mutually loved. It was an emotional moment. He was right in many ways, and none of us could see Bobby as our enemy. Hal Prince appeared, gently helping his partner down from the chair. "If you keep on like this, you'll kill yourself, Bobby," Hal said. And that's what happened. That moment began a downhill slide for Bobby's health and his broken heart. Equity won its cause, but within a year we had all lost Robert S. "Bobby" Griffith, one of the best guys of the Golden Age of Broadway.

scene viii: 1960-1961, New York City

Journal, June 20, 1960: So happy to be back at work again! Hey, aren't actresses in the same show supposed to hate each other? I love Ellen Hanley—impossible not to—a great woman!

Ellen Hanley played Thea, LaGuardia's first wife, in *Fiorello!* Ellen and I had no scenes together, but became close friends offstage.

The Fabulous Life of a Happy Has-Been

Pat Stanley and I had many scenes together, and in one we were plagued with the actor's ultimate nightmare: we couldn't stop laughing. It was a dramatic onstage moment, that scene, one in which our characters had come to warn Fiorello of a plot against his life, yet there was a trigger in it that somehow set us off. I can see Pat's earnest face looking up at me yet, and forty-odd years later, I smile. I suppose my intensity as Marie got to Pat, too. Whatever it was, and in spite of admonitions from the stage manager, Ruth Mitchell, night-after-night we suppressed giggles, held back tears, and in my case, resisted pressure on a weak bladder. Our voices shook from the strain. We were serious young women, dedicated young actresses, trained in concentration. We couldn't bear to be unprofessional, but for a period of time we couldn't help ourselves.

Our plight wasn't helped when Tom Bosley, who spoke our cue, burbled his lines during one performance. Marie and Dora wait outside Fiorello's office door as he speaks on the phone to his wife, Thea, who is very ill. Tom's line, and our cue to enter his office, was: "Now, you just stay in bed, sweetheart—the doctor says you need the rest." Pat and I pantomimed agitation outside the office door, awaiting that line, our cue to burst in on Fiorello.

One night, as Pat and I were finally getting our tendency to break up under control, Tom said our cue-line like this:

"Now, you stay in bed, sweetheart—the doctor says you need the *money.*"

Pat and I burst through the office door, as we were staged to do, but we barely got through the scene. Tom, not realizing his gaffe with our cue-line, looked perplexed as the lights went down at the end of the scene, and we faced upstage in a full break-up.

In a favorite scene, Dora tells Marie she's in love with a cop, Floyd. Marie remarks that she has stopped on her way to visit Dora to enjoy "a Moxie."(Mr. Abbott explained to us younger folk during rehearsals that "Moxie" was a 1917 soft drink, a predecessor to Coke and Pepsi,)

"*Moxie!*" says a horrified Dora to Marie. "Don't you know Moxie is bad for your teeth? Floyd says if you put an ordinary molar in a glass of Moxie, and keep it there overnight, in the morning you'll find the tooth is completely disappeared!" Dora is sure of herself and the pronouncement by her new hero.

Marie answers, "Floyd told you *that*?"

"Yep," says Dora, proud.

Mr. Abbott directed me to walk s—l—o—w—l—y across the stage, pondering what Dora had said. It was the longest pause in the fast-paced first act, but Mr. Abbott allowed it, resulting in one of the show's biggest laughs as Marie finally says,

"W—e—ll, as long as you're happy, that's the main thing."

I've seen the show played several times, with different Maries. The long pause is not in the written stage directions, and the line never gets a laugh. It's the pause, the timing, that does it. That was George Abbott's comic genius at work.

Journal, July 18, 1960: If only I felt as strong offstage as I do on. My social life is a disaster. What's wrong with me? I wish I could talk to Dr. Braun. I'm sure he'd encourage me to find another therapist. I dread the prospect.

My dating life was negligible. The few times I allowed myself to go out, I couldn't wait to get home. Except when I was onstage, my self-esteem was at a low ebb, and in spite of the personal appearances I was making, I'd developed a painful shyness. Paradoxically, one of the few people I now felt comfortable with was George Abbott. He'd shrugged off my sexual rebuff of him and began inviting me to join him making the rounds of shows (mostly off-Broadway), those on different schedules from *Fiorello!*

"Just as intelligent company, Pat. I don't like going alone." George wasn't to meet and marry his wife Joy for several years. He never again made a pass at me, but became a comfortable friend.

And what a privilege to attend theater with George Abbott. I'd never known anyone so astute. He thought Hal Prince had the potential of being the great producer/director he indeed became. When we saw Carol Burnett in *Once Upon a Mattress*, which Mr. Abbott had directed (and which made Carol a star) he commented on Carol's "humanity." In his opinion that quality took her even beyond her gifts of comic timing and voice. We saw John Gielgud in Shakespeare's *Much Ado About Nothing,* which, except for Gielgud, neither George Abbott nor I liked very much.

George invited Tom Bosley and me to spend a weekend at his country home in Monticello, New York. He pointedly invited us both, and I gladly accepted. Tom had a new car, and we would drive to the country together. I received a note from Mr. Abbott:

"Dear Pat: I wrote Tom yesterday and gave him all the road map details, so I shall expect him to deliver you safely after Saturday night, the 22nd, or Sunday AM, as you decide. I wish you could be here now—it is so beautiful. The mountain laurel is still in bloom and everywhere you look there are blossoms. Amy and I went in the sailfish race yesterday and came in last. I don't think my grand-daughter has a high opinion of me as a skipper! It has been warm and lovely. I do hope it is as beautiful as this when you get here. I have a great series of golfers booked now, and shall devote myself to improvement in that treacherous game for the next couple of weeks. See you soon—Yours, George."

Friendly, straightforward, genuine. Qualities I'd come to respect and appreciate in George Abbott. All else was forgotten.

Tom told me the day before we were to leave that he was taking along Jean Elliott, a dancer from our show. I felt a moment of panic. Were Tom and George in cahoots? If Tom was pairing off with Jean, would that leave me vulnerable with George? It wasn't the case, and taught me yet another lesson—it was time for me to grow up.

Jeanie Elliott and I shared a guest room that weekend and became good friends. She was deep and serious, along with being adorable. And she was what Tom had longed for, someone special with whom he could enjoy his success.

George Abbott and I shared long talks and walks around the lake, the water a quiet mirror for the trees and blooms surrounding his country home.

"What do you intend to do with your life after *Fiorello!?*" George asked.

"Jule Styne is stumping for me to play the lead in his new show, and he ran through the score for me a few days ago. David Merrick will produce it." George and I laughed, because Jule had said to me, "Oh, Pat, you'll love it! It's my best score since *My Fair Lady!*"

"Well," said George, "We know what he meant, but let's not tell Lerner and Loewe that Jule thinks he wrote *My Fair Lady!*"

He grew serious. "It's wonderful that you might go from our show into another. But I hope you'll find a young man. You seem like a lonely kind of girl to me." What was my problem? Was I suddenly so shy because I feared a new relationship? Why was I only comfortable with George, more than twice my age? I looked at this remarkable man and sensed how lonely *he* must be. I never met the woman he eventually married, his widow, Joy, but I've heard from mutual friends that she made him very happy. They had many years together. George Abbott lived to be 107.

Ellen Hanley had been in *Two's Company*, which starred Bette Davis, a few years prior to *Fiorello!* When Miss Davis attended a performance of *Fiorello!* Ellen invited some of our cast to her apartment to meet the great film star. At the gathering, Bette Davis was complimentary and kind, telling me how much she liked the show and my "nifty performance." It was a thrill, for she was one of my idols.

During the evening, nausea and panic suddenly overwhelmed me. It wasn't physical, I knew. What was wrong? I couldn't catch my breath, sweat beaded on my forehead. I went to the powder room, and then took Ellen aside, telling her I was ill. I left quickly, without saying goodbye to anyone else.

Journal, August 2, 1960: I'm in trouble. I'd better do something. I'm the most successful I've ever been professionally, and the least I've ever been personally. I must find a new therapist.

Dour and expressionless Dr. Handman said very little, barely even "hello." I was used to Dr. Braun, who talked face-to-face, reacting to me, presenting me with information. Dr. Handman told me to lie on a couch and "free-associate," which I thought was interesting at first, but seemed silly after a while. Yet I threw myself into the experience. Analysis was expensive and time consuming, but I had to find out why I was so inconveniently shy. A dream convinced me I'd gotten to the bottom of my problem: A woman who was my twin was wearing the same dress I was wearing, (my then-favorite) white silk with brown polka dots. She and I were making love.

"That dream! It must mean I'm a lesbian!" I told Dr. Handman.

"No," said Dr. Handman, "You were screwing yourself in the dream, and your subconscious is telling you that you're screwing yourself in life."

Well, maybe Dr. Handman was wiser than I gave him credit for. I forced myself to look at my shyness, at my fear of socializing, particularly with men. I began going out again, not just to the theater, but to parties. I circulated, engaged in conversations. I realized this was the kind of talk therapy I needed. George Abbott was right. I was lonely. I missed Rick and being married. A good-looking doctor, eligible, in his late thirties, asked if we could have a drink together after a party, and then asked me for dinner the next night, and the next.

A journal entry from that era: *Wow! Dr. Handman is really helping me! At last I'm enjoying getting to know a man better!* On our fourth date, I mentioned Dr. Handman to my new friend.

"You're in analysis?"

"Yes—isn't it terrific?"

"Terrific," said the first man I'd felt close to in a long time, as we kissed goodnight. He was a great kisser.

The next morning an enormous floral arrangement accompanied by a note arrived at my apartment. It was from the doctor/great kisser.

"Dear Pat: No one is sorrier than I that I can no longer see you. As a psychoanalyst, I'm unable to date someone currently in therapy. I'm sure you understand. I wish you every good thing in life, and will be following your career with interest. With loving respect—"

He was sure I understood? *Wrong.* What the *hell*? What did my being in therapy have to do with anything?

I called Dr. Handman. "It's your fault!" I wailed. "I really like this guy!" Dr. Handman was very casual, very patronizing. *Very* annoying.

"Oh, he just doesn't want you talking about him to a fellow analyst," he said.

More anger and angst to deal with. *Up again, old heart.*

scene ix: 1961, Enter an Idol, Broadway

"Laurence Olivier just asked me who you are," said my Ohio State friend, Ken Diehl. Ken was now a Manhattan realtor, and as an old school chum, someone with whom I could be comfortable. "He told me he'd like to meet you, if I wouldn't mind. I told him I wouldn't mind." Ken and I were attending a Sunday night Actors Fund benefit performance together, and had hurried to the bar across the street during intermission. Ken was nursing a cold and in need of a brandy, I wanted to use the ladies' room in the bistro without waiting in line at the theater.

Ken chugged his brandy. "C'mon, maybe we can catch up with him!"

"Yes, of course, Kenny, and Queen Elizabeth just told me in the ladies' room that *she's* dying to meet *you*. Have another drink!"

"No, I'm serious, Pat, Larry Olivier was here, and he said he'd like to meet you."

"*Larry*? Please, Ken, I'm not in the mood!"

"Well, that's what he called himself!"

Ken grabbed my hand and we returned to the theater. The house lights were still on. He marched me to the fourth row, and leaned across two people seated on the aisle, Ruth Gordon and Garson Kanin. He said to the man seated next to them, "Larry, this is my friend, Patricia Wilson." Sir Laurence Olivier stood as the houselights were dimming, and murmured something unintelligible. He was only unintelligible. I was speechless.

Thereafter, on Sunday nights, throughout a season of Actors Fund benefits, I sat with Ruth Gordon, Garson Kanin, and Sir Laurence Olivier. Don't ask me how it happened that week after week our seats were together. The Actors Fund distributed tickets to its performances as it saw fit. No one asked for special seats. Logistics undoubtedly prevailed. Sir Laurence came with his friends, the Kanins, taking up three center seats. Ken was transferred to Washington, and I didn't feel like inviting anyone else, so I was usually alone, assigned the single seat next to the Kanins and Sir Lawrence. Serendipity.

One of the last Actors' Fund benefits I shared with the Kanins and Olivier was a drama called *A Taste Of Honey*. It starred a young British actress, Joan Plowright. Sir Laurence cried during her exceptional performance, taking out a large handkerchief, wiping his eyes, and blowing his nose. Weeks later, when his divorce from Vivien Leigh became final, he eloped with Joan Plowright to Connecticut. They were married until his death in 1989, and had four children.

I never saw him again. *Up again, old heart?*

scene x: Summer, 1961, Enter a love affair, Manhattan

Peggy Cass, the friend who introduced me to the Kerrs and composer Leroy Anderson to sing the *Goldilocks* auditions, became a household name in the late 1950s. Peggy had won a Tony for her performance as Agnes Gooch in the Broadway comedy *Auntie Mame,* and an Oscar nomination when she reprised her role in the film. She was hardly unknown when she appeared as a guest on the *Jack Paar Show* in 1958, but appearances on the Paar panel catapulted her into international stardom. The public fell in love with her. She was soon a regular on TV's panel quiz shows, *What's My Line* and *Match Game.*

Peggy had been married for several years to the company manager for *Fiorello!,* Carl Fisher, but they separated soon after *Fiorello!* opened. It was distressing to watch Peggy's success wear at their marriage. It was even more distressing when Carl began pressuring me for a date.

"Have dinner with me, Pat, I'm harmless!"

"Carl, I don't date married men, and I wouldn't date *you* if I did! You're married to my friend."

"Peggy and I are both dating other people!"

"Fine," I said, "but I'm not going to be one of them."

Other of Peggy's friends didn't feel the same way. One openly pursued Carl. She was a friend of mine as well, and I said to her, "Jan, how can you go after Carl? He and Peggy aren't divorced yet!"

"All's fair in love and war!" she answered.

Carl was a catch, I suppose. In his early fifties, handsome and boyish with graying blond hair and piercing blue eyes. Like his uncle, George Abbott. He called himself a "working stiff," but in truth, Carl Fisher had made a comfortable fortune investing in George's productions.

Carl delivered my paycheck every Friday night to my dressing room, saying, "Dinner between shows tomorrow?" or "Have a drink later?" I'd offer him a cup of tea and one of Brona's biscuits. We'd chat until the overture began, he'd say, "How about it?" and I'd say "No." It was a ritual that went on for over a year.

Dr. Handman was silent when I talked about Carl. I told him I saw no future with Carl as long as his marriage to Peggy was intact, separation or no separation. I didn't want to get involved in a casual relationship.

Brona knew how I felt. But she also knew I spent a lot of time alone at home with dog-pal Charlie. "It wouldn't hurt to have dinner with Carl, Pat."

"Hey! Carl's a great guy—and rich!" said Nat Frey. A theater company becomes a family. Everyone knew my business, and was willing to offer advice.

Then I ran into Peggy one night after the show in the ladies' room at Sardi's. "Oh, for heaven's sake, Pat, Carl and I are *done*. Our marriage was over a long time ago! I'm filing for divorce. He's pining over you. Give him a break!"

So it was after a year and a half of a professional relationship, Carl Fisher and I began a personal one. Because of the problems I'd experienced in personal relationships since my divorce, it was intense for me. I think it was for Carl, too. A day didn't go by that we didn't meet—lunch, dinner, after-theater supper—then his apartment or mine. Serious stuff. He was older by twenty years, fifty-two to my thirty-two, and had a grown daughter from his first, short-lived marriage, before Peggy. Still, he liked the idea of our having a child.

But I was concerned. I liked Carl very much. But was what I felt for him only loving friendship? *Where's the chemistry?* I didn't trust my judgment.

One day, as I discussed the possibility of going deeper into a relationship with Carl, Dr. Handman got up from his chair and paced around his office. He wiped his face with a handkerchief. *Strange.* I used the new-found self-assertiveness he'd instilled in me (or as Brona wisely suggested that time and tide had instilled in me) and asked,

"What's the matter, doctor? I get the feeling you don't like my talking about Carl."

"We must end our session now, Patricia. There'll be no charge for today."

Dr. Handman had told me several months earlier that he'd seen *Fiorello!* the night before.

"Hey, did you like it?" I said, like a kid with a parent after a dance recital. "Why didn't you come backstage?"

"Well, I'll put it this way, Miss Wilson. (pause) You didn't quite ruin the show for me."

So much for all that expensive work on my self-esteem. I discussed it with Carl.

"Could it be the guy has developed inappropriate feelings for you? It wouldn't be the first time it happened with a therapist and client."

That struck a nerve. A girlfriend had been seduced by her therapist. It took her years with another analyst to unravel her confusion. I spoke with Dr. Handman one more time.

"Yes," said Dr. Handman, "I think we've gone as far as we can with your therapy. It's necessary for me to terminate your treatment."

That's right, jerk, lay it in my lap. At last I wasn't so dumb. Leaving his office, I felt free for the first time in months.

Sometime during the next week, Carl and I were having a drink in his apartment when his phone rang. My knowin' told me it was Peggy, calling from California. My knowin' was right.

"Oh, God," Carl said, "I'll get there as soon as possible." Peggy and Carl had been separated for over a year, on the path to divorce, but they were still friends. She was now one of the hottest stars in the country, and was in Hollywood filming a new TV series.

"I'm with Patty," Carl said into the phone. "She'll understand." He hung up and began throwing things into a suitcase.

"Peg was driving home after a party," he said. "She'd had a few drinks, and was in an accident. She's—uh—not in a position to be caught driving like that. She needs my help."

"Was she hurt, Carl?"

"She's okay, just scared and stunned—but someone else may have been." That was all he'd tell me as he rushed out of my life to help Peggy. I heard a rumor that he took responsibility in California for driving the night of the accident, the night he was with me in New York. He and Peggy reconciled for a while, but the reconciliation faltered. He was soon on the available list again, but by a quirk of fate, I wasn't. On the available list, that is.

scene xi: 1961, Enter a man named Art, Manhattan

Journal, June 17, 1961: My birthday. I'm 32 with no fella, no kids, no prospects. But I'm making plans for the future. Do I stay or go? My Fiorello! contract ends October 18th.

"No actor should play a role for two years," said Uta Hagen, my acting mentor and friend. "Pat, you're in danger of becoming the character you inhabit for eight performances a week!" I had no desire to become a long-suffering female like Marie. I knew the real-life Marie would be the first to agree. Tom Bosley didn't mind his long stay in his role, but I was growing restless. My third grade teacher wrote on my report card: "Trustworthy, responsible Patty! She is the backbone of the class!" Though it was complimentary to be told over and over that I was the backbone of *Fiorello!,* that mine was the most consistent performance, I began to resent being responsible and trustworthy. *Good ol' reliable Patty!*

In a year-and-a-half of *Fiorello!'s* long run, I'd missed two performances. One, during the first winter, a Monday night after coming down with a severe respiratory infection. I'd barely made it through both performances the preceding Saturday. A friend told me about a doctor who loved theater people and treated President Kennedy. With a temperature of 103 degrees, I took a cab to meet him at his eastside office after the Saturday night performance. He gave me several injections, one directly into my ravaged throat. "Double doses," he said. Unlike those he gave many celebrities, the injections he gave me were only mega-vitamins and minerals. I was back onstage by Tuesday night, after having my one and only treatment with Dr. Max Jacobsen, the infamous "Dr. Feelgood" of the 1960's.

My second missed performance in the run of the show occurred late in the second year. I'd flown into Cincinnati to spend a Sunday with my family. Pop drove me to the Cincinnati airport on Monday afternoon to catch my flight back to New York. "That flight is cancelled," said the airlines clerk. "Engine trouble." We tried other airlines, other travel modes, but nothing could get me back to New York before the eight o'clock curtain that Monday night, and my understudy went on.

Changes were afoot anyway. *Fiorello!* had moved from the Broadhurst to the Broadway Theater at 52nd Street. Ellen Hanley left the show to welcome her new son, Julian. Pat Stanley left to make a movie, *The Ladies Man,* with Jerry Lewis. Margery Gray, who had replaced Pat in the show, became a pal offstage. "Margie" was the kind of loving, outgoing friend I needed. Her exuberance helped to force me out of my cocoon.

But the most important change was a realization in my own mind and heart: I could give nothing more to the role of Marie.

Television producer George Schlatter, the son of my mother's lifelong friend from their days performing on the Chautauqua circuit, was often in New York on business. George and I had been friends since childhood, as our mothers were like sisters. Though not blood-related, we laughingly called ourselves "cuzzins." George had been producing Dinah Shore's television show in Los Angeles, and developing what later became the hit comedy series *Laugh In.* Hoping for good advice and encouragement, I told George I was thinking of leaving *Fiorello!*

"I have a knowin', George—it tells me I should come to California."

He laughed. Grandma Daisy's Ohio expressions were a part of George's family vocabulary, too. "Your knowin' is probably on the money, Pat. Most all of television will be coming from California soon. You should definitely be in La La Land!" That was all I needed to hear.

It was mid-August, and I decided to leave *Fiorello!* at the end of my contract in October. I hired a public relations consultant to create a campaign aiming for a California career.

Journal, August 23, 1961: Damn! Complications. My new publicist, Jack Tirman, says he can't do my campaign justice. He has a replacement for himself, a guy the public relations industry calls "The Doctor." Jack says this guy ghost-wrote for Walter Winchell for years, then took a leave-of-absence to write a play. Now he needs one client to pay his son's school tuition. With no other clients now, I'll have his "individual attention." Or so Jack says. Hmmm. I think I'll call Betty Lee Hunt from supper club days.

The phone rang. "Patricia Wilson? This is Art Franklin. I'm told you need help with a public relations campaign." The richest basso-baritone I'd heard since Ezio Pinza in *South Pacific,* the voice was strong, reassuring. I agreed to meet Art Franklin for coffee before that day's matinee. The late summer felt like autumn, so I wore my new fall dress.

Coming out of sunshine, I stood for a moment at the entrance of The Spindletop Restaurant on 48th Street just off Eighth Avenue. It was dark, as most Broadway bistros are at noontime. While I waited for my eyes to adjust to the dim room, a strong hand took my elbow. There was no mistaking the voice.

"I knew you from your picture, Patty. I have a table here." Only my family and friends called me "Patty."

He'd ordered our coffee, and filled my cup from a pot on the table. Art Franklin was tall, broad-shouldered, with strong features and perfect white teeth. Thinning dark hair, grey at the temples. I guessed he was in his mid-forties. He wore heavy, horn-rimmed glasses. Boyish dimples on either side of his mouth seemed incongruent with the rest of him.

"Are you sure you want publicity?" he asked.

"Well, I'm sure I want to leave *Fiorello!* in a blaze of glory."

Art Franklin sighed. "Okay." He studied me so deeply I thought my bones must be showing. "Just what the world needs," he said finally. "Another celebrity."

I started to cry. Damn! *What's wrong with me?* We made plans for Art Franklin to see that night's *Fiorello!* performance, and I fled to my dressing room at the Broadway Theater.

"Brona! I just had the most intense experience! I need tea!" I told her about my meeting.

"You *must* have had a knowin'. Why did you wear your new dress? Sounds like love at first sight to me." Brona. My own personal "Jiminy Cricket," an ever-present diagnostician of the heart.

"Don't be ridiculous! I just thought he had an interesting voice." I gulped hot tea, and escaped to Tom's dressing room phone. I called Tony Angelo, an Ohio friend who was now a New York television producer.

"Art Franklin? He's one of the top creative minds around. They call him 'The Doctor' because he's done spectacular damage control for several celebrities. Kate Smith made an anti-Semitic remark publicly, and her TV show was almost cancelled. Art Franklin did such a masterful job of smoothing things over, that Kate Smith kept him as her public relations counsel for fifteen years. And your pal, Johnnie Ray? After he tried to pick up an undercover policeman in a gay bar in Detroit, his career would have been destroyed if it hadn't been for Art Franklin. I hear Art's written a play?"

"But I don't need damage control, Tony. I need career-building."

"Well, Art Franklin single-handedly brought stars like Ella Fitzgerald and The Ink Spots into the mainstream. Black performers couldn't get professional publicity in the papers until Art Franklin forced media guys into featuring them in articles and photos. He *made* their careers. He'll help make yours, too." Tony continued, "The guy has character, Pat, and integrity. He's a great PR man."

Stage manager Paul Phillips knocked on my dressing room door. "Places, Patricia!" The matinee intervened, and I hung up on Tony. But not on the things he'd told me about Art Franklin.

scene xii: Later that night, A walk around Manhattan

"Well, Mr. Franklin, did you like the show?" I asked after that night's *Fiorello!* performance. We walked to Gilhooley's Bar & Restaurant on Eighth Avenue. "I've heard some wonderful things about you today. Now it's your turn to tell me what you thought tonight." My conversation with Tony Angelo had made me eager to hear this man's opinion.

"George Abbott is a brilliant craftsman. You'd better start calling me Art. "

"Well, okay, Art. But do you think you'll be able to help me?"

"You're not talented, Pat," Art Franklin said. My heart clunked to the sidewalk. He stopped walking and turned to face me. "You're *gifted.*" The solid sincerity in his face made me blush. We arrived at Gilhooley's and sat in a polished wood booth. Art ordered beers from a ruddy-cheeked Irish waiter.

"I'm told you took a leave-of-absence from public relations to write a play," I said.

"You're changing the subject. Hasn't anyone told you that before, that you're gifted?"

It took me a minute to answer. "I think someone did, once..." I was remembering what Ruth Gordon had said: *"Yer the hahdest-workin' woman on Broadway, Patricia—ya carry the show on yer back—but ya fool 'em—ya come through at the end!"*

Art continued, "Whoever it was, you'd better believe it yourself. As far as my play is concerned, it was performed at The Actor's Studio, and I'm talking to Jed Harris about producing it on Broadway." I was impressed. Jed Harris was a theatrical icon, the producer of such classic plays as *Our Town* and *The Heiress.* "Trouble is, the son-of-a-bitch wants co-writing credit to produce it, and he never wrote a line! We're negotiating." I remembered that a book called *The Saxon Charm,* based on Jed Harris, was a dark portrait of the man, made into an even darker film starring Robert Montgomery.

Art and I left Gilhooley's and strolled up Eighth Avenue. The moon was a perfect silver orb. Street lights seemed superfluous. I listened to Art's story as we walked. He was a Brooklyn kid, he said, a skinny, myopic Jew raised in an Irish neighborhood, and had suffered bigotry all his life. He learned to fight, and became the captain of an otherwise all-Catholic basketball team. Some of his Irish friends, like Robert Sylvester and Nick Kenny, became New York journalists and columnists, and remained his allies. He'd been a writer since he was eight years old, and his friends began publishing his poetry and stories in their newspapers. At nineteen years of age he was offered a job as public relations director of The Gale Agency, which handled black artists. Art bristled at latter-day media resistance to publicizing black entertainers. He browbeat his friends into helping his new clients, demanding the same media coverage as that afforded white entertainers. Many years later, Ella Fitzgerald publicly stated, "I could never have been who I am without Art Franklin." So Art had championed black artists as a kid, and as his reputation grew, other artists and corporations as founder-owner of the international public relations firm, "Art Franklin, Inc."

As he told his story that August night, as we walked together, Art seemed to have a sense of humor about where his life had taken him, about life itself. His laugh was as deep as his voice, and his dimples telegraphed good nature, good cheer. My comfort with Art Franklin soon made me realize that Brona had been right: I'd had a knowin', and I'd met the second true love of my life.

ACT FOUR

SCENE CHANGES

"The big wheel turns!"
…..Nancy Fox

scene i: August 1961, Later that same night, Manhattan

"Fraud," Art Franklin said. "For twenty years of my life, I felt as if I'd participated in fraud."

"Fraud, Art? Why?" He ignored me.

"One day I just handed the public relations business I'd built over all those years to my assistant. I moved from an East 62nd Street townhouse to a coldwater flat on 48th Street and began writing my play. Now everyone thinks I'm a nut case, leaving all that success and money behind. Not that I didn't enjoy it myself, being a poor kid from a Brooklyn ghetto. I was able to get things for my family they never dreamed of having." Art's dimples disappeared. "I loved all the trappings of success, but the trappings became my trap. It felt as if my soul was being chased, and I simply walked away. I even gave my Porsche to my mechanic. My books and art collection were all that mattered to me. They nurtured me. My friends, my estranged wife, people I worked with—everyone thought I'd lost my mind."

Our walk had taken us to 57th Street. Crossing west towards the Hudson River, the moonlight followed us as we continued talking.

"Well, I hate to sound cynical, but they were all profiting from your success. They must have hated to see it end! And it was probably a thrill for you, Art, to be able to help your family. So if I'm not too nosy, why did the public relations business make you feel like a fraud?"

"The catalyst was the quiz scandals." His face darkened. "I was public relations counsel for Jack Barry and Dan Enright, the producers of *Twenty-One*."

"That show had such a following!"

"It was the biggest thing on television. Then one of the contestants, Herb Stempel, was defeated on the show by Charles Van Doren, remember? A Columbia University professor, very appealing? Stempel was a real *schlemiel,* a geeky kind of guy, and became insanely jealous. He trumpeted all around town that he'd been given the answers to questions before each show, and that Van Doren was also given the answers, in order to get him, Stempel, off the show. In other words, *Twenty-One* was 'fixed.' And he was exposing the fix."

"What did that have to do with you, though, Art? It wasn't you who fixed the show."

"No, it wasn't. But through it all, Barry and Enright consistently denied culpability. They said Stempel was a deranged blackmailer, and I believed them. The fight between Stempel and the producers and NBC lasted nearly three years, and led to two grand jury hearings and a congressional probe."

We crossed Ninth Avenue. Rather than take my arm, Art slipped his hand into mine. To my surprise, I was comfortable with the familiarity.

"I'm remembering bits and pieces that I read in the news. Didn't another contestant come forward to back Stempel's claims?"

Art nodded. "A guy named Snodgrass. He said he had been coached to win, too. He'd been afraid to tell the truth any earlier."

"So Stempel was vindicated?"

"Well, *I* began to believe Stempel. Snodgrass had a script he'd saved from his days on *Twenty-One*. It spelled out all the questions and answers. Stempel was telling the truth, and Charles Van Doren had been perjuring himself every time he was interviewed. That was unbelievable to me! The guy's father is a hero of mine—Mark Van Doren, a scholar and poet."

"I remember Charles Van Doren's repeated public statements of *Twenty-One*'s integrity, then his eventual admission of the truth in Congress. I was shocked at the time."

"My attorney advised me to jibe my story with my clients, Barry and Enright, when I testified for the grand jury."

"Now wait a minute—your own lawyer advised you to perjure yourself in front of a grand jury?"

"That's right. He said if I told the truth, no one would believe me. They'd believe Barry, Enright, NBC, and the esteemed Professor Van Doren." The word *esteemed* came out like a snarl. "I smelled a double cross. I knew I was being set up. They were going to blame the whole 'fix' on me. Their little plot could have landed me in jail, but they didn't care."

"Wow."

"Yes. A lot of other people were guilty of perjury, too." Art's grip on my hand tightened. "Do you see why I was disgusted with the whole 'image' business? I saw how fame and money and power corrupts people, even someone with the solid family background and opportunities of a Charles Van Doren. And my 'friends,' Barry and Enright? I defended them for two years and they were going to throw me to the wolves. I had to walk away, Pat. It was pure evil, and I didn't want my soul near it."

"Is your play about this, Art?"

"It's about a man's soul, yes."

It was four-thirty in the morning when we arrived at my building. The silver moonlight turned pink as it merged with eastern sunrise. I fumbled in my purse for a check. I knew Art needed the money for his fourteen year-old son's tuition.

"I can't take this now, Pat," Art said softly. "There'll be another way to help my son." He kissed me on the cheek and turned away. I was like ice cream in mid-July sun, melting indefensibly.

Early the next afternoon, Bill O'Malley, the doorman of my building, knocked at my door.

"I wasn't supposed to give this to you until noon, Miss Wilson," O'Malley said in his Irish brogue. He'd wakened me, but who could be angry at a man with such music in his voice?

"A tall gentleman with horn-rimmed spectacles dropped this by for you." He handed me a framed painting of a young woman with huge, bewildered eyes. "The gentleman didn't want me to wake you up, so I been lookin' at this all mornin', Miss Wilson. It's a lovely paintin', isn't it? Her face—she kinda haunts me! And for the last several hours I been thinkin'—she looks just like you!"

scene ii: Late Summer- Autumn, 1961, Exit Marie from Broadway

Journal, August 25, 1961: There's an item in Robert Sylvester's column this AM: "Patricia Wilson leaves her starring role in Fiorello! when her contract ends in October. California calls."

It could only have come from one source. I phoned Art Franklin.

"I want to help you, Pat," he said. "I want you to have a good send-off, a dignified one. But I don't want your money."

Within minutes, Carl Fisher was on the phone.

"Are you really leaving the show, Pat?" he asked.

"I think it's time for me to move on, Carl."

"We're good for another year! We're moving to The Alvin Theater on November 1st."

For my friends in the cast I was happy to hear there was a plan to move *Fiorello!* to the Alvin. I'd heard we were losing the Broadway Theater to another show, and I knew losing a theater and incurring the expense of a move was often a death blow to a long-running show.

That night several cast members came to my dressing room. They had read the item Art planted in Robert Sylvester's column about my leaving for California. I assured them I'd been told the show was continuing its run in another theater, but that, yes, I'd be leaving.

Since *Fiorello!* would run another year, I wanted to give producer Hal Prince as much official notice as I could to replace me. "Boy, I wish you'd stay on," he said.

"Hal, you know I love this show. But I'm honestly weary." There was no argument for that.

On Wednesday October 18, 1961, I played Marie for the last time on Broadway. To my astonishment and everyone else's, a closing notice for the show went up that weekend, effective for October 28th. The show would not move to The Alvin Theater after all. I called Carl Fisher.

"If the show is closing in ten days, Carl, of course I'll stay to the end! You told me it was going to run for another year!"

Carl's voice was ice. "The part has been promised to your understudy. She'll play Marie for the last ten days on Broadway."

Rusty Bonaccorso, who had ably managed our show's period hairstyles for two years, stood in the back of the theater watching my understudy's first performance after I left *Fiorello!* Director George Abbott stood next to him. He turned to Rusty.

"Pat is irreplaceable," Mr. Abbott said.

scene iii: Autumn, 1961, Manhattan

Journal, September 14, 1961: Charlie's in love with Art Franklin. I think I am, too.

To our friends, Art and I were an unlikely pair. Twelve years older than I, worldly even for a New Yorker, he affectionately called me "Patty-from-Cincinnati." His friends were mostly journalists. Peter, a tall, heavyset man with a jolly fat-man smile, seemed to magically appear wherever Art happened to be.

"Is he in the news business?" I asked.

"Peter? No," Art said. "He's my genie." He offered no more, and I didn't press the subject.

Art was an avid reader and a museum devotee. If he read or saw something he liked, he set out to meet and know its creator. Unlike me, he had no fear of people. He introduced me to psychologist/author Andrew Salter, who wrote *Conditioned Reflex Therapy*, and to Richard Condon, whose chilling book, *The Manchurian Candidate,* utilized Salter's theories. He enjoyed long conversations and correspondence with famous author Theodore Dreiser, and argued with him after he announced, shortly before his death, his intention to join the Communist Party. "I told him I thought it was a lousy idea," Art said.

Robert DeNiro's artist-father, well-known for his work in the '40s and '50s, sketched a contemporary, abstract portrait of Art. The celebrity photographer, Richard Avedon, had recently taken a classic portrait of actress Greta Garbo devoid of makeup, and when Art told him how much he admired it, the photographer presented it to him. Among the things I was finding I loved about Art Franklin, this streetwise Brooklynite: he was a cultured, refined man, a diamond-in-the-rough.

Together we studied the portrait of the young woman with bewildered eyes he'd given me after we met.

"O'Malley the doorman thinks she looks like me!"

"Yeah, she's got those big, haunted eyes, too."

Journal, October 10, 1961: Difficult to keep up with Art, he's so smart. Maybe someday I'll be able to introduce him to John Steinbeck.

Art and I met with Joseph Stone, New York's assistant district attorney, who had pursued the quiz show case against NBC and producers Barry and Enright.

"I want to marry this girl. I want her to know exactly what happened," Art said. Joe Stone sat in my apartment living room until dawn, explaining how the infamous quiz scandal story unraveled through years of obfuscation and legal manipulation.

"When contestant Herb Stempel began accusations that the show *Twenty-One* had been 'fixed,' Art was loyal to his clients. Then, even after the irrefutable truth surfaced— that the show *was indeed* 'fixed'— he remained loyal. He focused on doing his job for producers Jack Barry and Dan Enright, by attempting damage control. But he didn't know that behind his back they were plotting to abdicate themselves of responsibility by making him the scapegoat.

"They first set out to disparage him, with the help of the man he'd taken on as his business protégé and had promised a partnership to. They set up a kind of unholy alliance. When Art realized what was happening, he came to me."

As Joe Stone was leaving my apartment he said, "You've thrown in with a good man, Pat. A tough one, but a decent one with a lot of courage. His testimony in Congress was the straight, unvarnished truth, and received a standing ovation from the gallery. It was well deserved. He helped right a moral wrong, one that nearly scarred our national sense of truth and honor."

The quiz scandals might seem small potatoes amidst the rapidly changing cultural markers of our present times, but as I've said before, things were different in those days.

scene iv: Later that Autumn 1961, Enter more Sturm and Drang, Manhattan

As *Fiorello!* closed, I wrote in my journal: *I hope Art will go with me to the closing night party. He's not much for musical comedy get-togethers.*

A young woman named Sheila crashed the *Fiorello!* party, admitting she was there hoping to see Art. He stepped from my side to speak with her privately, and said later, after the party, "Patty, I've saved a lot to tell you. It's serious stuff. It could even mean I lose you."

We sat on my green sofa together, a pot of jasmine tea on the table in front of us. I sank into the familiar comfort of squashy pillows, Art's arm around me. He sighed.

175

"The girl who crashed the party tonight, Sheila? She was able to crash because she knows Linda, one of the singers from your show. Sheila was married to a guy who did undercover work for the government. She was terrified of her husband and what he did. She wanted out of the marriage with her two small kids, but she needed money and a guarantee of safety for herself and her children."

"Safety? Why?"

"She *knew* too much. She knew she couldn't get out of the marriage and stay alive without some guarantee of protection from the government."

"But what could she know? What kind of undercover work did her husband do?"

"I'll never tell you what he did. Or who he was. That information could put you in harm's way. Believe me, it was the kind of stuff the word 'nefarious' was invented for. I'm sorry, Patty."

I took a sip of tea. "Keep going."

"Sheila and Linda came to talk to me because they wanted the press on Sheila's side. They knew of my close relationship with Walter Winchell, and thought if I brokered a deal for Sheila with her husband and the government, she and her kids would be safe. Winchell would be ready to break the story if anything went wrong. So I rode in on my white horse. I brokered the deal for Sheila, a very fair one. She accepted it at first, and then later decided it wasn't enough. She got greedy and double-crossed everybody. Went behind my back and demanded more! Damn near got herself killed and me along with her. It wasn't the money—the government's deal-makers felt she couldn't be trusted."

In today's world, post-Watergate, post so-many-other–gates, government subterfuge might come as no surprise. But in the world we knew in the apple-pie 1950s, our government seemed above reproach. Like all organizations dependent upon public approval for its survival, it wanted to protect its image. Walter Winchell was enormously powerful. He could have done damage to any soft underbelly.

"I'm not going to tell you any more, Patty, except to explain that the reason Sheila crashed the *Fiorello!* party tonight was because I've refused all her calls. She wanted to talk me into getting involved again," Art said. "Don't worry. I won't."

"But don't leave me hanging! At least tell me what happened!"

Art's smile was bitter. "I walked away from Sheila and the mess she created, but they've run surveillance on me for over a year. You know Peter?"

How could I not know affable, charming Peter. The man Art called his genie. He seemed to be everywhere Art and I went together. Many times I invited him to have pot-luck supper with us in my apartment.

"Peter's with the government," Art said. "I was his assignment. He was to make sure I kept my word that I wasn't going to reveal anything to Winchell, or anybody else, that the government didn't want made public. He would have pushed me in front of a bus a year ago, but since then he's put his own career and reputation on the line for me, because he knows I keep my word. Of course, it helps they know I've written the story in a letter to be delivered to Winchell if anything happens to me. It's in everyone's best interest to keep me alive. When you and I met, Peter had to know who you were. That's why he's been around so much. Your phones have been tapped. Haven't you noticed the clicking when you talk to people? They wanted to make sure you're not blabbing secrets I might have told you."

My stomach somersaulted, and I nervous-giggled.

"Sorry, Art. Do you think some CIA guy might be listening to the conversations I've been having with my girlfriends?" Art, solemn, ignored me.

"Peter tells me it's over. My life isn't in danger any longer. I'd walk away from you if I thought otherwise. But I won't tell you anything more. You're so open." He reached over and brushed the hair away from my eyes. "It's one of the nicest things about you, but you might say something to someone without meaning to."

Charlie stretched out on the sofa next to me and sighed. I retied the ribbon in his terrier topknot, searching for something routine that would ground me.

"A lot has been done to smear my reputation, Patty. Both the government and the *Twenty-One* gang want me discredited, swept under a rug somewhere, if not dead. My assistant for years was hired to ruin me. This is the same guy I taught everything I know about public relations, and handed my business over to when I decided to leave. His assignment? To make the world think I'm crazy. He cried when he told me, but he took the job anyway. He said the money was good, and he had his family to think of."

"But what about *your* family? Your son?"

"You're asking the same question I did. The guy's known Jeff since he was a baby. He just shrugged." Art looked sad all over again. "See why I wanted out of public relations? The power of it, the power to have such influence over public thinking, can twist a man's heart and soul." He took my face in his hands.

"Patty-from-Cincinnati, it sounds melodramatic, but you had to know. Can you handle it?"

"Maybe I don't have a choice." I felt as if I'd swallowed a bowling ball. "You say I'm transparent. You must know—" I could feel the blush start. "I think I'm falling in love with you."

"Yes." A simple affirmation. "I may have trouble starting my business again, and it may be a while before my play gets produced. I have only a few allies left in my old world. I allowed my former assistant, and the other guys out to destroy me, to nearly succeed. Honestly I was beginning not to care, until I met you."

"Why would you go back into public relations anyway? You hate it."

"It's all I've got to offer you, Patty. At this point it's not what it used to be." He smiled, the dimples in his cheeks deepening. "But I have to try to dazzle you, to keep you from running off to California!"

"Couldn't we go together? Wouldn't it be easier for you to start over in a new place?"

"I'm a New Yorker, Pat. I'm miserable in California. I have to stay in my home territory to feel authentic, and I can't feel like I'm running away. I have enemies everywhere, but the few loyal friends I have left are here. So I'm going to ask you again: can you handle this?"

Weeks earlier, I'd made up my mind that I wouldn't be able to leave Art Franklin for California. Could I handle this? I smiled to myself.

"What are you thinking?" Art said. "That's the sickliest smile I've ever seen."

It was my turn to ignore him. I leaned back, closed my eyes, and parroted Scarlett O'Hara's thick Southern accent:

"W—e—ll," I drawled, "Ah'll just have to think about all this tomorra'."

For the next forty years, that's what I did.
"Damn actress!" Art said, and held me tight.

scene v: Autumn, 1961, Enter a Life-Decision, Manhattan

In *Carousel,* Julie Jordan sings to her girlfriends about Billy Bigelow. In Oscar Hammerstein's and Richard Rodgers' beautiful ballad, *What's The Use Of Wondrin'?* her love for Billy was a simple fact: Billy was her fella, she was his girl.

It was that simple for me, too. I was Art's girl. He was my fella. So I didn't leave Art and New York to go to California. Hadn't I already lost my career momentum two years earlier by signing a long *Fiorello!* contract? I was no longer Broadway's fresh, new leading lady, with TV and film opportunities in Hollywood eagerly awaiting me, I rationalized. I was yesterday's mashed potatoes.

Art and I settled into life together in The Big Apple. I loved him as wholly as I'd loved anyone, ever, even Rick. I didn't fall often, but when I fell, I fell. And what of the rest of Oscar Hammerstein's lyrics for Julie Jordan, who loved Billy Bigelow, a man as different from herself as Art Franklin was from me? Common sense told Julie she perhaps should run away while she had a chance, that perhaps her relationship with Billy would have a sad ending. For Julie—and for me— there was no common sense. There was certainly no running away.

And no one on God's earth could have convinced me then that the ending would be sad.

scene vi: 1962-1963, The next two years, Enter Mrs. Franklin, New York City

Journal, February 14, 1963: Valentine's Day. Art and I were married this morning at The Community Church at 35th and Park. A simple Unitarian ceremony. Jeff was with us—my new son!

A Valentine's Day wedding to Art, the real-life "very next man."

We'd had to wait a year. Art was legally separated from June, his Irish childhood sweetheart and first wife, Jeff's mother, for nine years, but they'd never divorced.

"I thought someone would have to put a gun to my head to get me to marry again," Art said.

"If only it had been that easy!" I laughed.

In the preceding year, while we waited for Art's freedom, he'd rented an empty apartment next to mine, using it as a home and office for his new public relations business. It was the closest we could come to living together. He worked for Universal Pictures, and took on a young artist-client he thought had great potential, Peter Max. It was not like the old days of *Art Franklin, Inc.,* with long-term clients keeping him on fat retainers, but his new schedule gave him time to write.

He was drafted as the drama critic for The Long Island Press, and we went to opening nights in the theater together. We walked in Central Park, safe in those days, a magical place. I never tired of its generous green in the summer, or of the snow crackling crisp and cold under my boots in winter. We fed seals in the park zoo, and Art introduced me to his favorite tiger. He loved animals as much as I. He cuddled one of the kittens of the mother tabby at the corner delicatessen.

"We'd better adopt him, Patty. Charlie could use a pal." We took the kitten home and named him "Herman," after the deli owner. It took months to realize Herman was actually "Hermione."

During that first year after Art and I met, it was wonderful to just be alive and in love, with no half-hour calls to meet, no entrances to await in the wings. I wasn't upset when producer David Merrick defeated Jule Styne's campaign for me to play the lead in his new show, *Subways Are For Sleeping.* Merrick decided on Carol Lawrence for the role.

But one day Jule called me from the *Subways* out-of-town try-out in Boston.

"Please!" he pleaded. "It's hell up here! Can you come to Boston this weekend?" He had a train ticket and a script delivered to my door. By the time I got to Boston, whatever the brouhaha was had been resolved.

"Someday you'll sing a score of mine," Jule said happily. It never happened.

As Art and I walked the neighborhoods of New York, holding hands like going-steady teenagers, we visited the hangouts of newspapermen, restaurants like Pen and Pencil, pubs like P.J. Clarke's. I understood why he hadn't wanted to leave New York. We ran into his pals everywhere, and everyone commented on his quick wit.

"Say, didja hear this one about that guy of yours?" I was asked. One story has been repeated in print many times. I had the opportunity to check it out with Ernest Lehman, a former press agent turned writer and producer. (Ernie wrote *Sweet Smell of Success*, and produced the film versions of *The Sound of Music* and *Hello, Dolly.)*

Ernie and Art were young New York publicists together in the early '50s. One female columnist—oh, well, hell, it was Dorothy Kilgallen—kept a bench outside her office, where publicists lined up, waiting to be honored as if by the queen. In order, they entered her office, one-by-one, to present their daily press offerings. It was a humiliating ritual, despised by all. One day Ernie and Art sat on the bench with a few other resolute supplicants, each awaiting his turn, A large New York-style cockroach scurried across the floor in front of them.

"Hey, *you*," Art snarled at the beast, "*Get in line!*"

Shortly before his death, Ernest Lehman and I met at a California party. "Yes, I was there when it happened! Art Franklin was the wittiest man I ever knew!" Ernie said.

Art's sense of humor included the ability to laugh at himself. Once we stood together on a Fifth Avenue bus, holding hands, talking quietly. A stranger pushed past us, giving us the once-over, the freckle-faced gentile girl with the Semitic fellow she plainly adored.

"Dirty Jew!" hissed the man.

Art looked startled and swiveled his head in all directions. "Oh, my God!" he cried. "*Where? Where?*" Passengers laughed and broke into applause. The man slunk off the bus at the next stop.

Art's wit, his charisma and ease with people, were marvels to me. My shyness gradually dissipated. I felt safe. I became domestic, happily trying out new recipes and redecorating my apartment. But reality intervened, and it was important that I keep working. My former manager Gus Schirmer called, early in 1962.

"Pat, do you think you could brush up on your tap dancing and do *Gay Divorce* with me?" Gus, now producing and directing most of the time, had had great success with his off-Broadway revival of *The Boyfriend.* It ran longer than the Broadway original. He followed it with Cole Porter's musical, *Gay Divorce,* done all in black-and-white, as if it were a 1930's film. The Royal Poinciana Playhouse in Palm Beach, Florida, wanted the production for its winter season.

"Gus, I haven't tapped since I was eight!"

"Well, try. This is the Ginger Rogers role, one tap dance solo in the first act, and the rest duos with the Fred Astaire character. I know you can fake those fancy ballroom steps to *Night and Day.* I can visualize you in those '30's costumes! All that marabou!"

"I think you should do it, Patty," Art said. "I can be with you part of the time, and you love working with Gus. I'll get out a couple of press releases. It's a good story, you and Gus together, since he used to be your manager."

So I became Ginger Rogers. A real dancer in the cast, Frances Martin, tapped up a storm, making up for my lack of talent in that department. Frannie was (and is) Mrs. Hal Linden. They were an unusual theatrical couple: they stayed married. They had three little girls and were ready to stop, but their fourth was a boy. Hal needed a hit TV series to support that brood, so he became *Barney Miller.*

Beatrice Arthur, later TV's *Maude* and then Dorothy in *The Golden Girls,* was also in that production. The musical was intended as a spoof, and one of the critics pointed out that Bea and I seemed to be the only ones in the company who got the joke.

Howard DaSilva called me in Palm Beach.

Bea Arthur and I in Gay Divorce. *We got the joke.*

Marabou and a blonde wig and I became Ginger Rogers. Walter Lang was Fred Astaire.

"Pat, I'm directing *Fiorello!* for the Papermill Playhouse. Tom Bosley has agreed to do it, and I'd like you to reprise Marie. We open the end of April. I know you'd just about make it from Palm Beach, but how about it? I hate the thought of doing *Fiorello!* without you."

The Papermill Playhouse in New Jersey, prestigious and close to New York. The money was good, and Howard understood I wanted to play Marie with more leeway than George Abbott had allowed me. I found I wanted to take the job, as tired as I'd been of the role only a few months earlier.

"This is a good opportunity for you to wrap up that character, Patty," Art said. "And you can commute from home."

But as the straw hat circuit began operations for the summer, we were booked into other theaters after The Papermill, a touring production of a Broadway hit, complete with its original stars. Art traveled to visit me for the main part of the summer.

During that summer of 1962, there arose the only glitch in my long friendship with Tom Bosley. Howard DaSilva allowed me to play a freer, more abandoned Marie. He let me progress in the character, as we both felt she should have, in the sixteen-year period covered by the show's story-line. George Abbott's direction was that I play Marie "as if you are scared to death of the man," from beginning to end.

"Unrealistic!" Howard said. "Marie wouldn't be such a wimpy kid after working with Fiorello for sixteen years!" The evolution of the character, as Howard and I saw her, allowed her to sing *I'll Marry The Very Next Man* as a tongue-in-cheek belter, rather than as a throbbing torch song. I never clowned it, but now I sang it like the thirty-five-year old woman with a sense of humor I felt Marie was meant to be.

The changes in Marie didn't please Tom. He threw a protective cloak around the show that had made him a star, I continued to evolve Marie. After harsh words, we spent the summer in uncomfortable silence. To his credit, with Jeanie Elliot, now his wife, by his side, Tom made a touching tribute speech at our closing night party. He broke the back of our feud, enabling us to continue the friendship that began with *Guys and Dolls* in Dallas six years earlier, one that has lasted for over forty-five years since.

scene vii: Late Summer- Early autumn, 1962, Enter Jackie Gleason, New York

Journal, August 17, 1962: Home again! Don't know who is happier, Charlie, Herman, Art, or me! Art says Charlie misses me so much when I leave that he lifts his leg on the furniture. Oh, I said, I thought it was YOU! I have a new manager, "Fats" Farber. He's an attorney, not fat at all. Nicknamed for his big handle-bar mustache. He manages comedians, and wants to branch out with theater people.

"You have an interview tomorrow morning, Patricia," Fats said.

"A new show?"

"Television. Jackie Gleason is doing a new hour-long variety series, *The American Scene Magazine* for CBS. They'll be doing a *Honeymooners* segment on each show. Joyce Randolph doesn't want to come back as Trixie Norton, Art Carney's wife. You're a perfect Trixie."

The funniest of Gleason's sketches, *The Honeymooners*, and working opposite Art Carney. It was the answer to my prayers. I would be home in New York, catching a breather from touring and the loneliness I felt on the road. Fats had tentatively booked me for the next six months on a national supper club tour, a tour I was determined not to take.

"Patty, Art Carney will like you," Art said. "Gleason's a difficult guy, but be yourself. You'll be okay with him." The next morning I said my prayer, *"Let your light shine through me, Lord,"* knowing it was the best way to dispel my ego and fears at the same time. I left in high spirits for the interview at CBS.

The writers read a scene with me, then walked me into Jackie Gleason's office across the hall. The big man sat at the head of a conference table, next to an open bottle of wine. I assumed I was going to read for him, but he looked up and said, "Say no more! She's exactly right!" Less than fifteen minutes after I entered Gleason's CBS offices I was the new Trixie Norton in *The Honeymooners*. I skipped home, ecstatic.

Art picked me up and swung me around. "Hooray! My 'goil' is staying home!" Erudite Art used New York-ese to poke fun at his

Brooklyn roots. Charlie caught our excitement and did a doggie-marathon through the apartment. We all celebrated with a walk in Central Park.

Within a couple of days I reported to the CBS Studios to rehearse the first new *Honeymooners* episode. Art Carney and I introduced ourselves, and stood talking with his manager. The writers handed out scripts. We waited for Jackie. And waited.

"This is how Jackie is," Art Carney's manager said. "He's always late, if he shows up at all." I learned that during a live performance of the original *Honeymooners*, before millions of viewers, Jackie was late making an entrance into a scene. He left Art Carney onstage alone, in the familiar seedy apartment set of Alice and Ralph Kramden. Unflappable, Carney improvised action for Ed Norton. He looked around, scratched himself, then went to the Kramden refrigerator and peered in. He pulled out an orange, shuffled to the table, and sat down and peeled it. Meanwhile frantic stage managers raced to find Jackie. Art Carney sat onstage peeling and eating an orange, and the audience convulsed in laughter. It was Ed Norton free-loading, smacking his lips, and picking his teeth. When Jackie/Ralph finally made a belated entrance, Art/Norton hastily gulped the last segment of orange. The audience roared.

"You have to be ready for anything with Jackie," Art Carney said. I hoped I would have his presence of mind in playing scenes with Jackie, who hated to rehearse. Jackie had a photographic memory and learned a script in one reading. The rest of us rehearsed, when we could, with his stand-by, Barney Martin. (Barney later played Jerry Seinfeld's father in the Seinfeld series.) In Jackie's mind, we were all professionals. We'd come through for him.

When we finally saw him, it was shooting day. We were in the CBS Theater on Broadway at 50th Street, where Ed Sullivan's *Toast of the Town* was broadcast, and where David Letterman today does his *Late Show*. I was comfortable, because this was a regular theater, with a proscenium stage and an audience, the cameras set high in front.

We watched *American Scene Magazine* unfold in rehearsal, the popular Glea-Girls, the sketches (never with Jackie), and a young discovery of Jackie's named Wayne Newton. Sixteen years old, working with his brothers on guitars and banjo, Wayne rocked the theater like a California earthquake. I've never seen him in Las Vegas, but there couldn't have been a greater performer than Wayne Newton on Jackie's first edition of *The American Scene Magazine.*

Jackie invited us all to his dressing room in the theater just before show-time, to toast the first show of the season. I was the last to file out of the room. He called me back.

"Patrick," he said (his version of Patricia) "it's an honor to have you on my show."

"Thank you, Mr. Gleason. I'm honored to be here."

"Come to the office tomorrow morning around ten. We'll seal a deal for the season."

"Wonderful! My manager has booked me for a supper club tour, but I'd much prefer working with you!"

"Can the tour," Jackie said, making a face. "See you in the morning."

Watching the show from the wings, I was concerned for Jackie. He fretted over lights, sets, costumes, music, and then threw himself into performing. He was brilliant, but came offstage exhausted and breathless. I was the best Trixie I knew how to be, rehearsal or no rehearsal. Art Carney gave me a hug. His manager whispered to Fats in the audience, "Your girl is a winner! Carney thinks she's great." I felt like the luckiest woman alive.

As nerve-wracking as Jackie was, I respected his talent. "He deserves respect," I told Art, and he agreed. "I was worried about the rumors about his drinking during shows. But he came through like gangbusters, so even if he does all the stuff they say he does, at least he can handle it."

Promptly at ten the next morning I was in Jackie's office at CBS. "I have an appointment," I said to his secretary, who told me he hadn't arrived yet. I waited. Endlessly. "He didn't leave a message for me, or a paper to sign?" I asked.

"Sorry, Patricia. I haven't heard from him since the show last night. I have nothing in my book about an appointment." I explained that Jackie had personally made the appointment with me the night before. She nodded. I went home, assured I'd get a call as soon as Jackie arrived at his CBS office. I called Fats.

"Pat, I haven't heard from anyone to discuss business, but it's great that Jackie wants to sign you for the season."

Art warned, "Patty, Gleason is a busy guy. Go pin him down." I did, sitting at CBS for the afternoon. I wrote a note, finally, at five-fifteen, as the office employees left for the day.

"Rehearsals for next week begin tomorrow morning," Jackie's secretary said, " He'll be here then."

"Oh, okay," I said, tearing up the note. "I'll be here for rehearsal, too. I'll find a minute to talk to him."

When I arrived the next morning, Jackie was sitting at the head of his table, the ever-present bottle of wine next to him. "Hey, Patrick! Didn't anyone tell you we're not doing a *Honeymooners* segment this week?"

"No. I—uh—just assumed—well, I guess I should have waited for a rehearsal call." I could feel myself flush with embarrassment.

"That's right, Patrick!"

"Mr. Gleason, I was here yesterday. You asked me to meet you to discuss a deal for the season. Should I have Fats Farber call you?"

"Not necessary, Patrick," Jackie said, holding out his hand, "Here's your contract for the season. It's all the contract we need!" He shook my hand. "See you next week."

"What do you think, Art? He's a man of his word, isn't he?"

"It's rumored he's on something all the time, booze or God-knows-what, but I can't tell you not to trust him, Pat. I've worked with people for twenty years on a handshake. Look, wait, and see what happens next week."

Fats agreed with Art. "If I run in there demanding a written contract, Gleason will be insulted. That's the kind of guy he is."

But there was no phone call to report for work the next week. Again, I sat in Jackie's office waiting for him.

"Patrick!" Jackie said, surprised to see me. "We've scheduled a *Honeymooners* segment for next week's show. See you then!"

Several days later, walking Charlie on West 57th Street, I ran into Jackie's assistant. "I'm on a break," he said, scratching Charlie's ear. "Why aren't you in *The Honeymooners* this week?"

"I am, Michael. I'm waiting for my rehearsal call."

"But we're in rehearsal today, Pat. You're not in the script."

Jackie was nowhere to be found at the studio. *Of course he's not here, dammit—why would he be? For a mere rehearsal?*

Back at our apartment building, I knocked on Art's office door. He was having a drink with a friend, a TV columnist, Sid. One look at my face and Art knew something was wrong. He invited me in.

"It's okay, Pat." Sid waved his hand. "Art and I are just shooting the breeze. You look angry. What's up?"

"Angry, Sid? That's not even the word!" My rage emerged from wanting to stay in New York with Art. I hated the thought of being on tour again. Worse, I wasn't positive the supper club tour, cancelled when Jackie offered a contract, could be re-booked. But if Jackie Gleason wasn't a man of his word, I'd have to find other work.

"I'd like to track Jackie Gleason down! I know just where he'll be!" I vented.

"That would be Toots Shor's," said Sid. The restaurant was Jackie's favorite hangout, where he ate and drank with his buddies.

"Exactly! And when I find him, I'll give him a piece of my mind! He's a performer—how dare he treat another performer this way? What, because I'm a woman, I don't deserve to earn a living? I'd like to pop him one!"

Sid chortled.

"Sid, it's not funny. He's irresponsible, and everyone just tippy-toes around him."

"I know, Pat. But aren't you on a weekly salary? Whether you perform or not?"

"I thought I was. Jackie said his handshake was a contract for the season. But I haven't seen a paycheck except for the week I worked."

Sid shook his head. "Then you've got a right to be mad. He's wasting your time." He smiled again. "Sorry! I just got a mental picture of you walloping Gleason in front of his drinking buddies. I'd like to be a fly on the wall for that one."

Art joined the chuckling. "That's my 'goil' Sid," he said. "Get it out, Patty. I don't want that anger taken out at home."

I fed Charlie and Herman their supper, then dressed in my classiest black silk cocktail dress. I clipped on outrageously long earrings, applied complete glamour makeup, and grabbed a cab for Toots Shor's restaurant.

"I'm looking for Jackie Gleason," I told the headwaiter. "I'm from his cast."

"Yes, Miss Wilson. Mr. Gleason hasn't arrived yet. Shall I seat you at his table?" I thought for a moment. "No, thank you. I'll come back."

I walked around the block, not once, but several times. A long block. My feet hurt. When I returned to the restaurant, the head waiter shook his head.

"Mr. Gleason is still not here, Miss Wilson. Are you sure you wouldn't like to wait for him at his table?" Kismet. The walk and the night air had cooled off my anger. I thanked the waiter, hailed a cab, gratefully shucked off my spike heels, and headed home.

"Mine warrior," Art said. "Wanna talk about it? Sid's gone."

"All I want is *sleep*. Fats and I will figure it out tomorrow, Art." I slept badly, dreaming of a scene between Jackie and me. In the dream, Jackie punched my nose.

The next morning a headline screamed from the TV page: "ACTRESS FUMES AT GLEASON!" The accompanying story detailed my tirade in front of Sid the night before, right down to my desire to smack Jackie. The words insinuated that it was a *fait accompli*. The column didn't carry Sid's byline, but it was plain he'd been the source.

"Why would Sid do such a thing, Art? I didn't treat him like a TV columnist. I thought he was a friend!"

"That was your first mistake, Pat. You haven't learned a thing from me."

A familiar, sour-tasting gorge rose in my throat. "But, Art, I didn't *do* anything. Nothing happened! I came home."

"I know that, and you know that, but Gleason doesn't care. You've embarrassed him. The worst part is, I can't fix this thing, Patty. I have no power anymore. I can go smack Sid down for being a heel, and I just might, but that won't help you with Gleason." It was a harsh tone of voice. "My dear, dear Patty-From-Cincinnati! You're in trouble, and I can't help you."

"Art, even you said my anger was justified. You encouraged me to get it out!"

"It *is* justified, Patty, and you should have gotten it out, but not in front of a newspaperman! You and Gleason are news. Sid's job is to report it."

Art had chuckled all through my tirade the night before. I took it as his benign approval. He'd lectured me about being more assertive. By God, I was going to show him that I was a tigress worthy of my mate. Life didn't seem fair at that moment.

Professionally speaking, Art was right. I tried calling and wiring Jackie, to somehow connect with him, talk it out with him, tell him how sorry I was that my private disappointment had erupted into public headlines. He refused to see or speak with me. It was his basketball, his court. The media tore at the story. My phone rang like an incessant, insistent alarm.

Art tried to comfort me, then disappeared into his apartment/office next door. I knew he was heartsick that he, once so powerful, could do nothing to help. I wrote in my journal that night: *"This is the most alone I've felt in my life."*

Jackie Gleason attacked me in the press, telling columnist Jack O'Brien that I couldn't be trusted. That statement dug deep. I'd made a contract with Jackie on a handshake, and he'd broken the contract, but was telling the world that *I* couldn't be trusted? It was my first experience with someone so brilliantly talented and so damaged by personal demons. Others dealt with him by bobbing and weaving, and I should have done the same thing. Had I ignored the fact that he left me hanging for several weeks, had my personal anxieties not pushed me, and had I not blurted my feelings out with Sid, there might have been a different outcome.

CBS announced *The Honeymooners* segment was being dropped from *American Scene Magazine*. Art Carney opened on Broadway in a new play, *Take Her, She's Mine*. I visited him backstage in his dressing room at the Biltmore Theater.

"Art, I feel so guilty. Did my brouhaha with Jackie cancel *The Honeymooners?*"

"No, Pat. Jackie didn't want to repeat *The Honeymooners*. CBS insisted. You walked into the middle of the whole controversy, just in time to become Jackie's fall guy."

He could see my distress. He leaned over and took my hands in his as I sat opposite him. "Jackie has had a kick in the pants coming for a long time. You're not the first one he's hurt. You're the only one with the guts to confront him, and a lot of people have wanted to, me included."

He made a stage entrance, and his manager continued the conversation.

"There's a back-story to this, Pat," he said. "Carney was a free-lance player on Jackie's old Dumont variety series, an underdog. But as soon as he became Ed Norton on *The Honeymooners,* he was a star. Fans adored him. They demanded more and more of him, and the writers were ordered by the network to feature Ed Norton, to give him more laugh lines. They began stealing Jackie's lines from future scripts and transferring them to Carney. Jackie burned up with jealousy and resentment."

"So I walked right into a one-sided feud?"

"That's exactly what it was. Jackie wanted to get rid of Art Carney and *The Honeymooners.* He wanted to prove he was The Great One alone, and CBS, understandably, wanted to repeat the success of *The Honeymooners* on their new variety series."

"But I still did a dumb thing."

He shrugged. "Maybe so. The outcome would have been the same, sooner or later. And like Carney told you, Gleason had it coming to him a long time ago. It was about time somebody ripped his cover away."

A few years later CBS produced a musical version of *The Honeymooners,* filmed in Miami. Art Carney was Ed Norton, for the fans had made him as much a part of the series as Jackie Gleason's Ralph Kramden. There couldn't have been a *Honeymooners* without Art Carney. Jackie may have been jealous, but he knew which side of his bread held the butter.

Art Carney died in 2003, at the age of eighty-five. I received calls from news services, asking for a quote about him. The words that came to mind were Art Carney's words, or perhaps they were Ed Norton's, but they filled the bill:

"Art Carney was a gent," I said. "A real, first-class gent."

That was the truth.

scene viii: Spring, 1963, Fire Island, New York, and Ohio

Journal, April 16, 1963: Had lunch with Gus Schirmer today— so good to see him! And great news! His office has two bookings for me.

"You're not afraid of me, Gus? Because of all the Gleason publicity?"

"Afraid of you, Pat? *I cried* for you. You were beyond your depth." Gus didn't say it, but I knew he felt my new manager, Fats Farber, had let me down.

Art was in his office when I arrived home.

"Gus has come through for me, Art. I'll be opening The Club Atlantique on Fire Island in late May, then I'll go on tour with Merv Griffin in Neil Simon's play, *Come Blow Your Horn.* We'll play Columbus and Dayton. I'll be able to see my family!"

The ashtray on Art's desk contained a small cigarette stub.

"Have you started smoking again?"

"This? No, Patty, it's just pot. You know, marijuana. I use it when I'm writing. It helps me get my mind into a creative zone." I'd heard of pot, but I knew little about it.

"Oh, okay. They say with F. Scott Fitzgerald it was booze. I was afraid you'd started smoking again. They've come out with all kinds of stuff now, about how bad smoking is for your health."

"No way would I start smoking, honey! Pot is harmless. Don't worry!"

"Okay, I won't." And I didn't. But I should have.

Journal, May 27, 1963: It's beautiful here on Fire Island. We rented a cottage for the month I'll be working at The Club Atlantique. Art, Jeff, Charlie, and Herman are all with me. A happy time.

"Patty, don't do the old supper club act," Art said. "Let me help you with new material. You're an actress as much as a singer. Why not try characterizations like your mother did in Chautauqua? Do your own characters, but blend characterizations with your singing."

The Atlantique was the perfect place to try such an act. Its sensitive, theater-wise audiences knew what I was aiming for, and encouraged me. My characters included Tommy Twiddledorfer, a young man with braces on his teeth, saying goodbye to his girlfriend in *Toot, Toot Tootsie.* And a beauty contest winner (her talent was blowing bubbles) anxious to please her stage mother in *Keep Smiling At Trouble.*

Classical musician and Columbia University professor, Karl Otto Westin, reviewed the new act, then wrote a song for me called *The Clown.* A haunting ballad, its theme was universal: we can laugh on the outside while crying within. It was so well received it became a theme song for the act. I interspersed new material with old arrangements, *Lucky Star, I Got Rhythm,* and *Limehouse Blues.* I was a guest on ABC's nighttime show with Les Crane and Nipsey Russell, and NBC's *Today Show* with Hugh Downs and Barbara Walters.

Gus was more than pleased. "They want to interpolate a song into *Come Blow Your Horn* for you. Your part is that of a singer, and Merv Griffin plays piano. You two will break into a song during one of your scenes." It was worked out that I would sing *I Didn't Know The Gun Was Loaded* to Merv's accompaniment in the first act. I'm sure the interpolation didn't make sense, and I never asked if anyone had gotten Neil Simon's permission. Probably not. It was corny, but audiences loved it.

Journal, June 17, 1963: My birthday. I'm 34! Rehearsals are great. I like Merv Griffin very much, and William Bendix is a hoot. He's full of Hollywood stories, many about his best friend Alan Ladd. We open in Columbus next week.

(Later, after rehearsal) Finally met the legendary Jed Harris. Art and I were walking down 57th St. and a guy pops out of a Bentley and waves the driver away. Jed Harris, theatrical icon, Mr. "Our Town" himself, followed us home like a puppy and invited himself in! We'd planned my quiet birthday dinner alone. Turned out to be a birthday celebration for three.

We opened *Come Blow Your Horn* at the Kenley Players in Columbus, Ohio, the next week.

Journal, July 6, 1963: Celebrated Merv Griffin's birthday. I gave him a cake during curtain calls— lit it with sparklers instead of candles and almost burned up the backdrop carrying it out to him! Now I'm yawning. Couldn't go out tonight. God, I hope I'm not coming down with mononucleosis again. I'm so tired lately. Maybe I'm overdoing seeing friends here— old pals from WBNS-TV, Delta Gammas, OSU buddies. So good to see everyone. But all ask about Rick. And then everyone wants to know about my "new husband." Oh, dear. Sounds as if I've had so many.

Journal, July 7, 1963: Mom is here. We drove to where Grandma Daisy and Grandad Ben's farm used to be. It's now a freeway off-ramp, gas stations on two corners. Made me sad. The farm was so beautiful. Still fatigued. I'll catch up on rest next week.

"You look tired, Pat," said character actress Mae Questel. She stood behind my dressing table chair, her hands on my shoulders, staring at me in the mirror. Mae played the Jewish mother in *Come Blow Your Horn.* She fascinated me because she was not only the voice of Olive Oyl in the *Popeye* cartoons, but had voiced Popeye himself on occasion. Then, as the cartoon industry grew, it took a look at tiny, adorable Mae, with her piquant round face, Cupid's-bow mouth and huge eyes, and developed her into a cartoon, *Betty Boop.* I'd grown up with Popeye, Olive Oyl, and Betty Boop. Mae was a true star to me.

"Well, Mae, I've been out every night after the show with family or friends. I love it, but I'm exhausted!"

"Take care, Bubbala, we don't want to lose you." Mae cracked me up every time she opened her mouth, for out came squeaky Betty Boop.

Journal, July 12, 1963: Am I pregnant? This terrible fatigue and backache. I can get used to the idea, but how will Art feel? He loves Jeff, but Jeff is ready for college. I'll keep this to myself until I'm sure.

Journal, July 15, 1963: I'm sure! Threw up this AM. Nauseous all day—yep, I'm sure!

Journal, July 21, 1963: Art is 46 today, and about to become a father again. Haven't told him yet. I must do that in person.

Merv Griffin gave me a lift in his limousine when we arrived back in New York. I felt woozy when we finished our run of *Come Blow Your Horn.* Merv whispered in my ear as we hugged goodbye, "I'll bet you're pregnant, Pat." I whispered back, "I think I am—does it show?"

"Only in your eyes, honey, only in your eyes," he said. Merv was the first to know.

Art and I sat quietly together as I told him my news. We calculated how long I'd have to work, and how Art could accelerate his business for when I'd be out-of-action. As we discussed the practical side of things, I saw a glow come over my husband. It had finally struck him that he was going to be a father again. He was tender.

"My God, Patty, this is wonderful! It's just what you need!"

A momentary hitch in my joy.

"But what about you, Art? Is it what *you* need? I've never stopped working long enough to think about having children, but oh, honey, I have to admit—I'm thrilled!!"

"Patty, me, too. I can't believe it, but me, too." When I saw Art's eyes fill with tears, I knew all would be okay.

There's an old Spanish proverb: "Every baby brings a sack of gold on its back." The day after I got home from the tour of *Come Blow Your Horn*, Ann Wright, a bright young agent, called. I knew her slightly. Her office adjoined Gus Schirmer's.

"Pat, I wonder if you'd be interested in doing commercials? They're wonderful for theater people between jobs. I heard you going over songs with Merv Griffin in Gus's office. You have wonderful energy. I'm sure there would be a lot of commercial work for you." She explained what commercials paid, and how one day's work could stretch into months, even years, of re-run payments —"residuals."

It was the answer to a prayer, another opportunity to stay in New York. I've always believed things happen for a reason, guided by something larger than ourselves. If we follow without questioning too much, our lives work out for the best. I didn't care that my theater friends looked down on commercials. I wasn't above doing them. Within a couple of weeks, I'd joined the Screen Actors' Guild and filmed two national spots, one for Lux Liquid detergent, another for Downey fabric softener. Once again my Ohio persona worked for me. In those days commercials were geared to middle-American house-wives in their thirties, and I was one of them. When my first residual check for several thousands of dollars came in, I knew it wouldn't be long before my elitist actor friends would change their minds about doing commercials. I wasn't wrong. Soon even major stars were scrambling to sell detergents and cheese.

Art and I settled in to await our baby. I had three months before I'd have to stop working. The way luck was going in my new field, I'd make another two or three commercials in that time. They would more than carry us through a maternity leave. I shopped for a layette. I hugged Charlie and sang lullabies to him. He licked my face as if to say, "I'm happy for you, Mom." I could hear Art whistling in his office next door.

On a hot August day, without rhyme nor reason nor warning, the baby was gone.

"We never know exactly why, Mrs. Franklin," the doctor said. "It wasn't anything you did, it could be that it was an imperfect fetus. It could be because you're an elderly primipara."

"I'm a *what?*"

"A first-time mother past the age of thirty." Damn. It was useless to brood. My tears were wept in secret.

Up again, old heart.

scene ix: 1963-1964, Enter Katherine Beatrice, Manhattan

Later that year, in the fall of 1963, Art said, "The Bon Soir wants to book you, Patty. Interested?" I knew Art had probably gone to one of his friends for a favor, someone who could arrange for me to play the popular Greenwich Village nightspot. He wanted to distract me, to lift me out of my depression over the loss of our baby. The Bon Soir had similar audiences as The Club Atlantique on Fire Island: young, hip, theater-oriented, largely gay. A new singer named Barbra Streisand had been performing there with great success.

"I'd need some brush-up work, Art."

My friend Silver Saundors from *Fiorello!* had recently opened a new club, *The Improvisation,* with her husband, advertising executive Budd Friedman. They let me use their club as a workshop, and Art and I honed my act with helpful suggestions from Silver and Budd. The "Improv," legendary now, seemed destined to be something special.

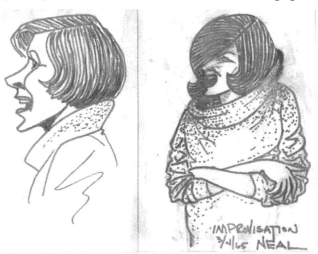

The "Improv" artist gave me quite a ski-snoot.

Karl Otto Westin, who'd written my theme, *The Clown*, brought a young actor friend to see me—Martin Sheen. And yet another young actor, as yet undiscovered, was the waiter who brought us our drinks, Dustin Hoffman.

When I opened in the Bon Soir in October, I was well-received and reviewed in an entirely new mode. The owner signed me for five return engagements. And I was pregnant again.

Journal, November 16, 1963: Another miscarriage. My heart is broken. What's wrong with me?

Journal, November 22, 1963: John F. Kennedy was assassinated in Dallas—too much sadness to bear all at once.

"I'm worried about you, Patty-From-Cincinnati." Art's arms were around me.

"I'll be all right." But I couldn't stop crying.

Mary Bryant, my publicist friend from *Fiorello!,* called.

"George Abbott's autobiography is coming out, and *Life* magazine is throwing a party for him. Can you come? We want as many of his friends around him as we can gather!" It was just before Christmas. After the national ordeal we'd all endured, and Art's and my personal ordeal of losing a second baby within a few months, I wasn't ready for the holiday, let alone a party.

"You must go, Patty. It'll be good for you to get out and remember who you are!" Yet Art declined to come along. It was difficult not to have him with me for things that were important to me. But I was growing up. I appreciated that we were not joined at the hip. I kept seeing Dr. Braun in my mind's eye, his two hands held close together, not tightly clasped.

So I went to Life magazine's party for George Abbott alone. George was happy to see me, to see us all, from many of his shows, gathered in his honor. So many friends I loved were there: Ellen Hanley, Tom Bosley, Jerry Bock and Sheldon Harnick, Howard DaSilva, Bob Fosse. It was good-old-home week, with bonus people thrown in. I met Lillian Gish, the silent screen star, so beautiful, still active as an actress. I said hello again to Claudette Colbert. I met my teen idol, Van Johnson, though I didn't have the nerve to tell him of my girlhood crush, and the prize-winning letter I'd once written to *Photoplay* magazine about him.

Carol Burnett attended, visibly pregnant. I hugged her for luck, saying, "Carol, by the grace of God, me next!"

Journal, January 30, 1964: I can't believe it, but I must be pregnant again. The signs are there: fatigue, nausea, back ache. I'm not telling Art right away. Dear God, let me keep this baby.

Jean Kerr once told me she knew she was pregnant when her waist thickened. Jean was a plus-sized lady, tall and big-boned. "The first thing that happens when I get pregnant? I lose my waistline," she said. "I square off until I look like a refrigerator. Bingo! I know."

This time around I noticed the same phenomenon in my own body. So did Art.

"Patty, are you putting on weight? Where's your waist? *Uh oh—*"

"This time it's going to be okay, Art. I promise." I took excellent care of myself. I indulged my craving for cold soups: gazpacho, cucumber, watercress. And there was a mixture of my own invention that I glugged down by the quart: tomato juice, buttermilk, and brewers' yeast.

"You deserve to have a great kid with that junk you imbibe," Art teased.

We moved to the penthouse at 325 West End Avenue, with a thirty-foot living room, three bedrooms, and a fifty-foot L-shaped terrace overlooking the Hudson River. It sounds glamorous, but it was just spacious and comfortable. There were unused rooms, formerly servants' quarters, adjoining the apartment, and Art set one up as his office. Nothing can compare to those old Westside pre-World War II buildings in Manhattan. It was a wonderful home for us, and I'm sure it still is, for whoever is lucky enough to be living there now.

A few weeks earlier, I'd made the last commercial for the duration of my pregnancy. A pregnant actress was needed by the Grey Advertising Agency. Their client, Proctor and Gamble, had developed a new disposable diaper. Thus I, along with my unborn baby, made the first Pampers commercial.

Weeks went by, and my baby stayed with me. I thrilled to every move and kick, every heartbeat heard on the doctor's stethoscope. I wasn't about to risk anything happening to the baby during delivery. I'd read about the Lamaze method of natural childbirth. Women in Great Britain and Europe were swearing by it, no drugs or anesthesia for the mother, no forceps to drag out the child. The mother was prepared with body and mind exercises for weeks before delivery to work through labor and childbirth. I was already psychologically and emotionally prepared for anything that would ensure the safe entry of my child into the world. *It's not as if women haven't been doing it this way since time began—what's the big deal?* I talked Art into going to Lamaze classes with me.

"I know you love me to do this!"

"You'd better believe it," grumbled my husband. "This is not the real me."

Yes it is, Art. I smiled to myself. *More than you know, tough guy.* I watched the dimples deepen in his earnest face as he counted my laboring breaths.

Elizabeth Bing, the New York nurse/practitioner/advocate for the method, taught Lamaze classes in her living room. "It'll be good for this movement to have women like you publicizing natural childbirth, Pat."

Publicize the birth of my precious baby? No, not even for a good cause. Weeks after I gave birth, another Broadway leading lady was not so superstitious. She birthed her baby with Elizabeth Bing's coaching, and great accompanying fanfare. When interviewed in the hospital, she cooed, "I feel blessed to be the first Broadway mother to have my baby the Lamaze natural way. I want to shout from the rooftops!" Shout she did, but she wasn't the first.

Few doctors were willing to deliver a child naturally in the mid-60's. What I encountered when I said I wanted to have my baby without drugs or anesthesia were condescending pats on the head, and such responses as, "Of course, my dear, whatever you wish. You'll feel differently when those labor pains start."

I needed a doctor I could trust to believe me when I said, "I want to be awake! I want my baby to enter this world fully aware!" Young Dr. Fred Tanz was game to go with my plan. He even got permission from Lenox Hill Hospital for Art to be in the delivery room to play his role as a birth coach. Like Elizabeth Bing, Fred was a pioneer.

On October 5, 1964, at 10:04 AM, after a total of five hours of labor, my daughter Kate, seven pounds, eleven ounces, entered the world, without the help of drugs or anesthesia. I was thirty-five years old. I felt God and I both giving the finger to those who labeled me "elderly primipara." Kate looked like a small Apache with strawberry blonde hair, and the sweet smell of her new-babyness made me dizzy.

"You're the most beautiful sight I've ever seen," I sang to her. She squeaked out her protest at the rudeness of her new, brightly-lit world. "Yell away, my darling," I said. "It's like the overture to a hit show to my ears!"

We called her "Katherine Beatrice," after my mother, and Art's friend Kate Smith. The maternity nurse had a different idea for her small charge.

"'Katherine Beatrice?' For such a tiny thing? She's just a wee 'Katy-Bee,' that's all."

Poor Kate. The name stuck.

Once home in our penthouse, all I wanted was to stay with my latest, greatest production, my baby. I wrapped myself in Art's thick cabled cardigan, and Katy Bee in her pink bunny suit and blanket. I sat for hours in the warm sun on the terrace, rocking her, watching the boats on the Hudson River below.

Momma flew in from Cincinnati, carrying a folding bathinette and a suitcase full of baby clothes. She stayed with me until I wasn't afraid to lower Kate into her bath. It took some time. In the afternoons she and I sipped peppermint tea while Katy Bee napped.

Art and me and Katy Bee make three.

"I like Art, Pat." He'd been making her laugh since she arrived. "He's a good man."

"Yes. Momma, I'm home at last."

Eventually I had to think about working, but Art and I decided I should wait until the New Year.

We were invited to Cincinnati for Christmas, and I wanted to go, to show Katy Bee off to my girlhood friends, to my brothers and their families. And most of all to my father. My father, clinging to his anti-Semitism, had refused to attend my small, informal wedding to Art.

"You should go, Pat," Art said. "You need to see your Dad, to introduce him to Katy Bee. Christmas doesn't mean much to me. When I was a kid we were always either too poor or too Jewish—I was never sure which!—for Christmas. I'll stay here with Jeff."

"But Mom loves you, Art! She'll be disappointed!"

"And I'm crazy about your mother. But your father hates me, without even knowing me." He smiled his sardonic smile. "It could get worse when he meets me. Please go!"

So I went, not knowing what to expect when I got off the plane in Cincinnati. Would my father meet me, or Mom, or one of my brothers? My father stood at the foot of the stairway, as one could in those pre-terrorist days, waiting for me to deplane. He took the tiny pink bundle that was my daughter and held her close. Katy Bee peered at her grandfather, her perfect bud-mouth turning into a gummy smile. My father cried. The old Spanish proverb was right. Each baby *does* bring a sack of gold on its back. But it isn't necessarily the shiny, metallic stuff.

scene x: 1965-1966, The next year, New York City

"Patty, you can't sit on your ass anymore. Katy Bee is more than a year old now. You've got to get back into action." Art's harsh words startled me. I'd first noticed changes in him during the long strike of New York's newspapers by printers and engravers, which began in late 1962 and lasted until mid-1963. Several New York newspapers folded, among them *The Mirror*, which carried Walter Winchell's daily column. The world that had once made my husband so powerful was rapidly disappearing.

Motherhood had made me cavalier about my career. I received calls to audition for shows, and turned them down. Eight performances a week are a full-time job, and my new job as mommy was more important to me. I didn't fault my friends who couldn't wait to get back to their careers after their babies were born. With commercials, I needed to work only a few days a month to bring in a good annual income. I was grateful I had what was, to me, the best of both worlds. And perhaps I felt that my success in *Fiorello!* had already fulfilled for my mother what my father had denied her.

"Did you hear me, Pat? I said it's time to get off your ass and get back to work!"

"Don't you consider the big campaign I did this year work, Art?" Twenty, thirty, and sixty-second versions of my pain-killer commercial were running in prime-time TV. A print campaign lifted from the commercial had appeared in every magazine in the country.

"I'm talking about your *real* work, which in case you've forgotten, Patty, happens to be as one of the finest singing actresses around." *Angry.* I confronted the near-snarl in his voice.

"Okay, Art, what's wrong?"

"A club is opening on Central Park South called The Penthouse. They want you to appear as their opening act. And if you do it, I'll handle their publicity."

One's heart can sink and leap at the same moment—that's what mine did then. Discovering what disturbed Art was a relief, for it had nothing to do with the CIA, or government shenanigans. Art was demoralized. From somewhere, an angel whispered in my ear, giving me the right words to say:

"Art, how wonderful! The Penthouse Club lucked out! We can work together!" I hugged him. Katy Bee laughed and clapped her hands. We grabbed her up and held her between us.

Journal, February 14, 1966: Our third wedding anniversary. I open tonight in The Penthouse— pretty place, overlooking Central Park. Katy Bee is playing with the feathers on my opening-night outfit as I write—I tickle her nose with them. She's precious! Am I biased? You bet. She helped me get my voice in shape. Practiced scales with me every day. Art said, "God, I have another singing actress on my hands!"

We'd found the perfect outfit for *The Clown* theme of my act. It was a one-piece ivory crepe jumpsuit with a ruff of dyed-to-match marabou feathers around the neckline, and more marabou at the bottoms of the culotte-type legs. The opening night audience laughed and applauded when I entered and made a small curtsey. I knew I was

203

In marabou again, in my new act for The Penthouse Club.

home free. It was a spectacular evening. For The Penthouse Club, for me, and for Art, who'd given it his considerable all.

The new act, now a full-on combination of characterizations and standard songs, was billed as "High Camp, Low Vaudeville, and Plain Singing." My favorite review? William A. Raidy:

"....Miss Wilson, who has a talent strictly her own, has a gamine-like look until she raises her voice. Then a rare feeling comes over you—this little girl has a wisdom, a phrasing, and a taste of repertory that comes along once in a decade." From *Variety*: "Miss Wilson combines thespics and singing—she is good in both." And Dan Lewis told the backstage story in his review in the *Daily News*: "Patricia Wilson gave up a Broadway career to become a wife and mother—it has been a number of years since she has appeared before a live New York audience, but she has lost none of her stage presence. Her arrangements are strong, every number skillfully delivered, her Toot Toot Tootsie a positive delight."

Representatives from several television shows appeared for the opening. Walter Winchell carried the story: "Patricia Wilson's four big weeks at The Penthouse Club got her the J. Carsoncast and a *Today Show* stanza with Hugh Downs."

Art gave me a single red rose for the combination opening night-and-third wedding anniversary celebration. The card said, simply, "More and more——"

scene xi: Two weeks later, March 3, 1966

My brother's voice was strained. "Are you alone, Pat? Is Art there with you?" David asked.

"No, you just missed him, Davey. He went for a walk. Katy Bee's taking her nap. What's wrong?"

"It's Pop."

"Is he sick? He's been so much on my mind. Did he get the Penthouse reviews I sent?"

My father, six weeks past his seventieth birthday, had died of a cerebral hemorrhage an hour earlier. Death was so sudden that my mother continued chattering away as they sat together in their family room. When he stopped answering her questions, she thought he'd fallen asleep.

"Poppa, I wish you peace at last," I whispered to my father. His difficult life, the difficult life he'd imposed on his family, had ended so simply. I strongly felt his presence. My father, close for maybe the first time.

When Art came home, I told him what had happened. He put his arms around me, his warm, familiar breath against my ear. Within a few minutes, he went to call the owner of The Penthouse. The club was sold out that night.

"Art, I want to sing. I'll go to Cincinnati tomorrow." The show must go on, and it did. It was a private father/daughter joke, between a couple of troupers. I dedicated my show that night to my father, the man who hated show business but was proud of his daughter's success. I flew home to Cincinnati the next day, to my mother and brothers, to bury Ross Howard Wilson with military honors. Art didn't go to Cincinnati with me.

"I didn't know your father, Patty, and I hate funerals. When I kick off, just wheel me to the curb and let 'em haul me away." Why didn't my husband realize I needed him? Why did he consider my wanting to lean on him a sign of weakness? I ached with pain and rejection.

March 4th, 1966, was a dreary and still wintry day. I took a cab from the airport to my parents' house in the Cincinnati suburb of Hyde Park. A gray half-rain, half-snow flicked against the cab window, the windshield wipers diligently pushing at falling slush. My mother, brothers, and their families were gathered at the funeral home for the evening visitation of Pop's friends. It was pre-arranged that I meet a neighbor, a volunteer baby-sitter, at the family house. I would put Katy Bee to bed, and after she was asleep, join my family at the mortuary.

With seventeen-month old Kate in my arms, I let myself into the house my parents had owned for twenty-seven years, the house that had been my home base from age eleven. The babysitter hadn't yet arrived, and the living room was nearly dark in the Cincinnati twilight. A sudden, sweet scent washed over me, so powerful that I sat down with Kate in my arms. Her small face lit up as she looked into the dim room. She reached out her arms and dropped to the floor.

"*Poppy!*" she cried. Her name for my father. Goose bumps burst forth on my arms. There was no doubt she was communicating with her grandfather. She'd loved him from the first moment he held her, for what was inside of him, not for the gruff, complicated man life had made of him.

The sweet scent of lilacs. That was the smell I recognized washing over me in the dark room. There wasn't a bloom anywhere in the icy March outdoors, and flowers delivered to the house had been carried to the funeral home earlier that day. My father hated the scent of lilacs. It reminded him of the May day in a convent when he'd been told of his father's death, and of later hard times during the Depression on my grandparents' farm, where a grove of lilac bushes sweetly tormented him, telling him his life had reached a new low.

I leaned against the familiar upholstery of the couch Pop had been sitting on when life deserted him.

"You're telling me something, Poppa. I'm listening. I'm trying to hear you. What is it?" Katy Bee turned to me with her angel-smile, the curve of her upper lip so like my father's. She made a small circle with her chubby thumb and forefinger, the family sign that all was well.

"Don' cry, Momma," she said. "Poppy's okey-dokey!" She climbed on my lap, snuggling close. I held my daughter tight until the doorbell announced the arrival of the baby-sitter.

scene xii: Spring, 1966, Home in Manhattan

Journal, April 12, 1966: A realization today: Art is becoming as controlling as my father ever was. It's as if nothing I did professionally before The Penthouse Cub means anything. Why was I successful before I met him? I bite my tongue. Am I taking the same road to peace that Momma did with Pop?

Art was neglecting his own work. He rarely sought new clients for his public relations business. "Clients come to me," he said, a new bitter-arrogance in his voice. "It's the only way they respect me. Otherwise I'm like some frigging ambulance-chasing lawyer."

The real meat of our future, in my mind, lay in his writing, but rewrites of his play sat in piles, gathering dust. He accepted an advance from publisher Lyle Stuart to write a memoir of his celebrity-packed life. The advance was a comforting nest-egg, but when Lyle Stuart Publishing came out with a bonanza book, *The Sensuous Woman,* Art returned the money.

"Runaway best-seller?" he said of *The Sensuous Woman.* "It's nothing but pornography."

I couldn't fault my husband for his high moral standards. I wanted such values instilled in our daughter. But I was worried about our future.

"We'll go with *your* career now, Patty. I have as much invested in it since The Penthouse as you do," he said. His tone was disturbing. *What had happened to the reassuring self-confidence of the man I fell in love with? When had it become arrogance?*

"Then we should reconsider California, Art. There I could do television as well as commercials. Maybe films. Broadway has changed since *Hair* and *Jesus Christ, Superstar.* It's been six-and-a-half years since *Fiorello!* I'm yesterday's mashed potatoes."

"No! Never California! I mean it. I hate the frigging place!" One more time I ignored my knowin'— when I should have heeded it.

Art sold an idea to a Columbia Records producer for a subsidiary label to be called *Theater For The Ear Records.* I was to record its first album, using characterizations and songs from my *Clown* act. *Fiorello!'s* lyricist, Sheldon Harnick, who had married my friend Margery Gray, agreed to write the liner notes for the album.

207

Sheldon and Jerry Bock wrote the phenomenally successful *Fiddler On The Roof* after *Fiorello!,* and Sheldon was doing me a great honor to write liner notes for my album.

I recorded two advance sides for the project, *Toot Toot Tootsie,* and an original song Art had written for The Penthouse called *Champagne Blues.* In it my character was a tipsy lady. The recording ends with a huge hiccup. The purpose of advance-recording two sides was to see how the idea would play with Columbia executives, but to our surprise, when Art and I walked into a restaurant one evening, my recording of *Toot Toot Tootsie* was playing on the jukebox.

"Well, as we used to say in Brooklyn, ya puts in yer nickel, and out comes yer music!"

We learned bootlegged copies had made their way into several jukeboxes around the city. Rather than get legal and demand they be withdrawn, we reveled in the fact that people were curious about them. They were getting plays. We prepared other material for the album.

Then one day our liaison with Columbia Records disappeared. Columbia had thinned out its creative staff, Art's producer/connection along with them. As Art began a campaign to re-sell the idea to other Columbia executives, I knew it was time to tell him my secret.

Journal, October 16, 1967: I'm pregnant again. Art hasn't guessed, even when I got dizzy and nauseous recording "Tootsie."

I rationalized that I didn't want Art to know until I was past the danger of miscarriage, but that wasn't the truth. The truth was that I didn't want him to be angry.

Journal, October 18, 1967: Will I ever understand this man? He's as thrilled as I! It's as if I turned back the clock and got my beloved Art back again. I can only admit it to you, Journal, but I hope we have another girl. Katy Bee won't be alone in the world. I dare only admit to myself and God how much I want this child—

This was the late 1960s. Pregnant performers were not so public in those days. I wasn't Angelina Jolie, or Britney Spears, or any of today's celebrity mothers. Columbia Records calculated I'd be out-of-commission for several months, and shelved our Theater For The Ear project until a "later date." As often happens in show business that later date disappeared from the calendar.

Katy Bee and I flew to Cincinnati for Christmas. My brothers said Momma was not doing well without Pop. A lifetime of control was gone from her life, and she was bewildered.

"Momma, look, I'm having another baby!" She touched my swelling belly.

"Another *mitzvah*," she said. I'd never known my mother to utter a Jewish word.

scene xiii: Early spring 1968, Enter a new dimension in Greenwich Village

Journal, February 14, 1968: Our fifth wedding anniversary. We're invited to celebrate at the Bon Soir in the village. I look as if I've swallowed a basketball!

Italian family man Ernie, the Bon Soir's owner-manager, my old boss and friend, laughed when he tried to hug me. "Come back after that baby arrives. I can't get close enough to kiss you on the cheek!"

When Art and I left the club at one-thirty AM, snow was falling in angry swirls. Art ensconced me curbside, stomped a pathway through a deep drift to the street, and waited to flag down a taxi.

"Don't move, Patty. I'll help you across the snow when I get a cab."

The flakes dimmed the glow of the streetlights as they fell. I watched them thicken on the top of Art's Russian-style hat, and shifted my numbing feet inside my boots. There were no cabs. We waited in the growing storm.

At last a taxi appeared, its off-duty light signaling that it wasn't picking up passengers. The driver slowed when he spotted a highly pregnant woman and the frantic man waving him down. We were lucky. The cabbie was a family man and empathized with our predicament. Art opened the door, spoke to the driver, and smiled as he turned back to me. He had secured our ride home.

From out of nowhere, a young man hurtled through the drifting snow and the open cab door. He slammed it in our faces. The cabbie looked at us, dismayed. Art spoke quietly to the young man.

"Buddy, this cab is off duty, but the driver agreed to get my wife home. As you can see, she can't be out in this storm."

"Tough shit," said the young man.

Things happened very quickly. Art reached into the cab and grabbed the young man by the lapels, lifting him out of his seat. He casually evaded the man's flailing fists.

"Get in, Patty!" I did, and the cab driver and I watched my fifty-year old husband calmly lift the young man, half his age and twice his weight, and throw him across the hood of the cab. It was like watching a programmed machine doing its job. From the cab's hood, he picked the stunned young man up again, tossing him like a rag doll into the curbside snowdrift.

"The next time you pick on a guy that looks helpless because he's old and wears glasses, make sure you can take him! I would've offered to share the cab uptown! Now you can damn well sit there and freeze your ass." We sped away.

On the trip up Eighth Avenue our driver laughed, shaking his head in disbelief, pounding his big fists on the steering wheel. "Man, oh man! I was raised in Harlem, and I never saw anything like that! How'd you do that, mister?"

"You have to understand leverage," Art said. "I didn't want to hurt the guy. I just wanted to put him in his place." He turned to me. "The little *putz* got me mad, Patty. He swore in front of you!"

A peculiar set of contradictions, my husband. I guess most of us are. I'd never seen Art violent before that incident. Nonetheless, I was watching changes occurring in him. I sensed, with some dread, what they foretold. It was a knowin': our lives would be different.

scene xiv: Spring 1968, Enter Penelope, New York City

Journal, April 1, 1968: Art and I make beautiful babies! Penelope Elizabeth was born last night at 10:58 PM, an hour before midnight. No April Fool, this girl!

Though birthing babies commanded a limited audience, I sensed the presence of God and angels around me in the delivery room, as I had all my life in creating characters on a stage. Perhaps both acts of creation were my calling.

One balmy mid-April day, needing a prescription refill from the pharmacy on the corner, I decided to take my children into the fresh spring air. Out I went without makeup, in a pair of wrinkled slacks and an old workman's shirt, which I rationalized covered my post-pregnancy pounds. I'd be gone for no longer than fifteen minutes. I hummed happily as I pushed the carriage with tiny Penelope, holding three-and-a-half year old Kate by the hand.

Howard DaSilva was standing on the corner, waiting for the light to change. My mental once-over told me I was out of my mind to leave the apartment looking as I did.

"My God, Pat, it's you! What beautiful kids!" Howard was a diplomat. We talked for several minutes, turning away with a hug. I realized too late that I probably smelled like baby spit-up.

"Oh, Katy!" I wailed to my three-and-a-half year-old daughter, "That man was someone I haven't seen for a long time. Do I look just *awful?*"

"You look like poo-poo, Momma," she said.

scene xv: Later that spring, 1968, Manhattan

Journal, May 30, 1968: Money is tight. Must get back to work, but dreading it. I love being home with the children. Art is more and more hostile. Does he hate seeing me domestic? He loves the kids but has little to say to me. I still have a few pounds to lose, but I'll call Ann Wright. Back into the commercial cauldron.

We were notified that our apartment building was going co-operative, as many New York buildings were in mid-1968. We could buy our penthouse for the insider's price, $40,000.

"No way!" Art said. "We're not buying this or any other real estate!"

"But Art, we've already spent so much to make the apartment the way we want it. The floors alone cost over a thousand. Forty thousand dollars is a fair price."

"Forty thousand? That used to be *nothing* to me," Art said. "I grossed that every month!" I didn't want to hear it. I bit my tongue to keep from saying that now it would be my money invested in our home. This was a new feeling for me. From the beginning of our marriage, everything each of us made went into a family bank account.

"Then you know how easy it would be to buy this place," I reasoned.

"Yeah, well, Jews hate owning real estate, anything that might keep them from picking up and escaping in a hurry!" I knew his fears ran deep. His father had watched from a secret hiding place as his brothers, Art's uncles, were slain by Cossacks in Russia. My own father's nightmares about the Ku Klux Klan tarring and feathering actors had reached out to haunt my childhood. I could only imagine how his father's dreams had haunted Art's growing years.

Nonetheless, most of my Jewish friends owned their own homes.

I was sad as the couple who bought our penthouse came to take measurements.

"My, this wood is nice," commented the lady buyer, appraising the Spanish-oak-stained floors I'd had sanded and refinished just the way I wanted them. I said nothing. I scoured the *Times* for a rent-controlled apartment in our neighborhood, so Kate could stay in her nursery school, near her friends. I found a ground-floor apartment in the building next door, at 333 West End Avenue, a sharp contrast from our penthouse. I missed our terraces and view, and the play-yard I'd had built on the side terrace for the kids, but I set about making the new apartment our home. I hired our superintendent, who'd been a master carpenter in his native Hungary, to do the remodeling. He built walls to create two smaller rooms out of one large one, and a loft bed for the children. Beneath the loft I set up a mini, indoor play area, complete with a swing.

In 2002, I was in New York and passed by 333 West End Avenue. The windows of our former apartment, those facing West 76th Street, were open. I peeked into what had once been my children's room. The swing was gone, but the walls and structures I'd built for my family in 1968, thirty-four years earlier, were still intact.

Our penthouse, $40,000 in 1968, is worth millions today.

scene xvi: 1968-1969, New York City, Western New Jersey, and Canada

Journal, June 17, 1968: I'm 39 today. Filmed an American Airlines commercial. The actor I worked with is from California, and itching to get back. He has a house there, a yard for his kids, and works all the time. He says what am I waiting for? Even commercials are shifting west. Art says go without him. He knows I won't. Is that what he wants?

Margit, the wife of our Hungarian carpenter/superintendent, a loving woman with a seven-year old son, became our nanny. The situation was ideal. Margit could be home with her family when she wasn't needed in my apartment, and Art and I didn't have to provide a room for a live-in caretaker.

Nonetheless I was anxious when I had to be away from my small daughters. Penelope was three weeks old when I was hired to play a party hostess (wearing my Penthouse Club clown culottes for the character) in a commercial for a national line of floor tiles. I kissed my baby on each rosy cheek, and nuzzled my nose into her dark curls.

"Momma has to work," I said, handing Penelope to Margit, and turning to hug Kate.

Work-report time was seven AM, and I was camera-ready, costumed and made-up, by eight-thirty. The producers, clients, and representatives from the ad agency supervised the laying of floor tiles to be featured in the commercial. They supervised. They bickered. They did all but contemplate their navels. I drifted on set and watched them, amazed that ten grown men could come close to blows over thirty square feet of flooring. The director rushed to my side.

"Not long now, Pat! We're almost ready for you!" His whisper was conspiratorial. "This should have been taken care of yesterday. They didn't want to pay for an extra studio day."

Minutes and hours ticked away. Nothing suited all of the geniuses at any one time. I fidgeted in my dressing room. A day that began at seven, one that would normally have ended at five in the afternoon, didn't get around to camera work until six that evening. I was accustomed to the vicissitudes of creative people, but this eleven-hour wait to film a commercial was beyond nerve-wracking. I was like a racehorse snorting at the start-gate.

Actors often complain of being treated like pieces of meat. Once I heard an assistant director say to Hugh Downs's manager, "Okay, get your gorilla over here *now*!" That young man was knocked on his disrespectful behind, and I didn't blame Hugh's manager. I've known and worked with gorillas in my day, and gentlemanly, intelligent Hugh Downs was not one of them.

When the makeup lady returned from her break at four that afternoon, she smuggled two airline-sized bottles of Scotch into my dressing room.

"You'd better drink these, kid," she said. "You're gonna explode!" I accepted the warm, calming liquid, the one and only time I'd ever had a drink while working. It enabled me to begin the filming that carried us long into the night. But oh, the danger I ignored.

"Wow! Thanks! I feel relaxed," I commented to the makeup lady. I improvised actions in the commercial, throwing myself onto the floor, bicycling culotte-ed legs in the air. *Why not?* Marabou feathers went flying. I giggled, extolling the virtues of the flooring.

"Amazing! Isn't she creative!" the delighted agency producers said. They left my shenanigans in the final cut of the commercial, and it was later nominated for an award. But looking back at myself, taking a drink while working scared the daylights out of me. As it should have.

Later that summer I was on location, filming a toothpaste commercial. The script called for a camping scene, which was set up on the New Jersey side of the Delaware River, complete with a tent and a hot dog/marshmallow roasting fire. As a young wardrobe apprentice helped me into costume, a red-plaid flannel shirt and jeans, a summer thunderstorm broke. The girl and I ducked into the tent on the river bank, laughing as we tried to keep my wardrobe dry. Summer storms passed quickly. Shooting would soon resume. The crew scattered for shelter in camera vehicles and trucks.

The tent the apprentice and I ducked into was no match for the storm. The ceiling sank from the heavy downfall, the weight of the water on the canvas literally forcing us to double over inside. Water simultaneously rose above our ankles. We were attempting to fight our way through the soggy, heavy tent flap when a flash flood swept us, tent and all, down the river bank.

"*No!*" shouted the little wardrobe apprentice, "I'm only nineteen!" We thought we were going to drown. By God's grace, a stagehand glanced back as he ran for cover in the downpour. He saw our tent was seconds away from being carried into the swirling river. He ran to us, snatching up a coiled rope, yelling for help as he ran. He didn't take time to anchor himself. He clambered down the river bank, and with the strength that only God and adrenalin can impart, yanked us out of the tent. There's no doubt that he risked his life to pull us up and out. The crumpled canvas that raced down the river bore no resemblance to the tent we had just evacuated. One of my costume hiking boots, torn from my foot by the rigging as it broke away, traveled next to it. The stagehand put an arm around each of us. The wardrobe assistant murmured, "Thank you, sweet Jesus, thank you!"

I wept with relief. "I have two little girls! My baby is five months old!" I told the stagehand. He handed me a tumbler of something warm and alcoholic. I swallowed it in one gulp. "Then what the hell are you doin' here, lady?" he said in a thick Bronx accent. I wondered myself.

For the months after Penelope's birth, I felt as if I were on a treadmill, making money, but not rebuilding a career. A knowin' screamed, "California, dope!" Why couldn't Art see it? How soon would I age past playing nice housewives in commercials? Where would my family be when that happened?

"Art?" He was not in his office. I stood next to his desk. The ashtray next to his typewriter held little, hand-rolled cigarette stubs. I turned and walked out.

Later that year I went to Canada for a quick two-day shooting of a coffee commercial. Up to Toronto, back the next day, at triple-pay-scale. On our second day of filming, a Canadian blizzard developed, halting all transportation in and out of Toronto. Our cast and crew were stranded for three days. I was safe in my hotel, but unable to return to my family in New York. Penelope was less than a year old. I communicated with home by telephone, and Art's voice on the phone became surlier with each conversation. He was rumpled, angry, and distant when I returned. Even with Margit taking care of the children, he felt put upon. "What were you doing up there in Toronto, Pat? Screwing your director?"

Dear God. I was stunned by the vitriol in his voice.

"Art, what in hell is wrong with you? Don't you listen to the news? Don't you know what happened in Toronto? A blizzard to end all blizzards, even for Canada!" He turned away.

"Art! Don't you dare walk away from me! How could you say anything so cynical?"

"Easy," he said. "You're an actress, aren't you? I've never met one yet who didn't screw her director."

scene xvii: Spring 1969, Manhattan to Columbus

Journal, May 28, 1969: Kids and I are going to Ohio this after-noon. Am I running home to mother? Maybe. I ache with hurt. I'm infuriated. Art is in his office all day, anyway, so I'm going home for a week. I want—no, I NEED— my mother.

"We're going to visit Grandma!" I told my children. Mom was now in Columbus, close to my brother Donn and his wife, Joan. She was in a convalescent home, where she could be medically supervised for diabetes and congestive heart issues. We'd hired a home nurse for her in Cincinnati, but she insisted on smoking, and the nurse caught her lighting up close to an oxygen tank. She was no longer safe at home.

I called her on a Saturday morning. "Momma, the girls and I are coming to see you! We're flying in this morning. Donn is meeting us. We'll be there after lunch!"

"Oh, Patty-Cake!" My mother hadn't called me that since I was five. "I'll take a nap! Maybe the doctor will let me come to the air-port!" But when Donn and Joan met our flight, Momma wasn't with them.

"The doctor wouldn't let her come with you, Donn?"

"No, Sis, that's not it," he said. "It's just—you've arrived about an hour too late."

Momma's loving heart had simply stopped beating during her nap. The nurse went to wake her, to help her dress for the trip to the airport, and found she'd slipped away in her sleep. She was sixty-nine.

Donn took fourteen-month old Penelope from my arms. I leaned against the wall, the familiar throat-gorge beginning to rise. Joan put her arm around me, supporting me into the ladies room. Katy Bee was on our heels. "Oh, Momma! Momma!" she cried. "What's wrong?"

"It's Grandma, honey—a heart attack—"

"Did she die, Momma?"

"Yes, Katy, she died," Joan said.

Katy turned to the stranger in the ladies room. The sympathetic woman was wetting a handkerchief for me to wash my face.

"It's my grandma," Kate explained. "She stepped on a heart 'tack and died!"

Momma would have loved that. She was full of humor, kind, beautiful, and so uniquely talented. I was sure God and His angels were already applauding her gifts, laughing and crying from fluffy cloud bleachers.

There wouldn't be a dry seat in Heaven.

ACT FIVE

HOLLYWOOD

"Life has got to be lived…that's all there is to it."
Eleanor Roosevelt

scene i: Spring, 1972, Hollywood, California

Journal, May 2, 1972: I'm in Los Angeles, ten years late, but the future is here, and I put my foot down with Art AT LAST. Gus Schirmer is moving from NewYork, too, and will handle my career again. He has an associate here, Jack Molthen. I'm set up with The Wormser Agency, the best for commercials on the west coast, and casting people at Paramount and CBS. For now, I'm alone. Difficult to leave the kids, but Katy Bee needs to finish her school year.

I took an apartment in the old Montecito Hotel on Franklin Avenue, a block north of Hollywood Boulevard. It had seen better days, as had most of Hollywood proper, but the apartment was large and bright, with two bedrooms and a kitchen, the location convenient. Driving west on Santa Monica Boulevard, I passed through Beverly Hills, in 1972 like a quaint village, and ogled the pink-and-green Beverly Hills Hotel at Sunset and Beverly Drive. I meandered on Sunset Boulevard all the way to the ocean. On the return trip I wound across Coldwater Canyon into the San Fernando Valley. I loved every sunlit inch of southern California.

Journal, May 5, 1972: This seems right! It's exhilarating to be here.

Hollywood had plenty of aging leading ladies, gorgeous film stars with name recognition, so I decided not to compete in my new career locale as one of them, but to present myself as a character actress and comedienne.

"I'm forty-two, Gus, ancient for females in Hollywood. This isn't theater."

"But you still look young," Gus argued. I stood my ground. Again, I needed to trust my instincts, my *knowin.'* It was one of the best decisions I ever made, a difficult pill to swallow, but the pill was only leftover leading lady ego. That decision was to give me a thirty-year run in character roles in Hollywood.

Two commercials came up quickly, and an industrial film. Then I was sent to Paramount Studios to audition for the popular series, *Love, American Style.* The role was that of the pregnant sister of hero Bill Bixby. Bill was yet to become *The Incredible Hulk,* but had done *The Courtship of Eddie's Father* and *My Favorite Martian (*with my New York friend, Ray Walston.*)*

220

Who better to play a pregnant sister than me? For my audition, I added hiccups to the pregnant lady, something from my own life-experience. The producer laughed, and I got the job.

On a break during filming, I confessed to Bill Bixby that I missed my children.

"Bring them here! You're going to do just fine in Hollywood, Pat." The next weekend I flew to New York and returned with seven-and-a-half-year old Kate and four-year old Penelope. They settled into The Montecito with me, spending every day playing in the big pool with their new friend, a little boy from the touring company of *Oliver.* His name was Bobby, Robert Downey, Jr. He was eight or nine years old then, displaying all the talent and presence later seen in the movie actor he became. Robert Downey, Jr. is a genius actor, his *Chaplin* one of the more brilliant performances extant on film.

We missed Art, who had decided he still wasn't ready for California. He was calling west coast friends, wanting to join us later with established business connections. We spoke with him daily. He seemed enthusiastic about all of us reuniting in a new California home.

"You guys are trailblazers," he said. "I'll be along soon!" I knew leaving New York was a struggle for Art. He needed plenty of latitude.

Gus Schirmer settled into a little house on Orange Grove Avenue in Old Hollywood. The girls and I visited him frequently. He had several adorable dogs they played with, and Gus loved having children around. He cooked extravagant gourmet dishes for them, things they'd never eat at home, but devoured out of love for him. They drew pictures for him, and when he had them framed to hang on his wall, they were thrilled and impressed.

One day Jack Molthen called. "Remember your meeting with the head of CBS casting last week? Ethel Winant?" Jack asked. Of course I remembered. I'd met with Ethel for a general interview, and liked her immediately. She was a down-to-earth, reality-based lady.

"Well," Jack continued, "she thinks you're perfect to replace Patricia Neal in a television series version CBS is planning of *The Homecoming.* The rest of the cast will remain intact, but Pat Neal doesn't feel up to doing a series."

The Homecoming, a lovely made-for-TV movie about a family in Depression-era Virginia. The series would be called *The Waltons.*

The girls, "Melpy" (L) and Katy Bee(R), and I roughed it in Hollywood without Art.

The producer, writer Earl Hamner, Ethel Winant, and Pam Polifroni, the casting director for the series, were present for my interview the next day. I recognized a few actresses in the lobby at the casting call, among them former Miss America Lee Meriwether, later of *Barnaby Jones* fame. Mostly the interview consisted of conversation. I was asked about my family, my children. This kind of interview was right up my alley. The producers asked me to return on the next day, which I thought strange, for it was a Saturday. That day they had a camera rolling for yet another interview.

Two days later, on Monday, *The Waltons* began filming its first episode, with Michael Learned in the Patricia Neal role of Olivia Walton. Ethel Winant had explained to me earlier that things moved rapidly in television. *Wow—ain't that the truth,* I thought when I heard the news. I shrugged it off as just another lost role, for I had no idea *The Waltons* would become the historic television series it became, and Olivia a life-changing role for a non-star actress.

A year or so later I attended a small New Year's Eve gathering and was reintroduced to Pam Polifroni.

"Oh, I already know Pat," she told our host. "Patricia Wilson was one of the last two actresses we considered for Olivia. Casting Olivia was one of the toughest decisions made for *The Waltons.*"

It was the first I knew how close I'd come to being a TV star my first few weeks in California. Today I can't see how anyone, including me, could have been a better Olivia Walton than Michael

Learned. But it is one of those life events, or non-events, however you look at it, that I ponder now and then. How would it have changed my life, and the lives of my husband and children, had I played Olivia on *The Waltons*?

The way things worked out, I can only imagine.

scene ii: Later that summer, 1972, Re-enter Hal Prince and Follies, Hollywood and Beverly Hills

Journal, August 16, 1972: Art arrived in California, and is already restless. Should we hang onto our New York apartment? He threatens to go back. I must face that possibility. I bought a pretty new nightgown and he went into a rage—accused me of only wanting him here for sex. Dear God! I'm so confused! What's wrong with our marriage? I can't seem to do anything right.

Journal, August 18, 1972: They're bringing Follies to open in L.A. with the original New York cast, and I'll stand by for Dorothy Collins in the role of Sally! Funny—they turned me down in New York for Broadway as too young. Guess I've aged! And I'm right to get into character roles. Whatever. A chance to work with Hal Prince again! And to sing Stephen Sondheim's gorgeous score. A blessing.

We needed a more permanent place to live than the Montecito Hotel, within a good school district. Art delayed his threatened return to New York. "I want to know where my children will be living," he said. I could only ride the emotional roller-coaster with him.

We found a bright two bedroom apartment in a Spanish fourplex on South Elm Drive in Beverly Hills, across the street from The Beverly Vista School. I bought a new white Datsun station wagon, and turned in the rental car I'd been driving all summer. The church on the corner had a nursery school for Penelope, a year too young for kindergarten at Beverly Vista. The children skipped up and down the sidewalk, delighting in the freedom they felt in the dappled sunshine of Elm Drive.

ABC and Martin Tahse Productions hired me to play Paul Revere's wife in a musical special that would be completed before *Follies* rehearsals began.

"I'd better stay here until you finish filming," Art said. "You'll need help with the children."

Art took over one of the bedrooms in our new Beverly Hills apartment as an office. I still loved my husband dearly, and believed that being with the children and me was what he needed. But on reflection, I should have asked Art see a marriage counselor with me then.

"Might as well sell a coupla scripts while I'm here," he said.

"Wonderful, Art," I said. "But you can't smoke marijuana in this room. It's too close to the kids." After that Art began taking long walks, disappearing for long periods of time.

The floor in the children's room was worn, and I made a deal with the landlord to lower the rent if I refinished it myself. I painted it cornflower blue, then stenciled it in red-and-yellow flowers. To outsiders, we were a happy family settling into a new California life. I fervently prayed that was how it would be. Then I set about earning a living for all of us.

Follies opened the new Shubert Theater in Century City late that summer. The theater was barely finished when we began rehearsing, with piles of construction debris in the parking structure and crews frantically working to finish up the beautiful interior. All involved were certain the visual beauty of the show *Follies,* plus the appeal of film actors in stage roles, would play well in Los Angeles. Stars Alexis Smith, Dorothy Collins, Gene Nelson, Yvonne DeCarlo and John McMartin settled in for what everyone anticipated would be a long run, at least a year or more.

As a stand-by, my job was to rehearse before Wednesday and Saturday matinees on the Shubert stage, then phone in each night before the performance to make sure Dorothy Collins was present in her dressing room. It left me available for TV and film auditions and daytime work, with the understanding that I'd be free by seven-thirty each evening. In the beginning it was also part of my job after day-long rehearsals to watch Dorothy Collins perform each night. I was rushing home to Beverly Hills after rehearsals to cook dinner, help the girls with homework, bathe them, and then rush back to the theater.

"What is this, a twenty-four hour job?" Art was in his snarling mode.

"Sally's a difficult role, Art. I need to prepare myself in case Dorothy can't go on."

"Well, I don't like it. I can't baby-sit kids while you're off with your musical comedy pals. I have work to do."

Off with my musical comedy pals? My work now wasn't considered work.

Rehearsing the Stephen Sondheim score and James Goldman book for *Follies* both challenged and invigorated me. My self-imposed exile from theater rebounded in enthusiasm for this extravagant show and complex character. Sally, a one-time dancer, is restless in her marriage, and longs to re-live her youth with her old flame, the man she's dreamed about for twenty years. She is ultimately rejected, disillusioned, and borders on madness, singing Stephen Sondheim's haunting ballad, *Losing My Mind*.

Kate and Penelope, ages four-and-a-half and eight, went with me to the theater and watched me rehearse every Saturday morning. Then we'd lunch together and return to the theater for the matinee. The stage manager added my daughters' names to the sign-in sheet, so they'd feel like part of the company. They solemnly signed in every time they attended, then sat in the theater with me during performances, mesmerized by Florence Klotz's beautiful costumes and the Sondheim score, as I took notes on Sally's onstage blocking. Not once did the girls complain.

Unfortunately, the Los Angeles opening-night critics did. The sound system broke down in the middle of the opening performance. Though it was quickly fixed, the mishap falling short of disaster, *Follies* seemed a problem for youth-conscious Los Angeles, which didn't want to be reminded of growing older, or of the death of innocence and illusion, serious themes presented in *Follies*. We closed in a month, on the first of October, 1972, to the dismay of thousands of its loyal fans. It has since become almost a cult favorite, and I'm proud of even a short association with *Follies*. It, like *Carousel*, is a masterpiece in the world of musical theater.

scene iii: Later in 1972, Enter a Hollywood Agent—and new friend

"If I had your opportunities, we'd be rolling in money," Art said. Each jab from my once-supportive husband poked another hole in my self-esteem. My batting average for an actress was high, but Art's growing insecurities made him more and more critical of everything I did. Or didn't do.

My manager, Gus, called after *Follies* closed. "Patty, I'll oversee your career, but we have to find you a hands-on agent," he said. "Sandy Duncan is very hot now. I'm needed with her all the time." Actress Sandy Duncan, also Gus's client, took off in Hollywood films and TV in 1972.

An actor friend told me about Pat Amaral, an old-fashioned Hollywood agent. Pat personally made rounds every day, visiting the studios, schmoozing with producers, directors and casting people. She was respected for her ability to spot talented actors and match them with potential roles. Her limited number of clients usually became her friends. She told me when I called that she couldn't take on anyone new, "But drop a picture by when you're in the neighborhood," she said. Her office was in the Bob Hope complex on Riverside Drive in Toluca Lake.

Pat was sitting at her desk when I walked into her office the next day. I introduced myself, handed her my picture, and turned to leave.

"Wait, would you like tea?" she asked. "I've just made a pot." We chatted over Earl Grey for the next half-hour. I thanked her, thinking how much I liked her. Like Ethel Winant, she was a no-nonsense, no-Hollywood–b.s. kind of lady. "Why did you wait ten years to come to Hollywood after you left *Fiorello!?*" she asked. "You'd have done well here."

"My husband hates California." Pat Amaral looked surprised, then nodded.

The next day I received a call from Bob LaSanka, the casting director of Universal Pictures.

"Patricia, I have a small role in a new picture we're doing with Paul Newman and Robert Redford. Could you come to my office today to discuss it with me?" I certainly could.

"How did you find me?" I asked Bob LaSanka. The hills behind Universal Studios were turning lavender in the late afternoon light, his office window a frame for the beautiful scene.

"Pat Amaral dropped your picture on my desk. She says we'd be lucky to get you."

"But Pat isn't my agent!"

LaSanka laughed. "Maybe she is and you don't know it!"

Journal, September 12, 1972: Universal Studios. I've wandered around, looking at cute bungalows that were once star dressing rooms. I'm as movie-struck as a teenager!

Two weeks later Bob LaSanka called again. "Can you report to the studio for wardrobe tomorrow morning at eight? You're hired. You begin shooting next week."

The Sting, even in a small role, was a nice way to begin in Hollywood. It's a film classic, and I smile when another residual check, thirty-odd years later, appears in my mail box. My role began a client/agent friendship with Pat Amaral, and a Hollywood career as a character actress that has lasted now for over thirty-five years.

scene iv: 1972-1973, Beverly Hills

Journal, October 31, 1972: A first Halloween in California for the kids. Boy, they are cute! Even Art is enjoying himself. He seems happier.

"Mom! I'm a gypsy!" Kate, joyful in a sequin-bedecked broomstick skirt and head scarf, with colorful beads around her neck.

"And I'm a butterfly!" Penelope, in a black leotard with chiffon scarves attached to her arms as wings, and pipe cleaners as antennae. *Yes, Momma, my mitzvahs.*

Max Hodge, who had written and directed the Oldsmobile show I had done with Bob Fosse years earlier, was one of the friends I contacted when I moved to California. Max produced *The Batman* series, and later was story editor for a spin-off from *The Waltons* called *Apple's Way.* He was a bachelor, and gladly accepted a dinner invitation. Over coffee, he invited Art to write a script for an episode of *Apple's Way.* When the outline Art submitted was rejected by producers as too metaphysical (ironically, it carried the same theme as a later Clint Eastwood movie, *Pale Rider)* Max offered to help revise and re-pitch his idea. Art refused.

"I knew I'd be too much for this stupid town," he said. It was a complaint and a theme that was repeated many times.

Gus announced a booking for me on *The Mary Tyler Moore Show.* Mary's show exemplified everything I wanted from a California career. The regular cast members had steady, well-paying jobs in one place, with regular hours and time for family.

Valerie Harper and I had met several years earlier in New York. "Do these producers know who you are?" she asked. I said I reckoned they didn't, since my life and career had changed considerably since *Fiorello!*

During dress rehearsal, as the scene I was to do was being set up, Valerie sat in the audience with producer/writers Jim Brooks and Allen Burns. I stood under the lights, waiting to rehearse. From the bleachers, Valerie sang out: "I'm Gon-na Mar-ry the Ver-y Next Man!" She explained herself to the cast and crew: "This lady was a big Broadway star when I was a chorus girl! Treat her right!"

"I remember, too," Ed Asner whispered. "I was off-Broadway in *The Beggar's Opera* then."

Not always are actors in Hollywood so good to each other. For a while, a story line was considered for me on the *Mary Tyler Moore Show*, as a possible love interest for Ed Asner's Lou Grant. It didn't happen, but I returned several times over the next three years, casting director Pam Dixon making me a part of a recurring stock company of players in Mary's timeless series.

One day writer Ed Weinberger called me in to look over a script he'd written for a new female character. He wanted to hear it read aloud.

"Gosh, Ed," I said to him, "This is Betty White to the fingernails!"

"I kind of thought so, too," Ed said.

"Well, for what my opinion is worth, she's perfect for this role."

And she was. Betty White was hilarious as Sue Ann Niven, the ambitious cooking lady.

Mary's show was taped at the CBS valley studio. I was called for an audition for another show at that studio, on a day Penelope was out of school. Art was gone, on one of his long walks, so I took my small daughter with me to the reading. I raced across the parking lot with Penelope by the hand, her legs pumping hard to keep up with me.

"*Hey!*" shouted a voice behind us. It was Ed Asner. He knelt beside Penelope, face-to-face with the little girl.

"I know your Mommy, but I don't know *your* name. Mine's Ed."

"I'm 'Melpy,'" said my daughter. She was completely comfortable, unusual for her when it came to strangers. "I couldn't used to say 'Penelope,' so I called myself 'Melpy.' It stuck on me," she explained. Ed smiled and stood up.

"I spotted you from the makeup trailer," he said, "Great kid. Gotta get back." He walked away.

"Bye, Melpy!"

Why was this incident significant to me? In that moment, Ed Asner made me feel as if I were part of the inner circle of popular television, secure in a new Hollywood career. Art's undermining of my every move at home was seriously eroding my self-esteem, far more than I realized. I dodged his verbal assaults as best I could, hoping to keep our family together. My motives were good. But the simple caring of others like Ed Asner so contrasted the growing coldness in my home, I began to see how seriously I could be affected by what amounted to abuse from my husband.

scene v: Early 1973, Re-enter Johnnie Ray, Hollywood

Journal, February 14, 1973: Our tenth wedding anniversary. Art doesn't remember. The kids home from school with Valentines, but he's clueless. I should be used to it, but I'm not. I'm hurt. Jack Molthen wants to know if I'd like to work in a new club, The Cabaret. It might open up opportunities for the TV season.

Art warmed to the possibility of my playing a club again. I opened in April, with supportive friends appearing on opening night: Shirley Jones and her husband Jack Cassidy, Tom and Jean Bosley, Ethel Winant, Pat Amaral, Gus, and Sandy Duncan. I was so nervous I fell downstairs as I made my way from the dressing room to the stage.

As in The Penthouse and Bon Soir in New York, I interspersed special material and song characterizations with straight singing. The theme of the act was again based on *The Clown*. Was the material out-of-sync with Hollywood audiences? Doris Day I wasn't. I worried, but people trouped in to see something different, and I was held over. Shirley Jones came back four or five times, with a different group each time. The reviews were 95% positive. The only reviewer who didn't understand the concept of the act was from the erudite *Los Angeles Times*. He was the opera critic, slumming, and reviewed my act as if it should have been the re-working of *Aida*. Thankfully, his review didn't hinder audiences from coming to see me.

One night I saw a familiar figure sitting alone at the bar. It was Johnnie Ray. We'd lost track of each other during my *Fiorello!* run. He'd moved west to a farm in Oregon, and though he still toured, had become reclusive in his private life. Johnnie was basically a farm kid, and a mutual friend told me he'd become disillusioned with his celebrity.

"I want to catch up on your life!" Johnnie said. "Did you marry your friend from Ohio State, the real estate guy?"

"No, John, but I'm married. I have two wonderful little girls."

"Oh! I can't wait to meet them, and your husband! Is he here?"

I knew that Art had handled Johnnie's career for many years. I didn't know the circumstances of their parting, but I knew it had been unpleasant. I'd asked Art about what happened.

"He's your friend, Patty, you don't need to know. Johnnie overstepped a boundary," Art said. "He was all wound up with his success. He believed his own publicity. I warned him his bubble could burst, but there was no stopping him from doing something really out of line. So I had to burst the bubble." That was all Art would say then about Johnnie Ray. The sadness I'd seen in Art's face at other times once again overtook his dimples, and I was sorry I'd asked. My friend and my husband shook hands that night, but the look on Johnnie's face told me I'd never see him again. I tried many times to get in touch with him at the numbers he left with me, but after that night Johnnie Ray never returned my calls.

scene vi: 1973-1974, Re-enter sadness, Beverly Hills

Journal, June 17, 1973: I toast myself with a glass of wine as I turn 44. Calls from Donn and Joan and David, adorable handmade cards from Katy Bee and Melpy. But Art has forgotten again. I'll survive. He is here, we're together, and a family.

Before we left New York, Art talked to an editor from Simon and Schuster about the project he had earlier begun for Lyle Stuart Publishing. It was his personal story, how a poor street kid from Brooklyn became protector of celebrities such as Doris Duke, the tobacco heiress, who hired him to keep her name *out* of the papers; and creator of stars like Ella Fitzgerald and Johnnie Ray. The book Simon and Schuster wanted was a rags-to-riches, celebrity-filled autobiography. "All I need is five chapters and your resume to sell it, Art," the editor said.

In spite of the long hours Art spent behind the closed doors of his office, I knew he hadn't worked on the advance chapters requested by the editor. Writing about the government secrets he carried was what *called* to Art, but I knew he also feared writing about those parts of his life.

"So write the celebrity stuff! That's what they want! Call it 'Scabby'," I laughed, invoking his boyhood nickname, a result of the street-fighting that left him with chronic healing wounds when he was a kid. "Metaphors for the wounds of your life! Very literary!" Simon and Schuster liked the title "Hey, I've got time on my hands, with Kate and Penelope both in school now. Can I help you with those chapters?" I asked.

"Sure, okay," said Art. We worked all night. He typed; I read and commented as he turned out pages. The next day I overheard Art on a phone call to one of his few remaining public relations friends in New York, "Patty stayed up all night with me, Les! She's a great partner!" My heart almost burst open.

Journal, September 15, 1973: Are Art and I back on track? God, I miss who we used to be!

Journal, September 24, 1973: I'm really tired. Fell asleep in the dentist's chair today. Embarrassing. Also feeling nauseous. Just checked my waistline. Oh, dear God!

I'd be forty-five on my next birthday, and I was going to have another baby. It was hardly good timing. But the words in my journal are happy: *Imagine! Another mitzvah, Momma!* My kid brother Donn had been her late-in-life joy. I loved my children. There would be a way to make room for another. *Wouldn't there, God?* I phoned my friend and OB-GYN in New York.

"Fred, I don't know how I'll tell Art!"

"We have four now, and the last two weren't planned," he said. "Tell Art I can't imagine life without them." I laughed. Fred had been a confirmed bachelor when he delivered Kate nine years earlier.

On Thanksgiving Eve, I put the girls to bed, and stood in the kitchen preparing pumpkin pie for the holiday. Art was reading in the living room. Pain tore through me.

"Call an ambulance, Art! Hurry!"

The young resident leaned over my hospital bed to answer questions.

"You'll be okay, Mrs. Franklin." The young woman hesitated before answering the last thing I asked. Then: "Your baby was a boy."

scene vii: Summer, 1974, Enter Gene Kelly, Los Angeles and Dallas, TX

"Patty," Gus said. "You're wanted to co-star with Gene Kelly in a tour of *Take Me Along.* They tried to cast the role in New York, but couldn't find anyone they like."

"No audition, Gus? Doesn't Gene Kelly want to meet me?"

"Nope, they showed him your current picture, and he remembered you on Broadway, so he's approved you. It's a done deal. Just say yes. It's a limited thirteen-week tour, with two weeks of rehearsal in Dallas. You'll meet Kelly and the rest of the company to rehearse there on June 5th. This could boost your film and TV work, Pat. You'll be back in time for the new TV season. Pat Amaral and I will run ads in the trade papers. I hope you'll accept!"

The call had reached me in Century City Hospital, where Kate and Penelope were recovering from tonsillectomies performed that morning. I touched the cheeks of my still-groggy children. Art returned from lunch in the hospital cafeteria. I relayed the news.

"We're almost broke again, Art, and we're facing hiatus. The studios are closed down until August. This is a gift from God. We could save a lot of money over the summer."

"Then I guess you'll have to take it." My husband looked grim.

Penelope blew a bubble in her sleep. I smoothed her hair. "It'll be a month before I leave. I'll be here to see the girls through their recuperation."

"And then what?"

"I want them with me."

"How will you rehearse and get through an opening with them around?" It was decided that I'd go to Dallas alone, to rehearse and open *Take Me Along*. The girls would join me in St. Louis, the second city on the tour.

On the night of June third, I put my daughters to bed. They snuggled in under yellow-and-blue patchwork quilts, Kate in the prized top bunk, Penelope underneath. Daughter-in-law Sharon, Art's son Jeff's wife, kept an eye on them while Art and I went to Century City Mall. I reached for his hand as we strolled from store to store, selecting rehearsal clothes, T-shirts and soft slacks to pack into a waiting suitcase. He moved away from me. We passed the Shubert Theater, where I'd opened in *Follies*. "I wish we were rehearsing and opening here, instead of Dallas!" Art was silent. We stopped in Clifton's Cafeteria for a late supper. I sat across the table from my husband, reminded of the day we'd met at The Spindletop in New York, thirteen years earlier. *Why had I put unappetizing meatloaf on my tray?* I picked at crestfallen fresh fruit.

"This is a wrench, Art. Please, while I'm gone, work on the book for Simon and Schuster! I can't be on the road anymore, leaving you and the children." Art said nothing.

That night I was aware that the place next to me in our bed was empty. I vaguely heard Art's heavy shoes thud-thudding around the apartment. Office, kitchen, hallway, living room. Office-kitchen-hallway-living room.

The alarm rang at six. I shuffled into the kitchen and put our ancient tea kettle on the stove. Art was leaning against the sink, still wearing his clothes from the night before.

"I'll have our tea ready in a minute." I put my arms around his waist, and laid my head on his chest. *God, I loved the smell of him.* He pushed me away.

"I don't want any damn tea." His eyes were cold and blazing at the same time.

"I'll take you to the airport this morning," he said. "But I won't be here when you get back. I hope you enjoy your new escapade."

"*Escapade, Art?* That's what you call this going-away that's tearing me to pieces? An *escapade?*" Something inside of me, far beneath the scruffy robe I pulled over my nightgown, grew small and cold. It was my heart, this time shriveling. "Someone has to feed this family, and it looks like it's always going to be me!" I moved the tea kettle to an unlit side burner.

Art's lips twisted into a bitter smile. The dimples at the side of his mouth were dark, ugly ditches. "Don't hand me any girly shit about how you've given me the best years of your life!"

I didn't feel girly. I felt a hundred years old. Dried-out skin sagging from powdery bones. My teeth started to chatter. I went into the bathroom to throw up.

At the airport, I scanned the boarding area of my Dallas flight for signs of Gene Kelly. *Please, God, let him be on a different flight.* My face was ravaged by tears and unspoken anger. I didn't have the strength to be charming. I wanted to get to Dallas and into my hotel room to have a private nervous breakdown. Rehearsals for *Take Me Along* began the next morning.

"There's your new *leading man*," Art said, his innuendo inescapable. "Don't you want to go over and say hello? Might as well get an early start!" Gene Kelly was standing off to one side with two other men, waiting to board the plane that would take us to Dallas. I enlisted the help of a sympathetic stewardess. She waited as I kissed my daughters one last time, then pre-boarded me onto the flight, hidden under a scarf and sun glasses.

scene viii: Summer, 1974, Re-enter the leading lady, Dallas, Texas

Journal, June 4, 1974: Arrived in Dallas exhausted. A devastating day. Is my marriage over? The paranoid man I left in LA today isn't the man I married. Thank God Sharon is watching the kids while

I'm gone. It's 9:50 PM, rehearsals less than twelve hours away. I must try to sleep.

The telephone rang like a Chihuahua bark in my ear.

"Patricia, this is Gene Kelly. I'm on the floor above you. May I come down to say hello?" I splashed cold water on my face and threw on my prettiest pink summer shift. This was, after all, a star among stars, and I was his new leading lady. He appeared at my door in a white polo shirt and chinos, a can of beer in each hand. A knowin'— something was wrong.

"Patricia," Gene Kelly said, "I'm sorry we didn't have a chance to meet before." He handed me a beer. I took it. My stomach flopped. *Well, might as well know now, before rehearsals begin, if I'm going to be replaced. A good thing my contract is secure. At least they'll have to pay me off.*

"Tom Bosley tells me you're a better singer now than ever," said Mr.-American-In-Paris. "But you're not a dancer. Are you, Patricia?" He settled himself on the bland, hotel-beige striped sofa. I settled opposite him on the bland, hotel-beige striped chair.

He knows damn well I'm not a dancer. "No, I'm not, Mr. Kelly." I hoped to halt the axe I sensed was about to fall. I evoked the name of my famous choreographer friend: "Bob Fosse tells me I move well. I've had training, but I don't classify myself as a dancer." I took a sip of beer. Gene Kelly sipped at his.

"Well, Patricia." The star cleared his throat. "I want to show you a few dancer's tips on—a-hem-m-mm—on how you can appear *shorter* onstage!"

So that was the problem. Gene Kelly was of average height, and feared my five-foot-six-and-a-half-inch stature might make him appear less-than-tall. I was silently furious with the man. *This tap dancer! My life is falling apart, and Gene Kelly doesn't want to look short! Ham actor!* I needed this job. But Gene Kelly and I needed good chemistry between us to play the mature lovers in *Take Me Along.* If the star was ill-at ease with my height, I was expendable.

Taking a big breath, and a *very* big chance, I said in a firm, respectful tone, "Does my height concern you, Mr. Kelly? I'm quite a good method actress." Another breath. *"How tall do you want me to be?"*

Gene Kelly's eyes widened, then disappeared into the crinkly half-moons of his familiar Irish grin. He laughed out loud, stood, and clinked his beer can against mine.

"We'll get along fine, Pat. You'll look great onstage, and that'll make me look good. Call me Gene. They've got a terrific pool here—wanna go swimming?"

That's what we did.

scene ix: The next morning, June, 1974, A Dallas rehearsal hall

The cast, assembling early the next day for rehearsal, made innocuous small talk to cover first-day nerves. Gene Kelly put everyone at ease. He was outgoing and energetic, endearing himself to the cast and imbuing the role of Sid with Irish charm. Knowing his audiences would be disappointed not to see him dance, Gene added choreography to the production. He interpolated a Robert Merrill piece called *Flings* from another of Merrill's Broadway shows, *New Girl In Town*, as a big second-act solo. Sixty-two year old Gene Kelly, in every performance of *Flings*, did the athletic stretch-bounce across the stage on all fours that he was famous for in films. Audiences went wild.

Gene and I had many scenes and three songs together. In my favorite of our songs, Sid suggestively reminds Lily of their young romance. They are now mature. She is a spinster living with her brother's family since she broke her engagement to Sid years earlier. Sid, the charming reprobate, reminds her of all they had together in their youth, and the joys they'd assuredly savor in their maturity. He makes the Victorian spinster blush. Their duet, appropriately titled *I Get Embarrassed*, concluded with a wild chase around the stage parlor furniture, ending with the two of them laughing and breathless together in an arm chair. The audiences whooped and hollered as our chase around the stage escalated, and Gene and I pushed the envelope a little further with each performance. One night I stumbled as I ran around the end of the love seat placed at center stage. Gene grabbed at me to keep me from falling, and as I fell backwards onto the love seat, he fell on top of me. The audience howled, thinking Sid had maneuvered spinster Lily into a compromising position.

"Milk it, kid!" Gene whispered, so I shrieked appropriately, allowing my long costume skirt to fly into the air and expose knee-length Victorian bloomers. During another performance, I hauled up the long costume skirt and petticoats and kicked Gene in the seat of the pants. Gene faked Sid's surprise, because we were ready for almost anything the other would do in the context of the scene. Gene Kelly and I both carried personal sadness that summer. Abandoning ourselves to the frisky fun of *I Get Embarrassed* had a healing effect on each of us.

Sid and Lily share a long embrace in an arm chair when the chase finally ends. Gene's comedic choreography landed him in my lap for the embrace, rather than I in his. It was a perfect capper to the scene. As the audience applause and laughter died down, Gene jumped from my lap, blew me a kiss and exited up the stage staircase, leaving me, as Lily, alone in her parlor. The lights and music softened, and I sang *We're Home*, a sweet ballad-soliloquy in which Lily envisions her happy future with Sid.

There was a transitional moment needed from the wild chase and embrace to the tender ballad. I was too winded to break into song. I asked conductor Jack Lee to give me a few moments before I arose from the chair to sing. As Lily, alone with her thoughts, I slumped back in the chair, legs askew in long skirts and petticoats, with a huge, vocalized "Phew!" The action was unlike the reserved Lily. The audience guffawed one last time.

"What do you do to get that big laugh when I leave you?" Gene demanded. "Drop your pants?" Actors are always competitive for audience approbation. I only smiled an enigmatic, Mona Lisa smile. The stagehands told me Gene tried to peek through the scenery every night to see what happened in that moment.

Later in our Dallas run, I approached Gene.

"You and I both know I'm not a dancer, Gene, and frankly, it scares me to bring this up, but shouldn't our characters dance together, at least once?"

"Pat, you're right! We should dance together, maybe in the second act. Don't worry. I'll keep it simple." My hotel room phone rang late that night.

Gene and I in Take Me Along. *Look, Ma! I'm dancin'!*

Gene and I laughed a lot, onstage and off. We both needed to.

"I've choreographed a section of *But Yours* for us. I'll pick you up at noon tomorrow to take you to the theater and teach it to you," Gene said.

The song *But Yours* reveals how Sid and Lily have changed over the years. She sings, "I'm a little older, a little gentler, a little wiser, but yours!" They're together, at last. The dance Gene choreographed for us was technically easy, for my sake, and sweetly romantic, for the middle-aged lovers. It enhanced the love story, and, again, our audiences were enthralled. They loved Gene Kelly. He could do no wrong for them, and I was along for the dance. Later, when Gene-as-Sid appears in a drunken scene, reviving Lily's doubts about him, their estrangement is all the more poignant.

The on-again-off-again romance of Sid and Lily is resolved at the end of the musical. Sid is leaving, painfully certain his final episode of drunkenness has finished off a future with Lily. The townsfolk gather on a trolley platform to wave him off, singing a rousing tribute, *So Long, Sid!* The music stops as Lily races onstage, breathless, hat and valise in hand, her hair flying in all directions. Sid is astonished to see her. Stunned silence as the couple stares at each other. Then Lily faces front and softly sings a reprise of the title song:

"Take me a-long! Take me a-long with you!" Sid hops off the train and sweeps her aboard. The trolley chugs offstage (thanks to two healthy stagehands pulling on ropes from the wings) as Lily and Sid embrace. Curtain.

The finale. In Columbus, the embrace became a little more intense.

My favorite review of the summer reflected the poignancy of that scene. It said: *"Miss Wilson is 'Lily'—a beautiful lady whose heart-warming rendition of Take Me Along in the final scene is gentle and meaningful."*

Gene read the review aloud to me. "You're back where you belong, Pat," he said, and I wept as I ran to the ladies room to throw up.

scene x: Summer 1974, Enter the littlest troupers, Dallas

"My children, Bridget and Tim, arrive tomorrow," Gene said. "They'll be touring with us, doing little parts. I didn't want to leave them for the summer. Their mother died last year."

"I read about it, Gene. What a terrible loss for you."

Tim, twelve, and Bridget, who turned ten that June week, joined Gene in Dallas. They were lovely, well-behaved children, unlike the spoiled, monster-progeny of many Hollywood stars. "Gosh," I said when I met them, "they're great kids. They make me miss mine. I won't see my little girls until we get to St. Louis."

"Why can't they come to Dallas? They'd be company for Bridget and Tim," Gene said.

Was it good taste that kept me from sharing my personal problems with Gene, even though we'd become friends? Fear of crossing a professional boundary? Probably. My personal life certainly colored my performance as Lily. I was confused about my role in Art's life, and Lily was confused about hers in Sid's. Yet the character Lily felt about the character Sid as I felt about Art: a star-crossed attraction to an audacious, charismatic man.

Our Dallas opening was a triumph. Bridget Kelly rushed to me when the curtain closed. She was an adorable little girl with huge freckles, looking much like her dad, her brown eyes twinkling and crinkling. Her face shone as she looked up at me, and we hugged tight.

"Hey, Bridget," Gene said, "Cheer up!" He was relieved the first performance was over, an obvious success. The audience had given him a standing ovation.

It was my birthday, but I hadn't mentioned it to anyone. The company milled around, hugging and laughing. I headed for the backstage phone.

"Art, it's me! I thought you'd want to know the opening here in Dallas went well. How are you? How are the girls? What does the doctor say? Are their throats healed?" I was babbling. Conductor Jack Lee passed by. He and Art had known each other in New York. Jack grabbed the phone from my hand, "Art? Hey, you should have seen your wife tonight! She was sensational! She and Kelly are *great* together, the *show* is great! When are you coming to see it?" Thankfully someone swept Jack away. He shoved the phone back in my hand.

"Art?" He'd hung up. I dialed again. "I need to know—have the girls' throats healed okay?"

"They'd be better off if I *cut* their throats," said my husband. He hung up again.

I called my daughter-in-law Sharon.

"The kids are fine, Pat, they're with me."

Director Ed Greenberg, the same Ed Greenberg who'd directed *South Pacific* with the knife-wielding Latin-Lover-Guy years before, was one of the producers of our *Take Me Along* tour. He'd flown in for the Dallas opening. Seeing my old friend, I broke down, telling him what Art had said to me over the phone.

"What's wrong with the man, Pat? Do you think he's capable of hurting the children?"

"No, Ed, I don't. I think he's more likely to hurt himself. God, I'm so scared!"

"Well, send for your kids immediately! They can go into the show with Tim and Bridget Kelly. I'll order costumes for them tomorrow. I'll tell the choreographer to put them in the picnic scene. Then they'll have to be with you in the theater every night. You and Gene can keep an eye on all four kids for the tour."

Journal, June 17, 1974: I'll bless Ed Greenberg forever. I'm 45 today, and my best gift will be to have the children with me.

I slept very little. The reviews in the morning paper were raves for Gene Kelly, and I was happy for him. I'd been worried that I hadn't performed onstage for a few years, but for Gene, it had been a thirty-three-year hiatus. He'd confessed to me that he doubted his decision to do even a limited tour at his age. But watching him from the wings on opening night, he was magical. He charmed our audiences wherever we went.

I phoned Kate and Penelope's pediatrician early, to be assured the girls were well and could travel. Then I called our company manager and asked his help in getting them to Dallas. Last, I phoned Sharon.

"But Pat, their clothes...I need to do a laundry!" I knew her protests meant she was going to miss the girls.

"Dump everything in a bag, I'll get it done here. Just get them on that plane this afternoon, Sharon." I met my bedraggled little girls at the Dallas airport later that day. I couldn't stop hugging and kissing them. I rushed them to the hotel for a bath, then out for a swim in the pool. There was time enough to indoctrinate them into the cast.

Gene's secretary appeared at the pool. Kate and Penelope had already made friends with the Kelly children.

"Gene needs to see you," Lois said. "He's waiting in the suite. Can you go up right away? I'll watch the children." I was reluctant to leave the girls, but I knew it had to be important for Gene to ask to see me.

"Pat," he said as he opened the door, "I want to go down to the pool and meet your girls, but first I need you to do something for me. I should have done this right after my wife died, but I wasn't thinking clearly. Would you witness my new will? I have someone coming up to notarize your signature."

"Of course! Gosh, Gene—you've made me think—" I wondered what would happen to my children now, if anything happened to me.

Gene interrupted me, his voice gruff. "Just get it done," he said.

scene xi: Summer 1974, Re-enter a family En Tour, St. Louis

"Look at those little hambones out there!" Gene Kelly grinned. He and I stood backstage, watching from the wings as our children romped through *Take Me Along*'s picnic scene. Six-year old Penelope, serious and responsible, was in her Victorian costume dress, awaiting her entrance cue, fifteen minutes ahead of time at every performance. Kate and Bridget Kelly, by now fast friends, were just as likely to be off making mischief somewhere as they were to be awaiting their entrances. Many a picnic scene in *Take Me Along* played without them.

Bessie, Gene's nanny/housekeeper, called early one day, wanting the girls to come to the Kelly suite to have breakfast with Bridget. Penelope returned to our apartment, distressed.

"Momma!" she exclaimed. "Mr. Kelly just got up, and Momma! All his hair fell out last night!" I couldn't wait to tell Gene how worried six -year old Penelope was when she first saw him without his toupee.

Take Me Along was a popular show, and we were inundated with requests for newspaper, TV, and radio interviews. That Gene couldn't do them all was a Godsend for me. I got the spillover. Along with performing and taking care of my children, the public relations work kept me blessedly busy, unable to dwell on Art and the future. Everywhere we went, we were invited to press parties. In Dallas, we met the Dallas Cowboys NFL team. It was fun to talk to them, particularly Lee Roy Jordan. At another event in Dallas Gene hosted a screening of the just-released film, *That's Entertainment!* As members of the cast, our children were often

Surrounded by kids! Bridget Kelly (L), Penelope and me (C), Kate (R) Singer Carol Trigg, (BG) helped keep the girls focused onstage.

invited to join us, making it convenient for Gene and me to attend social events. On other occasions, when Gene and I were invited without the children, Nancy Fox, the ingenue of the *Take Me Along* company, was happy to stay with Kate and Penelope. On hiatus from her TV series, *Temperatures Rising,* Nancy became like a sister to the girls. She wasn't much older than the children, and they adored her.

One of the TV interviews I was asked to do was in Cincinnati, on the popular Nick Clooney Show. I'd been in high school with Nick's sisters, Rosemary and Betty, and Nick and I talked about our families. His young son showed Kate and Penelope around the station. The girls confessed to crushes on the young man, though it would be twenty years before George Clooney surfaced as an international heartthrob on television's *E.R.*

The children and I couldn't wait to get to the Ohio leg of our tour. We'd be with family. My big brother David, now divorced, lived in Cincinnati. Younger brother Donn and his wife, Joan, were in Columbus, where we all anticipated our reunion. But David, playing hooky from his job, appeared the afternoon of our arrival in our first Ohio stop, Dayton, just as we were leaving the motel for orchestra rehearsal. I was comforted and happy to see my big brother. Kate and Penelope all but mauled their adored teddy bear-uncle. He, a musician, was thrilled to be able to go to orchestra rehearsal with us. Gene Kelly knew every instrument in every dance orchestration, and carefully rehearsed the musicians personally. Dissatisfied with the harmonies in a certain section, he asked for some of the strings to drop out. David couldn't get over his musical skill.

"The guy is brilliant!" he said. Spotting me with my brother, Gene took a moment to come off the stage to greet him. "I thought Gene Kelly was supposed to be such an egomaniacal sonovabitch," David said.

"Not in my experience, Davey. Maybe he's mellowed. I didn't know him before." I told David I'd once complimented Gene on his straight acting in the film, *Inherit The Wind.*

"So what did he say?"

"He said, 'I wanted to hide under the seat when I saw that film! I walked like a damn ballet dancer, turn-out and all!'"

"Well," David said. "there go the man's credentials as a megalomaniac!"

I knew David would ask the question on the minds of everyone in my family.

"What's the scoop? Is your marriage over or not?"

"I wish I knew."

"Well, to hell with Art, Sis. You're still damned attractive. I see the way men look at you—Gene Kelly, even—!"

"Spoken like a loving brother, Davey. I wish it were that simple."

Donn and Joan appeared on our closing night in Dayton to drive the girls and me to Columbus. We would stay with them in their beautiful Tudor home in the Arlington suburb of Columbus during the next weeks of our tour. The girls and I were not in a dreary motel, but in the loving arms of our family.

"Let's show 'em in your old hometown tonight, Pat!" Gene said at rehearsal. "Say that prayer of yours extra-loud, for both of us." To my amazement, in that night's opening performance, Gene didn't fake our embrace in the finale. Our kiss was long, lingering, and full on the lips. "That was for Columbus," he whispered in my ear as our trolley chugged offstage. The squeals of delight from my now middle-aged college girlfriends in the audience told me we had, indeed, shown 'em in the old hometown. The kiss made quite an impact.

As I contemplated our return to California after the Ohio performances, my fears about going home grew. I used the excuse of end-of-tour parties to drink—a glass of wine here, a beer there, a Mimosa or a Bloody Mary, then another. Anxieties about the future of my family made me ever-eager to join in glass-tipping, but I rationalized that I still drank far less than most people.

There were offers for us to continue our run, even one to open on Broadway later that fall, and another from the Greek Theater in Los Angeles. But Gene had proven to himself that he could still cut the theatrical mustard. He didn't feel compelled to push himself further.

The principals in the company, those of us who had been together since the beginning of the tour, were invited to Gene's hotel suite for a small gathering on our closing night in Columbus. Gene thoughtfully invited my brothers and sister-in-law, Joan.

"Your family is salt-of-the-earth, Pat," he said. The four children, much to their dismay, were relegated to a separate suite with

Bessie for the evening. We talked quietly and toasted each other until nearly time to take our respective flights the next morning. The evening was bittersweet for me, with a recurring thought:

Life will be different —Art has changed so—what will the changes bring?

Even my usually reliable knowin' didn't prepare me.

scene xii: Late August 1974, Columbus, Back to Beverly Hills

Art's brother, Dave, lived in New Jersey. Before our tour closed in Columbus, I called my brother-in-law.

"Dave, could you possibly come to California now?"

"What for?"

"Something is wrong with Art. Have you talked to him?"

A sudden chilly silence. "Of course there's something wrong with him! He told me you deserted him and ran away with another man, then took the girls!"

"That's not what happened, Dave. I've been working, on tour. The girls were out of school, and they've been traveling with me."

"Oh? Well, I can't get away. You and Art will have to work out your problems without me."

My stomach performed its usual rollover. I knew if anyone would have a positive influence on Art it was his brother. I also knew it would be difficult for his family to accept that Art's interpretation of our family dilemma was not factual. I suspected drugs were contributing to what was so deeply wrong with Art. He was no longer clear-thinking, and the vile utterances he was making were from some dark place I couldn't understand. His problems were beyond my depth, and I'd hoped his brother would be willing to help. Now I'd be returning to California to face my disturbed husband on my own.

Donn and Joan drove the children and me to the Columbus airport after Gene's closing-night party. In the boarding area of our plane, I sat thinking about how Layne Montgomery, my manager Gus's assistant, would be picking the girls and me up at the Los Angeles airport to take us home. Layne had been friendly with Art.

He'll be a buffer if I need one, I told myself, as I spotted Gene carrying two paper cups toward me. Being Gene Kelly, he'd talked the bartender in the closed airport bar to mix a couple of drinks for him.

"Here, I thought we could use these," Gene said, handing me a Bloody Mary. I smiled, remembering he'd brought me a beer at our first meeting. When a stewardess came to pre-board Gene, the celebrity on their flight, he said, "I'd like this girl boarded with me."

"*Girl,* Gene?" I teased him. "You know I'm forty-five."

"Well, you're a girl to me," Gene said. Take-off was delayed for an hour, and the older children and I, restless, wanted to deplane again to stretch our legs. Penelope had fallen asleep.

"You go ahead, Pat, I'll stay with Melpy," Gene said, gathering her onto a pillow in his lap. One more time I wondered why he was considered difficult. Gene Kelly was a kind man.

As my sister-in-law and I hugged goodbye in the Columbus airport, Joan whispered, "Are you sitting with Gene on the plane?"

"Yes."

"Good," she said. "You have your future to think of now." My future. *What did my family expect of me?* That I'd turn my back on my husband? On my marriage if it were salvageable?

For a period of time in their childhood friendship, Kate and Bridget plotted to become sisters through union of their families. They made no secret of it, exaggerating the similarity of their eyes that crinkled when they smiled, thinking it might impress upon someone that they were sisters. But Gene Kelly and I were never more than friends, each of us like a wounded pup kicked into life's corner. The empathy that accompanied that dynamic and our ability to laugh was the basis of our friendship. We were both insomniacs. We'd talk on the phone for hours in the middle of the night, about books, work, the children, and the sweet mystery of life. Penelope remembers waking up, hearing us quietly conversing. But for all of my husband's marijuana-induced paranoia at the time, insisting to all who'd listen that I'd left him for another man, I was never unfaithful to Art. Gene and I weren't lovers, either on our tour of *Take Me Along,* or at any time afterward. God and His angels as my witnesses, that is the truth.

On the day we returned to Beverly Hills, Kate and Penelope skipped up the stairs to our apartment. They waited by the door as Layne put a steadying arm around my shoulder and turned the key in the lock.

Art's paintings, books, clothes, and office equipment were gone. Barney, the little stray dog we'd found and adopted months before, was beside himself to see the children. They tumbled with him on the floor while Layne sat with me at the kitchen table. There was a note:

"The apartment you've always wanted across the hall is vacant. Call the landlord, unless you're moving in with some actor. Good luck, (signed) Art."

Layne shook his head. "My God, Patty, this is tragic."

Art had left our children and me, over an affair that never happened.

ACT SIX

JELLY BEANS

"Up again, old heart!"
Ralph Waldo Emerson

scene i; Autumn and Winter, 1974, Beverly Hills, CA

"I was wondering, Mommy, when is Daddy coming home? Will he know where to find us?" Six-year old Penelope and I were hanging wallpaper in the hallway of our new apartment. The children and I had moved to the larger, brighter apartment across the hall, one that wasn't laden with memories of our family life with their father.

"He'll find us, sweetheart. Do you think about Daddy a lot, Melpy?"

"Yes."

"Do you think about how much you miss him?"

"No. I think about jelly beans instead."

A litany of emotions filled my journals. I was angry, sad, bitter, frustrated, disillusioned, confused, frightened, in love with my husband, in hate with my husband.

Journal, November 28, 1974: Our first Thanksgiving without Art. God, I miss him. But I'm fixing a turkey dinner for the girls and me. Where are you, Art Franklin? What are you doing? I'm drinking too much wine.

Journal, December 24, 1974: The girls and I are in La Jolla for Christmas, invited to Gene and Nancy Klein's beautiful home converted from an old Spanish mission. Peaceful and spiritual. Girls inspect tide pools and gather shells on the beach, I try to meditate and relax. Grateful we didn't have to spend Christmas at home.

Journal, December 31, 1974: Or should I say January 1, 1975? It's past midnight. New Years Eve. Can't celebrate, not even with old friends. I've had a split of champagne by myself, and plan to open another. Thank God the holidays are over.

My comfort was not in parties, nor was it in the arms of another man. The medicine for what ailed me, as Grandma Daisy would have said, was the one constant of my life: *work.* And acting was the work I knew. A stage or set, fellow actors, a script. Lights, camera, action! I, too, had to think about jelly beans. Money. I sat in front of the picture window of our new apartment, staring at the trees of Elm Drive with a glass of wine in my hand, considering my options.

The Fabulous Life of a Happy Has-Been

Maybe I should take the kids back to the warmth and roots of Ohio, to home. But not much acting work there. Back to New York? I'd been careless with the momentum of my stage career. Why had I let myself become yesterday's theatrical mashed potatoes?

Why had I let it happen? Throughout our marriage, I'd believed in Art's achievement in his writing. He'd been successful in everything he touched in business. He would always take care of me and our family. And in spite of my upbringing with a tyrannical father and a saddened mother, I was nonetheless a good, old-fashioned codependent product of my era. Young women today, thanks to the social and cultural changes of the past forty years, are more autonomous in their thinking, more respectful of their talents and choices in developing and utilizing those talents. It doesn't occur to them to turn their lives and options over to a partner, no matter how loving the relationship. Yes, I kept working, but from the moment I married, it was for the common financial good, not for personal achievement. Success was my husband's realm. As confusing as it was to me then, as long as it has taken me to unravel the mystery of codependence, I had to take responsibility for the decisions I'd made, for the "second banana" position I'd relegated myself to, in both life and work.

Luckily for me, the 1970s and '80s in Hollywood were prolific years for episodic TV and TV films. There was good work for us "second bananas." A stable home life for my kids was in my work in television and film, not in my beloved world of live theater. As the character actress I'd declared myself to be, able to shift from comedy to drama, I could grow old with no pretense of youth and beauty; a comfortable old shoe playing the next-door neighbor, the corner shopkeeper, the nurse or nanny. During those years the family jelly bean jar didn't overflow, but it stayed filled. I played, in episodic TV, everything from a distraught mountain mother whose daughter is kidnapped by a witches' coven (*Starsky and Hutch*) to a sex-starved bowling alley hostess with built-in bosoms of huge proportions, a mile-high beehive hairdo, and a foot fetish. It was actor Gerald McRaney's feet I obsessed over in that episode of *Simon and Simon*, and Gerald's reactions made for some very funny scenes. I was a regular on NBC's ill-fated series, *Misfits of Science* (as Mrs. Willis, a telepath who couldn't stop herself from finishing people's sentences), and had running roles in two soap operas: On *Santa Barbara* as witchy, wild-haired Cajun villainess Mabel, and later, on *Days of Our Lives,* as empathetic housekeeper Mrs. Miller. My life consisted of work, the girls growing up, and more work. And mind-boggling, soul-numbing depression.

"Honey," Pat Amaral said over lunch, "word is coming back from industry people that you're looking sad. You're an actress—you have to find a way to keep your personal life from showing in your work."

"Of course you're right, Pat. I'll watch myself, don't worry."

But my agent did worry, as did my friends. And my doctor. Black holes of sleeplessness engulfed me each night. My legs and feet were numb, and simple walking from one room to the next felt as if I were slogging through cement. Thoughts and clarity scrambled away from me.

My speaking voice cracked and shook during a recording session for a commercial, and the session had to be cancelled. I'd raise my voice to call the children in from play, and a croak that would do a bullfrog proud emerged from my throat. Private practice of singing scales mocked me: "Hey, star! What makes you think you can sing anymore?" *Dear God, what will I do?* My voice was our livelihood. And my soul. And I'd lost it. This was codependence rearing its ugly head. *You see?* I cried out to my absent husband and an uncaring world, *I can't exist by myself! I'll lose all I am without you! Even my voice!*

"You're fine physically, Patricia," my internist said. The depression deepened. And then the Face-on-the-Hill smiled at me again.

scene ii: Early 1976, Beverly Hills, CA

"Damn! I'm late!" I snatched up the paper with the casting office address from the car seat next to me, and veered into an open parking lot to study my Thomas Guide. *A helluva time to get lost.* The door of a small stucco building opened onto the parking lot, and a tall, silver-haired man stood in the open doorway. *Good! Help in finding my way!* I got out of the car.

"Excuse me, but I can't seem to find this address. Do you happen to know where it is?"

The man studied the piece of paper I handed him. I peered past him, past the open doorway into the cool tranquility of a church. Warming light from a stained glass window poured over a well-worn oak altar. My audition was forgotten.

"This is a church? Would it be all right if I came in for a moment?" I asked.

"Of course," the man smiled. "Sit down, be peaceful." *Peaceful? Who, me?*

"I think I need to pray," I said to the total stranger.

"Then you should." He smiled. "But remember what St. Ignatius said."

"St. Ignatius? Is this a Catholic church? I'm not a Catholic."

"It doesn't matter. What St. Ignatius said is good advice for anyone. He said, 'Pray as if everything depends on God, but act as if everything depends on you.'"

Long before I'd come to believe there are no accidents in life. In my mind and heart that day, I'd driven into the parking lot of that little church for a reason. I was lost in more ways than one. I needed sanctity, prayer, healing. I needed to stand like a woman and take back my life. The kindly, silver-haired man with the right words to say at the right moment that day was Dr. Bill Hart, the minister of the church. Dr. Hart became my spiritual mentor for the next several years. I joined the congregation, and began attending Dr. Hart's private, eclectic classes on philosophy and theology: Mary Baker Eddy and Christian Science, Joel Goldsmith and The Infinite Way, even Buddhism, Ernest Holmes, and Ralph Waldo Emerson. Here was what I needed. The wisdom of the ages. Involvement in philosophies larger than myself and depression. I told Dr. Hart about the experience I'd had when I was three, about the Face-On-The-Hill my brother David and I had decided was God.

"Maybe I missed my calling. Maybe I should become a minister."

"No, Pat, don't do it," Dr. Hart said. "Don't become a minister. The church is a corporate boondoggle in itself, and dealing with it would negate your idealism, your faith."

"But you deal with it just fine. And you gave up a big corporate career to become a minister!"

"That's just it—I came from corporate life when I realized the ministry was my calling. I already knew how to deal with corporate thinking. For you, your work is your ministry."

"I once heard a famous actress say that we give our souls onstage, that our performances are spiritual gifts to an audience. Remember Helen Hayes? She said that. My mom said it, too."

"I agree with your mother and Helen Hayes. I suspect God does, too."

So there went my calling to the ministry. Nonetheless faith replaced depression. A good thing, for soon I would need all the faith I could muster. Yesterday's mashed potatoes were showing up on my plate once again.

scene iii: Summer, 1978, Re-enter past players, San Francisco, CA

Journal, June 12, 1978: Kate and Penelope are out of school, and we're in San Francisco. I'm doing Carol Burnett's TV film version of Erma Bombeck's book, The Grass Is Always Greener Over The Septic Tank, on location in Marin County. Playing another ditzy lady, Dolly Sullivan, Carol's neighbor who talks to plants. Thank goodness I can use a ditzy voice. Always the clown, laughing on the outside, crying on the inside. But it is wonderful to see Carol again!

When filming finished, Kate and Penelope and I stayed on as tourists in the City-By-The-Bay, visiting Fisherman's Wharf, riding cable cars, eating glorious food. My young daughters were terrific companions.

I monitored our home phone number for messages.

"Pat," said a voice I hadn't heard in years, "it's Tom O'Donnell in Columbus. Please call as soon as you get this." Tom, Rick's fraternity brother and best friend from Ohio State, an usher in our wedding, was now a prominent Ohio attorney.

Rick, my first husband, was terminally ill in a Princeton, New Jersey, hospice.

"He'd like to see you," Tom said. "He's estimated to have only a few weeks—four at the most. Please come." The girls and I flew back to Los Angeles that day, and Art called me at home that night. His voice on the phone was the voice I remembered from our good years together—strong, gentle, kind.

"The girls called to say they're back from San Francisco. They told me about Rick. I'm so sorry, Pat. You'll never forgive yourself if you don't go see him. Jeff and I will watch the girls. If you don't have the money, I have a little saved. I'll buy your ticket. But you must go."

Art and I had spoken only perfunctorily in the four years since he'd left our marriage. He was ghost-writing again, and had formed a business partnership with an attorney, Stan Stern. He'd begun sending money every month, to help with our daughters. The girls saw him as often as they wished. His kindness now, reminiscent of the man I'd loved so intensely, touched me.

The next night I was on a red-eye flight to Newark. There I rented a car to drive to the Princeton hospice where Rick, the love of my very-young life, had only a few weeks to live.

scene iv; July 1978, Re-enter Rick, Princeton, New Jersey

The unfamiliar humidity of a brewing thunderstorm sucker-punched me as I deplaned in Newark the next morning. The storm hovered close on the rental-car drive to Princeton, never quite managing to break free from the blackening sky.

Rick was dozing when I entered his hospice room. I sat by his bed, watching him sleep. The room was painted in cheerful yellow, with a big window overlooking a grove of green-leafed maple trees. There was an insipid paint-by-numbers landscape over the bed. I placed fresh daisies on the bedside table.

When Rick's eyes fluttered open, he smiled and reached for my hand. For the next several days we reminisced: about Ohio State, about the school shows we'd done together, about Columbus and WBNS-TV, about our move to New York. A lifetime ago.

"Well, they say as you're dying, it all flashes before your eyes."

"Oh, God, Rick."

He studied pictures of my daughters. "They're not at all alike, are they?"

"No," I said. "My pal Nancy Fox says, 'Those two sure came down the chute different!'"

Rick laughed as he studied the photos. "Now, let's see: Kate is fun-loving, confident, outgoing and— look at those eyes!— supremely intelligent." He turned to Penelope's picture. "Penelope is more inward—artistic, empathetic, gentle. Is she psychic?"

"How did you nail them like that? Do you have a spy around my house?" Rick shrugged.

"When you're as close to God as I am now, you see things clearly. And don't forget, they were almost my children."

As if by a far-off stage direction, the brewing thunderstorm that had threatened since my arrival broke in banging fury. Lightning flashed through the hospice window. I flinched.

"It's only God taking our picture, Pat."

"Oh, sure, Rick... God. Where is The Big Photographer-In-The-Sky when you need Him?"

"Right here, right now. That's where He is."

"Maybe so, but Rick, this is unbearable." I blew my nose and collected myself. "You know, Kate was only four years old when Mom died, but she said something really profound."

"I'd like to hear it."

"She overheard the minister speaking. She asked me, 'Mom, what does he mean when he talks about the "after-life"?'"

"Oh, boy."

"Exactly. You should have heard me hemming and hawing. I finally explained that her grandmother had something inside of that big, sweet body she could hug, something called a soul. And I explained when that body got all tired out, the soul just went some-place else to live."

"Not a bad save."

"Thanks, but she wasn't done! She said, 'But Mom, *where* does it go?' Well, I said, that's the after-life. We don't quite know what it is, but we know it's something that's coming, something ahead of us."

"And?"

"And Kate said, 'Oh, I see, Mom! The after-life is like next year!'"

Rick smiled. "Tell Kate I said thanks. I guess that makes this New Year's Eve for me."

It was a solemn moment. We grew solemn with it.

"What happened, Rick? We loved each other so much."

"Yes. But we were immature, and I kept secrets. I was older, and should have been wiser. I thought it was okay because I cared about you. But there were things you should have known. "

"The dumb thing is, Rick, I love you so much—right now."

He nodded. "Me, too." Neither of us spoke for a moment.

"It's like Kate's after-life question, Pat. Some things are beyond our understanding. Maybe once you've loved, you always love. Love is never yesterday's mashed potatoes." He smiled. "Hey, isn't that what your Grandma Daisy would have said?" He reached into his bedside table, and handed me two small volumes. One was a book of Byron's poems. The other was a journal.

"Yep, my very own Infernal Journal!" he laughed. "I remember teasing you for keeping one. Read it later, when you get home. It'll help you understand."

It did.

After I returned to California, Rick and I spoke by phone every day. His voice grew weaker, and he died as was predicted, only weeks later, at the age of fifty-three.

An envelope arrived with a check, and a note written in shaky handwriting.

"For Katy Bee and Melpy," Rick wrote, "I was privileged to have known their mother."

scene v: 1978, Sherman Oaks, CA

"You've heard of gifts beyond price?" Dr. Hart asked. "That's what you and Rick gave each other."

"I couldn't believe his courage. But maybe I should have—he once married me, didn't he?"

"You're hard on yourself, Pat."

"He gave me his journal. He wrote about his feelings for me. I can't imagine how painful his life must have been!"

"Yes. Can you see now that Rick's leaving your marriage was an act of love?"

"Almost..."

"Rick knew you were on the brink of stardom. He worried about his past, and that he hadn't told you about it. Twenty years ago he felt he could have harmed your career! So beyond recrimination and judgment and bitterness, what's left?"

"Only love, Dr. Hart. Only love."

Early the next spring, I was rear-ended in an automobile accident. One more time angels surrounded me. I suffered a severe whiplash injury—the third vertebra in my neck was cracked—but in spite of the weeks I'd spend in the hospital, I wouldn't be paralyzed. Lying flat on my back in traction, with nothing to do but watch the holes in the acoustic ceiling above me widening, narrowing, widening, narrowing, thought became self-hypnosis, self-hypnosis meditation. *Love makes life fabulous. Not just romantic love, sweet as it is, but love that cuts deep into the soul, melting hate and fear,* I meditated. The healing that began with my neck injury found its way into my heart, and broke ground for deeper healings to come.

scene vi: 1985, Studio City, CA

"I'm saving a seat for your Mom," Kate's friend Gary said. Kate, now a junior at The University of Redlands, was home on a well-needed break. She and popular TV star Gary (not his real name) sat quietly talking in my living room. I flitted about getting ready to go out for the evening, a glass of wine always nearby.

"What the heck did that mean, that remark?" I asked Kate the next morning.

"Gary's an alcoholic, Mom. He makes no secret of it. He meant he's saving a seat for you in his twelve-step meetings. He thinks you're an alcoholic, too. Penelope and I have thought so for a long time. You have no idea how much you drink."

I sputtered black coffee. "What? *I'm* an alcoholic? It's your father who ingests anything liquid or solid to make himself high!"

"I lost Dad a long time ago, Mom," Kate said. "I don't want to lose you, too." The sadness in her voice shredded my heart.

"Well, you, Penelope and your friend Gary—you're all wrong! I'll prove it! I'll go to one of those twelve-step meetings, the first one I can find. Me, alcoholic? Just because I have a glass or two of wine to relax and help with back pain now and then?" *Wait until they have to face life's problems like I have!,* I thought, bitter with my daughter's truth.. Denial. Narcissism. Two of alcoholism's enduring companions.

The first meeting I found to attend was in a men's rehabilitation house early the next morning. I looked around the room at bikers in black leather and heavy chains, a roomful of facial hair, tattoos, and testosterone. *How could I belong here? Little Patty-From -Cincinnati?*

"Hello, ma'am. Why don't you take that seat back there? There'll be other ladies here soon." He was clean-shaven and wore a pressed denim shirt. His smile was gentle as he handed me a cup, his eyes deep. "Have some java? Hope you take it black. It's fresh. I made it myself." I muttered a thank-you-kindly, and sat plotting my escape.

The man with the gentle smile sat at a small desk facing the group, the leader for the meeting. I missed my early-on chance to escape, for when he shared his story, I sat rooted in my chair. He spoke quietly about having killed someone in a drunken rage years before, but murder wasn't in his soul. Alcoholism was. I sniffled, listening to his testimony. A small, sweet-faced woman, about my age, seated a few rows away, sneaked glances at me. She passed me a note: "My name is Jeanne. I cried a lot, too."

When the speaker finished, other men and women in the group shared stories of their battles to shake the hold alcohol had on their lives. I learned females metabolize alcohol differently, and may be more at risk than men to developing alcohol addiction. In fact there's no such thing as "a woman able to drink like a man." The "glass ceiling" of addiction is a truth women cannot afford to ignore.

And I learned that alcoholism is progressive. I was a "functional" alcoholic. I worked. I got up in the mornings. I had not yet become like one of the Skid Row women I heard speak at that first meeting. The bottom I hit, the motivator urging me to face my addiction, was not the degradation of living out of a dumpster. It was the recognition of a reality I had too long ignored: the daughters I'd

259

raised and loved with all my heart had faced every pain I had faced, right along with me, but drinking alone and isolated to anesthetize my feelings had dissociated me from helping them attend to *their* pain. And what about their father, the man I'd loved from the day I met him? Could I have helped him with the trauma he carried? I'd spent years with therapists, trying to root out shyness, codependence and depression. Those years might have been more successful had I understood the complex emotional and psychological pieces of the addiction-puzzle sooner. These were symptoms, all a part of this syndrome I was now hearing about called the disease of alcoholism.

I, who hadn't tasted alcohol until I was twenty-eight, against all odds identified with a group of twelve-steppers in that morning's meeting. By the grace of God, I got their message. Some in twelve-step meetings call sobriety "the gift," and that's what it was for me. Handed to me that day in a scruffy package. The humiliation of my daughter Kate's friend Gary saying, "I'm saving a seat for your Mom," saved my life. It is now twenty-four years later, and I am still grateful.

After that first twelve-step meeting, while Kate went job-searching, I called Penelope, who had been staying with Art. I invited her to join me for a walk in Studio City Park. As I sat on a bench in the warm, mid-June sun waiting for her, the aura of freshly-cut grass took me back to memories of my grandparents' Ohio farm. So much life lived since. So much sweetness drunk from a well turned bitter.

Penelope touched my arm. I looked up at her face, reflecting the beauty of my mother and the intelligence of her father, as well as the overlay of something all her own, something that spoke of an ancient, almost shamanic, wisdom. We shared a hug, and strolled around the baseball diamond together.

"Honey, I have something to tell you, something I've learned today." I cleared my throat of the husky tears gathering there. "I'm an alcoholic. From this moment on, I promise you—and Katy—and *myself*—I'm a *sober* alcoholic." A wild sparrow flew between us, seeming to carry away with it the burden of pain I felt I had brought to my daughter's life.

Penelope's soft brown eyes filled with tears. We hugged again, tighter than before.

scene vii: 1987, Enter Dennis the Menace, From Studio City to Traverse City

Journal, January 5, 1987: Here's an irony for you. I'm playing a rehab nurse! Working on the TV film Deadly Care with Cheryl Ladd. Boy, am I mean!! I offer Cheryl a razor blade to slit her wrists. I'm not so judgmental in life. I see Art through a new pair of glasses. I wish I could help him.

"Are you tired of playing sadistic nurses?" Pat Amaral asked. "They're doing a musical play based on the comic strip, *Dennis The Menace.* They need an older actress who can sing to play opposite Tom Poston." I confess to a heart-leap. It was a challenge. It had been thirteen years since I'd set foot on a stage in *Take Me Along,* and I was still dealing with a strangely unreliable set of vocal chords. But as appreciative as I was of the livelihood TV and film work had afforded me and my family, I felt unmitigated joy at the prospect of returning to live theater. Kate and Penelope were now capable young women on their own. I was free to tour. So I huffed and puffed every day, strengthening and limbering my now late-fifties body with the help of dancer and trainer/chorographer friend, Babs Warden Lebowsky, a friend from New York. I vocalized daily with coach Bob Gorman. The hard work paid off. I got the job in the Broadway-bound musical based on *Dennis The Menace,* as Martha Wilson, the grandmotherly neighbor to Dennis.

"Hey," said Hank Ketchum, the cartoonist/creator of *Dennis,* "You really ARE a 'Mrs. Wilson!' Can you bake cookies, too?" The cartoon Martha baked cookies for the cartoon Dennis.

Tom Poston was perfectly cast as Martha's curmudgeonly husband, George. Tom and I had the most successful song in the score, and its accompanying dance, a jitterbug sequence, garnered a standing ovation at every performance. Young actor Gary Beach, later a Tony winner for his outrageous performance as the cross-dressing director in *The Producers,* was wonderful as Dennis's father. We had a sweet, warm scene together. But a couple of good moments do not make a Broadway show. Though our reviews were mostly positive in the try-out location of Traverse City, Michigan, all lamented that the score was not up to other cartoons-turned-musical like *Annie* and *Charlie Brown.* We were not yet ready for Broadway, and closed down for a year-long period of music and lyric rewrites.

In the year of waiting for *Dennis* to resume, I lost several of my theatrical friends, including coach Bob Gorman, to AIDS. I loved Bobby. I was indebted to him for his help in the return of my singing voice. I decided to sing in his honor. Director Warren Lyons and musical director Shelly Markham helped hone the material for a new one-woman show, and in January of 1990, I performed it at Tom Rolla's Gardenia, a popular Hollywood cabaret/theater, donating the proceeds to Equity Fights Aids. The show was about my theatrical family, with some of my mother's material woven in, as well as pieces from my old cabaret act. Theater and Hollywood friends showed up for the premiere, dressed to the teeth, crammed in to the walls. I wore a full-length, black sequin Ceil Chapman gown, and had to laugh at myself. My costuming had come full circle from Village Vanguard

Tom Poston and I during rehearsals for **Dennis**

days nearly forty years before. Here I was in sequins again.

Art attended a preview with Penelope. *Why am I nervous? Just because he's here?* It was now sixteen years that we had been apart. Our children had grown into beautiful, responsible young women. I

262

PATRICIA WILSON

Forty years after my New York club debut, I was wearing sequins again.

had forged a successful career in Hollywood, a second career apart from Broadway. My soul, my voice, was back. I had purged myself, with spiritual help, of resentments.

And I felt the same flutters looking into Art's deep-lined face as I had felt on the cool August day in 1961 when I walked into Manhattan's westside Spindletop Restaurant to meet him for the first time. The Big-Scenarist-In-The-Sky had arranged for the heroine to enter the play at that moment to meet the hero, and through whatever angel's wing had brushed my heart that day, a part of me still loved what I knew was the best in the father of my children, Art Franklin.

On the night of the preview performance of my Gardenia show, Art suggested a chunk of monologue that resulted in one of the high points of the evening.

"Patty, remember how your mother loved that same kind of sequin dress you're wearing? How she once joked that she wanted to be *buried* in a dress like it?" I smiled.

"I remember, Art."

"Well, right at the beginning of your show, right after your first song, when you're talking about your mom, tell the audience how she wanted to be buried in a dress like the one you're wearing. Then take a deep breath and say, 'I hope I don't die in it tonight!'" When I opened the next night I added the line to the performance. The audience roared. It was a show business joke, and there wasn't a dry seat in the house. And it was another healing bond between Art and me. He'd made a successful contribution to a project important to me.

A busy spring, that spring of 1990. Tom Rolla invited my one-woman show for a return engagement at The Gardenia. I filmed a successful "M and M's" commercial in which I sang a boisterous version of *Happy Birthday*. I completed a Canadian film, *Martial Law,* with David Carradine, and immediately began another, *The Perfect Bride,* starring British film star Samantha Davis.

Dennis The Menace's producer called during the filming of *The Perfect Bride.* "We're doing another tryout of the show with a new score. Tom Poston isn't available—I hope you are! The rest of the cast is all New York theater people." He named the dates, and they just cleared the final shooting days of the film. I'd fly to Washington, DC to rehearse the new *Dennis* the day after *The Perfect Bride* wrapped.

I get murdered, after a terrible fight for my life, in *The Perfect Bride.* We filmed in an old Craftsman-style house in downtown Los Angeles, a spooky setting for my on-screen demise. Samantha Davis and I filmed the close-ups, fake-choking and fighting each other. Stunt-doubles then took over the choreographed brawl, wrestling across the floor and out into the yard. I shivered in a wide-eyed close-up as I stood at the top of a foreboding flight of

Another opening, another show. Director Warren Lyons and I at The Gardenia in Hollywood, 1990.

cement steps leading to the dark basement. Murderess Samantha hurtled herself at me, to topple my character backwards down the steps.

"Cut!" yelled the director, positioning a stunt-double in the place I'd been standing.

"Action!" he shouted, and down the stunt girl went, rolling down those cement steps, landing in a crumpled heap on the basement floor. She'd agreed to do just one take, and the shot was perfect. I replaced her, lying on the precise spot where she'd landed. The script called for me to whimper in pain, and I did so in empathy for the stunt girl. As young, agile, and padded as she was, she couldn't have helped but hurt herself in that fall. She said she was fine, but my hat is forever off to those people who do the dirty work of filming.

All that night, filming the fight/murder sequence, I half-sang to myself: *In the morning I go back to my roots! I'll be on the stage again!* I couldn't have been happier with the prospect that I'd be on a flight to Washington to rehearse and open in the new version of *Dennis.*

Unfortunately, the new version was not to be a joyous experience. Though all of Martha's original wardrobe was revised for this new production of *Dennis,* which was fine with me, I had to fight with the costumer to keep the original padding unchanged. Rather than padding myself with foam rubber, I wore undergarments filled with bird seed, a theatrical costuming trick passed down from Henrietta, my actress/grandmother. Bird seed moves like comfortable poundage. Foam rubber neither looks nor moves the same under a costume. The cartoon Martha Wilson is notably endowed in the bosom department, and I knew Martha's jitterbug with George was funnier because of that bouncy bird-seed.

The new jitterbug sequence was difficult for me to master, the off-Broadway choreographer impatient.

"I thought you were Gene Kelly's leading lady! Don't tell me you *danced* with him!" he sneered. I kept my mouth shut and worked harder to master the steps. Practically the only redeeming feature of that difficult few weeks was my dressing roommate, a cheerful, talented young triple-threat actress/singer/dancer soon to become a Tony-award winning Broadway star. Karen Ziemba. Karen is a great girl.

Karen Ziemba played Dennis's mother, I was neighbor Martha.

The new version of *Dennis* opened to lukewarm reviews, all acknowledging that *Dennis* as a musical was a viable idea, but expressing disappointment in the finished product. One reviewer said, *"Patricia Wilson fills the stage with the warmth and radiance of a summer sunbeam,"* and another stated I was *"right out of a Norman Rockwell painting."*

But another said, *"As sweet as she looks in her scalloped apron and flowered dress, Patricia Wilson can't sing at all...."* Ouch. Was I wrong that I'd gotten my voice back? Not necessarily, but I certainly wasn't that reviewer's cup of tea. I was from another era.

It was the last time I participated in *Dennis*. The show was tried out again with Gavin McLeod as George, and Marion Ross, from *Happy Days,* as Martha. The new producers felt it would surely succeed with an all-star TV cast. But once again, the show stopped short of New York and Broadway. Hank Ketchum died in 2001 without seeing his dream of Dennis-on–Broadway realized.

Scene viii: Autumn 1991, Enter baseball and Marla Hooch, Cooperstown, NY

Journal, October, 23, 1991: I'm getting around! Now I'm in Cooperstown, New York, working on a film called A League of Their Own, about the women's softball league during World War II. It stars Tom Hanks and Geena Davis. Directed by Penny Marshall. I play an old ballplayer named "Marla Hooch"—how's that for a name?

The character I'd tested for was that of Rosie O'Donnell's older counterpart. But Penny later decided I was better suited to play comedic actress Megan Cavanaugh as an older woman, so I became "Marla Hooch."

Marla was an original member of the team called "The Peaches." Flashbacks to the forties in the film relate the story of the league's origin, then flash-forward to the present, a reunion of the players at The Baseball Hall of Fame. We older versions of the young players had earlier spent several days in Evansville, Indiana with the company. There Penny Marshall filmed a few improvised scenes with us as we studied the mannerisms of our young counterparts. During that period, a small young woman bounded into the makeup trailer with a bright "Hi!" She talked in profane perpetual motion for several minutes before I recognized Madonna, the international singing star, playing "Mae," one of the younger ballplayers. Her reputation as a difficult diva and star notwithstanding, Madonna never appeared that way to me. During the filming she was professional, always one of the compatible gang.

Tom Hanks, one of the most accessible stars I've ever worked with, ambled over to introduce himself as Penny Marshall compared my eye color with that of my younger counterpart. Penny was so meticulous she decided I needed light brown contact lenses to change my dark brown eyes to match Megan Cavanaugh's. Tom gave me a thumbs-up sign.

"Gee, I've never worn contact lenses," I said. "Do they hurt your eyes?"

"No, Patricia," Tom Hanks said, uttering one of his more memorable lines from the film, "and don't forget—there's no crying in baseball!"

In the dressing trailer I shared with Bill Pullman. He forgave me for walking in on him.

The necessity for actors in the big cast of *A League Of Their Own* to share dressing room trailers by staggering their costume changes led to an embarrassing encounter with actor Bill Pullman. I opened the door of my assigned dressing room trailer just as Bill was pulling on his pants. "Oops! Sorry!" I said.

"It's okay," grinned the actor. "But who are you? The crew told me I'd be sharing this trailer with some old lady actress." What a gentleman! I love gentlemen.

Journal, November 5, 1990: Home again, after wrapping up A League of Their Own. And speaking of wrapping up, I realize I've now been working for more than fifty years.

As Grandma Daisy would have said, how do you like them apples?

scene ix: January 1994, Enter another shake-up, Studio City, CA

"Mom! Wake up! Brace yourself in the doorway!" Penelope's shouts awakened me, but I couldn't move. I was pinned to my bed.

Journal, January 17, 1994: Grateful to be alive after the earthquake—not everyone just north of here so lucky. Lost much of Grandma Daisy's hand-painted china, and was nearly hit by a flying TV set. Every aftershock rattled our nerves. No electricity. But Penelope and pets and I are okay. Stood in line for an hour at 7/11 to get

*water. In the twenty-two years we've lived in California we've expe-
rienced many jolts, but nothing like this.*

Penelope reached Art by phone a few minutes after the quake,
and drove to his apartment at first light. He was teetering on the brink
of disaster.

"The back of the building is destroyed! Dad's apartment is
lurching over the driveway! We've got to get him out of there." His
building condemned, Art had to be moved.

"Please let me stay with you and Penelope," he begged. Art's son,
Jeff, lived with his wife and daughters twenty miles west, in Agoura.
They were unaffected by the quake, and invited Art to stay with them.
But Art preferred not to be that far away from the area he knew.

Kate and her husband Mike, 3000 miles away, were safe. They
lived in a charming area on the Delaware River, Dingman's Ferry,
Pennsylvania. It was peaceful and rustic, yet only two hours outside
of New York City. Five weeks after the Northridge earthquake, I
bought a small red farmhouse in Dingman's Ferry, eight minutes
away from Kate and Mike. The house sat back from a country road
on a hill, surrounded by woods, fronted by a half-acre, meadow-like
yard. There were as many as five deer in the yard at a time, and a
black bear with her two cubs had to be rounded up and moved from
under the deck shortly before I took possession.

My agent of twenty-two years, Pat Amaral, retired and moved
back to her native Florida. Since I now owned a house in the east,
I signed with a prestigious bi-coastal agency, Ambrosio/Mortimer.
Penelope decided to move with me to the house in Dingman's
Ferry.

"We'll find an apartment for Dad in Milford," the girls agreed.

Art was now in his late seventies. Animosity between us had
eased long before. I only laughed when I learned he had assured teen-
aged Penelope years earlier that I'd forced him to leave our marriage
because I was a lesbian. His version of our history kept changing,
always to make him look like a victim. By this time the variety of
versions was only amusing.

"Well, Art, which is it? Was I a lesbian, or a slut who slept with
my directors and leading men?" It had been twenty years since our
marriage ended. In all those years I'd not met anyone else I wanted to
marry. Through twelve-step meetings, I'd come to understand that my

codependence was an addiction in itself. I also recognized that Art's addiction, not the man I'd loved with all my being, was the villain in our marriage. I talked Art into going to meetings with me.

"Sobriety has changed my life, Art. You should try it sometime."

"But I don't drink anymore, Patty," he protested.

"Addiction is addiction, Art. Substitute testimony from alcoholics for testimony from addicts." But he zoned out at meetings. Several friends who were dually addicted offered to take him to twelve-step meetings for those suffering from addiction to narcotics as well as alcohol.

"Nah, I'll pass," he said.

Art wasn't ready.

After the earthquake, Penelope and I left for the new house in Pennsylvania. We drove across the country, she in a small van with household belongings, her pick-up truck trailing behind. I followed in my sedan. Our animals were divided between the two vehicles.

"The Beverly Hillbillies are alive and well!" we laughed. The trip took a full week. I reveled in the scenery, marveling at this vast country, often reminded of my friend John Steinbeck's wonderful book, *Travels With Charley*.

Journal, July 8, 1994: What a way to go! Penelope and I arrived in Dingman's Ferry in one piece!!

Then: *Journal, July 19, 1994: The news today is unfathomable. Jeff had a massive heart attack—my stepson is dead, at the age of forty-eight.*

Art was devastated, overwhelmed by grief and guilt. Only weeks before, Jeff, under enormous stress, had come to his father to confess his marriage to his second wife was crumbling. He wanted to move in with Art to sort out his feelings.

"No! Go home, you stupid Irish prick! Don't make the same mistake I did!" Art could be harsh, even with his children. But after his son's death, Art felt if he'd allowed Jeff to stay with him, his son might still be alive. "Poor son of a bitch," Art muttered. "I should have listened to him. I should have helped him." Penelope returned to Los Angeles to be with her father.

Home is where the heart is, but it wasn't in Dingman's Ferry for long.

Within two years, we'd all returned, Kate, her husband Mike, and I. I rented a small apartment in Sherman Oaks, in the San Fernando Valley area where I'd raised my children after leaving Beverly Hills years earlier. Every summer, driving cross-country by myself, I locked up my apartment and visited the little red farmhouse I owned in Dingman's Ferry. I made the trip eight times over the next few years, sometimes meandering along on Route 40, sometimes on the 70 or 80, always reveling in the beauty of this country in all of its magnificent manifestations. Driving alone, with my dogs snuggled in the back seat, became a meditative, almost spiritual, experience. But when vandals threatened the Dingman's Ferry house in my absence, it was time to sell.

Separation from my family after their return to California wasn't the only reason rustic Dingman's Ferry, Pennsylvania, had to be left behind. I loved working on the stage, but Hollywood, too, can lay claim to your mind, heart, and spirit. As a young girl, I grew dreams through the dramatic films and musicals of the '30s and '40s. I never got over the thrill of working in the studios that turned out those films. The ghosts of movies and stars past still haunted sets and dressing rooms and hallways, and they all spoke to me. I never tired of our conversations.

271

scene x: 1996 , Enter Eddie Murphy, The Nutty Professor

In 1996, Universal Studios remade Jerry Lewis's classic comedy, *The Nutty Professor,* with Eddie Murphy. Tom Shadyac, Hollywood's new *wunderkind* of comedy, having directed Jim Carrey in the hit film, *Ace Ventura,* was director of the new *Nutty Professor.* I read for the role of Grace, the secretary to the Dean of the film's fictional college.

"Good audition!" Tom Shadyac said.

"Thanks, but if you're having callbacks, I'm leaving tomorrow to drive cross- country."

"That's okay, I have you on videotape. Where are you driving to?"

"I have a little house in Dingman's Ferry, Pennsylvania."

"Dingman's Ferry, Pennsylvania? You're hired! Just for having a house in Dingman's Ferry, Pennsylvania."

Two months later, on a Friday in late June, I was in New York City to read for a commercial. Posted above the sign-in sheet was an urgent message to call Kate.

"Mom," Kate said. "Universal is looking for you, for *The Nutty Professor!* When you didn't answer at your house, your agency called me." I was to report on Monday morning, three days later, to begin work.

"Where were you?" asked Tom Shadyac. I'd flown to California from Pennsylvania the night before. "The casting people wanted to shove someone else down my throat—what were you doing in New York? I kept visualizing you in Dingman's Ferry!"

You wouldn't know I spent three months working on *The Nutty Professor.* I'm not that visible in the final cut. My brother Donn teased me unmercifully. "Well, Sis," he scoffed, "I blinked and missed your entire performance!" That's the way it goes with movies. Even the hilarious scene with which I auditioned was never filmed. In that scene, a hamster escapes from the university laboratory and jumps into my character's hair. Stylist Beth Miller worked hours devising the updo I wear in the film, a pompadour in front to accommodate the hamster. Then other scenes cropped up that took shooting priority, and my hamster co-star and I never filmed ours. The hamster made a getaway, but I got stuck with the pompadour.

The opening day on the set I was hustled into wardrobe and makeup to film my first scene. I sat next to the set for an hour, waiting for lights to be adjusted. That, too, is the way it goes in film-making. It's a hurry-up-and-wait business. An obese gentleman passed by several times, smiling a polite "hello." I smiled back at him, saying a polite "hello" of my own. It was a full morning before I was introduced to the obese gentleman, Eddie Murphy, in his Professor Sherman Klump fat suit and makeup. Later in the film, if you've seen it, Eddie becomes his slim, real-life self, but the obesity makeup Rick Baker devised for him was pure genius. It sure had me fooled.

I spent a lot of time in my dressing room, waiting for the scene with the hamster to be shot. Every day it was scheduled as a possibility. Every morning I reported bright and early. James Coburn, who plays a rich university benefactor in the film, often reported to the makeup trailer at the same time. We'd settle into the high, barbershop type swivel chairs actors occupy while the makeup artists work their magic, and each morning Jim would greet me with, "Well, here we are again, Patricia. Imagine! Still making faces!" Jim suffered from painful rheumatoid arthritis. He went to great lengths to keep his distorted hands from being photographed.

In a large group scene, I was part of a crowd watching Eddie Murphy morph from his handsome self into obese Professor Klump. Extras, called "atmosphere" people in the business, were brought in for the day to be members of the crowd. That day, since I was not a star or player they recognized, the atmosphere people assumed I was one of them. It was the first notion I had of how competitive atmosphere people can be with one another. Extras supply their own wardrobe, unless it's a period costume film. One of the ladies eyed me up and down in the lovely electric blue gown bought by the costumer for my character, "Well!" she harrumphed "*I* was told *not* to bring anything blue to wear!"

Tom Shadyac hadn't directed me in any particular way, for I had no lines in the group scene. He asked me only to react as we watched Eddie undergo the painful morphing from his slim alter-ego to fat Sherman Klump. The camera filmed the scene with a long shot, encompassing the whole group. The crew prepared to move for the next shot on another set. Tom stopped them.

"No, we're not moving yet. Light *her*," he said, pointing to me, "I want a close-up on her face for this scene. *That's* the way it should be played!" This was off-schedule, and re-lighting and shooting a close-up would take an extra hour of precious production time. The atmosphere people around me shuffled and mumbled, for it meant they'd be on their feet for a long time. I was kidney-punched from behind, and heard a loud, whining whisper.

"That could have been *me*, if I'd brought *my* blue to wear!"

The Nutty Professor was a blockbuster. Later that year I was signed as the commercial "real-life" spokeslady, with spokesman Alex Trebek, for a life insurance company. A blockbuster in the commercial world. My children were raised, and I had, at last, what had long eluded me—a feeling of security.

scene xi: 1996-2002, Enter the role of a lifetime, Sherman Oaks, California

"So now you're an insurance spokeslady? Still working at your age. Well, I've always said there's no such thing as an ex-actress!" Art's jibes could no longer hurt me, and I gave back as good as I got.

"Yep, aren't you sorry? Think of what you missed by dumping me...a fortune in residuals!"

My friends had barely understood my relationship with Art in the beginning. Now they were baffled. "My God, Pat, I used to think Art was crazy. It wasn't Art. It was you all along!"

"You got that right!" What people thought didn't matter. Art Franklin, with all I now understood about codependence, was nonetheless, more than thirty years later, still the smartest, funniest man I'd ever known. What's the use of wondrin'?

He didn't feel well on Christmas Day of 2000, and was diagnosed with acute pneumonia.

"Art, do you smoke?" asked the doctor.

"Not for fifty years, Doc!" Art said, proud.

It was time to rip the veil away. "Doctor, Art doesn't consider his marijuana use 'smoking.' Please tell him it is!"

"Worse, Art," said the doctor. "You can't smoke *anything*, not with your impaired lungs. Besides, pot is a gateway to other drugs, particularly in the elderly."

"Did he just call me 'elderly'?" Art asked. I didn't laugh. The doctor continued.

"Art, if what Pat says is true, you must stop *immediately*!"

So Art quit smoking marijuana. Just like that. He was "scared sober," as people testify in twelve-step meetings, the gift of sobriety wrapped in fear for his life. Though he'd stopped abusing harder substances earlier, it was too late for his body. The sobriety miracle for Art was the return of his mind and spirit. Sobriety gave Art clarity. It had given me insight, and along with it, forgiveness.

Kate received an offer too good to refuse. But it meant she and Mike had to move east again, this time to Connecticut. Once more, after only four years back in California, Kate and her family moved 3000 miles away.

"Mom," she insisted, "You can't drive across country anymore." I was confident that I could, but it was my daughter's turn to play parent. I hung up my driving gloves, and hopped on a plane every few weeks for a visit to Connecticut. I carried a small bag and a case for Pete, my latest dog-pal.

"She has Chihuahua, will travel," quipped Art.

One day I received a call from his neighbors. They'd taken Art to the emergency room after he fell on their sidewalk. "He's okay, but he wants to know if you'll come to take him home."

"Why did he fall, doctor?" I asked the young intern.

"He may have had a small stroke. He shouldn't be alone for the next couple of days."

Art was annoyed that I stayed in the spare room of his apartment for two nights.

"God, a man can't have his privacy anymore? Why don't you go home? I gave up living with you years ago." I smiled and returned to my Sherman Oaks apartment. The next day the North Hollywood police buzzed me from downstairs.

"Miss Wilson, we have your ex-husband here in the car." In front of my building was a police car with Art sitting in the back seat.

"How did you know where to find me?" I asked the young policeman.

"He knew your name was Patty, and that you now live on this street. All he wanted was for us to take him to you." He grinned. "We have our ways."

Well, that's a little scary.

"We found him wandering," the young policeman said. "We always keep an eye on him. His neighborhood is our beat, and he seems pretty vulnerable. What a sweet old guy!"

Penelope was with me that day, and together we drove her father back to his apartment. Resisting family pressure that he should be in an assisted living residence, I had an identification tag engraved for him to wear around his neck. I knew the best senior residence available would crush his spirit. We engaged a loving Latino couple to tend to him and care for his apartment. With Gino and Carmen's help, all went well for the next year. Until Art began wandering at night, knocking on strangers' doors, rousing them out of sleep.

"Is Patty here?" he'd ask. One empathetic young man called me at two AM.

"My wife is so frightened she wants to call the police, but your number is around his neck," said the young man. "He doesn't seem like he'd harm a fly. He just wants to find you."

Retrieving Art from the living room of the kind strangers, I once again slept in his spare bedroom. The next morning, with his doctor's help, I located a convalescent hospital in Studio City.

"It's not a retirement home, Art. It's a place where you can be monitored 24/7. You seem to be having little strokes. If you fall without Gino and Carmen around I'm not strong enough to help you. Don't worry, I'm not deserting you. And I promise I'll never lie to you."

"I know, Patty-from-Cincinnati. That's not your style. This is great!" His new room overlooked a garden courtyard. I stayed with him until he fell asleep.

Journal, December 13, 2001: Art is now in a convalescent place. I slept for the first time in weeks last night.

Kate flew in from Connecticut to visit her father, and when she leaned over him and whispered, "Dad, it's Katy Bee!" he snapped his eyes open and asked for food.

"Art, you're eating!" exclaimed the nurse. "You've barely eaten for a week!

"I love my family," he said. He laid his head back on his pillow. "They're safe now. Nobody got killed." The last was barely audible.

"What, Art?"

He was asleep.

I visited him during the days, often bringing Pete the Chihuahua for him to hold in his lap. We sat together in the hospital garden, wrapped in wooly sweaters in the warm winter sun.

"Patty, I've always envied you that God-thing you have going— guess I'm just the cynical old Jew your Dad always thought I was."

"Cynical old Jew, Art? Where? Where?" I swiveled my head and looked in all directions, as he had done to make me laugh forty years earlier on a Manhattan bus. He smiled. His dimples were back, carving deep furrows into the gray stubble on his cheeks.

"Those were great days, Patty. Sorry it got screwed up. I tried to help with your career. I'd helped so many. But the damn government thing—I never should have—"

"Yesterday's mashed potatoes, Abner." Abner was his birth name. No one else dared call him Abner. He'd legally changed it to "Arthur" when he turned eighteen.

"You betcha, Daisy!" he answered. A private joke. He thought I should have been named after my maternal grandmother. "What a great stage name—Daisy Wilson! Patricia Wilson is so *boring*."

"She sure is."

"Aww, Patty, you were never boring onstage, just remember that. I'll bet you have your greatest role ahead of you, the role of a lifetime, even at your age—even with your fat ass!"

I could only laugh. He got that right.

The nurses in the facility spotted my insurance commercials on TV. "Art, you didn't tell us your girl is a star!"

"Yeah, well don't hold it against me," he threw back. He reached for my hand. A pink winter camellia peeked out from waxy leaves in the little garden.

"They keep telling me I'm improving, but I can't see, I can't hear," he said. "Now I can't even walk. You of all people know what walking means to me, Patty!"

"But you have your mind back, Abner! You got pretty crazy there for a while. You *are* doing better, Art. They say after Christmas you can go home."

"It's okay. I'll be fine here for as long as it takes."

Penelope visited her father a few days before Christmas and found him sitting in a wheel chair, gamely attempting *Rudolph The Red-Nosed Reindeer* in a group sing-a-long.

"I want to punch somebody," he said. She wheeled him outside, and held her flattened hands in front of him.

"Punch away, Dad."

Art said the next day, "Penelope's a really special girl, isn't she, Patty? Katy, too."

"They're remarkable young women, Art."

"Yeah. We did good."

Journal, January 5, 2002: Christmas has come and gone. Art still can't go home.

"You haven't seen the Connecticut contingent for a while," Art said on a late January day. The Connecticut contingent, Kate and her family, now included our first grandson. "You missed Christmas with them! You'd better go before they release me here, Daisy. Take pictures of everyone!"

I came to say goodbye with Pete in his airline travel case. "Have Chihuahua, will travel!" I said, wheeling Art to the corner 7/11 for his favorite ice cream.

"Yeah, poor damn dog was born in a trunk, too. I expect him to break into a time-step any minute. You'll miss the frigging flight," he fretted, stroking Pete's brown spotted back with one hand, holding onto Haagen Daaz like a tenacious three-year old with the other.

"Don't be silly. I'm on that flight so often they'll be afraid to leave without me."

"Just get outta here, Patty," he said. "You're driving me nuts! When you get back you can help me move back to my apartment. I'll be walking by then. Up again, old heart, right, Daisy?"

"Right, Abner."

He died in his sleep the next night. The nurses found him on their rounds, not breathing, his face and lips blue from the final, lung-paralyzing, oxygen-robbing stroke. The phone rang in Kate's Connecticut home at four-thirty in the morning.

"Miss Wilson, Art left a signed DNR with us. He didn't want us to try to resuscitate him if something like this happened," said the nurse on the other end of the line. "But we all saw how close you are, and he gave you a medical power-of-attorney. We have paramedics standing by. We wondered..."

The tufted chenille rows of the bedspread in Kate's guest room swam like waves in front of my eyes. I swallowed to keep my stomach from lurching into my throat. Kate and I held tight to each other. Beautiful, smart, successful Katy Bee, longing to redeem the memory-father of her small childhood, knowing he'd slipped away, slipped away. Long ago.

"Would he have any chance of recovery? I mean, without oxygen for so long?" I asked.

"Truthfully? I believe he'd have little or no cognitive sense. His blue color..."

"You're saying he'd be a vegetable?"

"No. Mom, no! Not Dad!" said Kate. Early in her career, Kate had been a cognitive therapist for brain-damaged accident and stroke victims.

"In my opinion? Yes, I'm afraid so, Mrs. Franklin." After thirty years, I was Mrs. Franklin again. My greatest role? Fat ass, advanced age, and all?

"Patty, I've always envied you that God-thing," Art's voice in my ear. "You know what's right, you sentimental bitch. Let me go."

I whispered a silent prayer. "Art can't be a vegetable," I said to the nurse. "I won't countermand his wishes. Please follow his directive."

I heard a sigh of relief from the heavens. I knew Art had deliberately dispatched me to Connecticut the day before. He wanted to spare me pain, but my hero was ready to be off now, on the latest, greatest adventure in the drama of life.

It wasn't the first time Art Franklin had left me alone on the stage, but this time around he did it right.

FINALE

"The song is ended, but the melody lingers on."
...Irving Berlin

Journal, June 6, 2003: (Good Lord! Did I just write that date?) I'm in Columbus, Ohio, being inducted into the Musicians' Hall of Fame. I, who have never been able to master reading music. Oh, well, I'm not about to tell them now!

Later that afternoon, at the induction ceremony, music historian David Meyers made a kind speech. I waited in the wings and heard him say, "...A star during the Golden Age of Broadway, a lady with a fabulous life—" and smoothed my once-auburn-now-silver hair for a walk to the podium.

Well, I thought, *here I am again, making another entrance. There'd been no escaping these genes I was born with, not in this lifetime, maybe not in the next. I'd tried to make a getaway several times, but DNA is powerful stuff. Maybe I'd always be waiting in the wings, humming along with the overture, like a firehouse Dalmatian leaping to its feet when the alarm bell sounds. Fair enough. But if I come back in another life,* I wondered, *will there be another Golden Age of Broadway for me to come back to? Probably not, the way things are going.*

"Patricia, I hope you've written a memoir," David Meyers said after the ceremony.

"Who, me? I think my life might read more like a Danielle Steel novel than a show business memoir," I said, laughing, to David Meyers.

But my mind reeled back to 1955.

"It's a helluva story, Patrish! Fun stuff! And it's the story that counts, trust me!"

So you told me a long time ago, John Steinbeck, so you told me.

Well, I've written it now. All of it, not just the fun stuff.

I have a knowin'. I'll bet he's somewhere smiling.

MUSIC SWELLS, UP AND OUT

LaVergne, TN USA
13 October 2009
160725LV00003B/4/P